Palgrave Hate Studies

This series builds on recent developments in the broad and interdisciplinary field of hate studies. Palgrave Hate Studies aims to bring together in one series the very best scholars who are conducting hate studies research around the world. Reflecting the range and depth of research and scholarship in this burgeoning area, the series welcomes contributions from established hate studies researchers who have helped to shape the field, as well as new scholars who are building on this tradition and breaking new ground within and outside the existing canon of hate studies research.

More information about this series at
http://www.palgrave.com/gp/series/14695

Ben Colliver

Re-imagining Hate Crime

Transphobia, Visibility and Victimisation

palgrave
macmillan

Ben Colliver
Criminology Dept, Curzon Building, C303
Birmingham City University
BIRMINGHAM, UK

Palgrave Hate Studies
ISBN 978-3-030-65713-0 ISBN 978-3-030-65714-7 (eBook)
https://doi.org/10.1007/978-3-030-65714-7

This Palgrave Macmillan imprint is published by the registered company Springer Nature Switzerland AG.
The registered company address is: Gewerbestrasse 11, 6330 Cham, Switzerland

Acknowledgments

First and foremost, I would like to thank every person who contributed and participated in this research. Thank you for trusting me with your stories, for giving me your time and energy and for being so honest and open with me. I hope that with this book I have accurately and authentically presented your stories and narratives.

I would also like to thank Dr Marisa Silvestri, Dr Joanna Jamel and Dr Adrian Coyle, who guided me through this research project, dedicated their time, energy and resources and always provided unwavering encouragement.

Finally, I would like to express my gratitude to my family and friends, who have supported me throughout the duration of this research project. They have given me so much of their time, patience and energy.

Contents

List of Figures

List of Tables

1

Introduction

The social positioning of transgender people in relation to rights, equality and legal protection have perhaps never been more significantly in the public spotlight than at the current time. Criminology has been slow to respond to the phenomenon of transphobic hate crime, particularly lagging behind the discipline's interest in homophobic, racist and Islamophobic hate crime. The publication of '*Transphobic Hate Crime*', authored by Joanna Jamel in 2018 marked the first book dedicated solely to transphobic hate crime. With this book, I hope to build upon the work of Jamel (2018) and offer an empirical account of hate crimes targeting transgender people. In doing so, I address a gap in academic literature, centring the lives and experiences of transgender communities. Whilst a significant amount of research has been conducted exploring hate crime on the grounds of race, religion and sexuality, incidents targeting transgender people has gained relatively little attention, particularly within Anglo-American literature. A number of factors have contributed to the historical exclusion of transgender identities from mainstream criminological research and academia more broadly. The exclusion of transgender people and communities is a theme that runs throughout academia, activism and society.

B. Colliver, *Re-imagining Hate Crime*, Palgrave Hate Studies,
https://doi.org/10.1007/978-3-030-65714-7_1

Psychological and biological studies have a longer history of engaging in issues affecting transgender people; however, they were largely influenced by essentialist ideas that reinforced a medical deficit model. Although there has been significant development within the social sciences over the past 15 years, existing research is not without critique. A noteworthy amount of researching exploring issues affecting transgender communities has been a result of Western, primarily American- or British-based interest. There is also a certain White, ethnocentric lens through which transgender communities are viewed within Western research. This has led to an under-appreciation of cultural diversity and a homogenising stance has been established. Indeed, Stryker (2006: 15) was 'struck by the overwhelming (and generally unmarked) whiteness of practitioners in the academic field of transgender studies'. I hope to address the dominant whiteness of research into transphobic hate crime by regularly challenging assumptions about who is transgender and 'transgender' as a category.

Issues of hate crime are gaining increasing prominence within Criminology (Awan and Zempi 2017; Chakraborti and Garland 2012; Healy 2020). Hate crimes are also gaining significant political and social attention as a result of annually increasing levels of recorded hate crime. Hate Crimes are a subset of crimes that the Home Office (2019) suggests represent around 2% of overall recorded crime in England and Wales. Incidents of recorded hate crimes are increasing annually with 105,090 hate crimes recorded by police forces in 2019–2020 (excluding Greater Manchester police), an increase of 8% from the previous year (Home Office 2020). Hate crimes targeting transgender people, or people perceived to be transgender, account for the smallest amount of recorded hate crime, accounting for 2% of all recorded hate crime (Home Office 2020). Despite only accounting for 2% of all recorded hate crime, this is increasing annually, with the year 2018–2019 seeing a 37% increase in transphobic hate crime from the previous year, and the year 2019–2020 seeing an increase of 16% (Home Office 2019, 2020). It is also key to note that police recorded statistics underestimate the prevalence and extent of transphobic hate crime, and other studies have shown much higher rates of victimisation (Chakraborti et al. 2014; Metro Charity 2014). High rates of victimisation targeting transgender people and communities have been well documented in research across the global north (Antjoule 2013; James et al. 2016; Turner et al. 2009). There are a number of political and social factors that may have contributed to the rising rates of recorded hate crimes. The Home Office (2019) attributes the annual rise in recorded hate crimes to two main reasons: the EU referendum resulting in higher levels of hate crimes being perpetrated and a continued improvement in the accuracy of police recording.

In relation to hate crimes targeting transgender people, there are a number of other issues that may have contributed to the rise in annually recorded transphobic hate crimes. Transgender communities have received significant social attention recently, with public attention focusing primarily on transgender women. Issues regarding gender identity have become a significant topic of interest within private, political and media spheres. In May 2018, Channel 4 aired a live debate show titled 'Genderquake', which brought together a range of transgender, non-binary and cisgender individuals to debate issues around gender identity. The live debate saw heckling from audience members shouting phrases such as 'you're a man' and 'you have a penis' at transgender women panellists. Despite requests from panellists to have hecklers removed from the building, Channel 4 continued to allow all audience members to remain throughout filming. Not only does this highlight the significant contemporary othering of transgender people, it also emphasises a much wider structural process that allows for the exclusion of transgender people. Moreover, the London Pride parade in 2018 was disrupted by a group of trans-exclusionary lesbian activists, who lay in the road to prevent the parade from beginning, covering themselves in signs displaying phrases such as 'transactivism erases lesbians' and 'lesbian = female homosexual'. This protest resulted in a Twitter trend of other lesbians, using the hashtag '#GetTheLOut', who agreed that transgender inclusion results in the erasure of lesbian identities. Again, not only does this illustrate the contemporary exclusion of transgender people, but wider societal and organisational structures that allow for this exclusion to prosper. However, it is important to note that there has been strong counter-movements, including the trending hashtags '#LwiththeT', '#GwiththeT' and '#BwiththeT', to signify lesbian, gay and bisexual people who are transgender allies and inclusive of transgender people.

In 2017, under Theresa May's government, an announcement was made that the government intended to streamline and demedicalise the process of changing legal gender to reflect that being transgender is not an illness. In 2004 the Gender Recognition Act (GRA) was introduced and has significantly 'improved the protocols ... [that] protect the rights of transgender people' (Jamel 2018: 43). Nonetheless, it is noted that the introduction of the GRA simultaneously reinforced the western gender binary and did not allow for alternative gender expressions. It did however, place a duty on criminal justice agencies to improve sensitivity when working with transgender individuals as the Gender Recognition Act prohibits the disclosure of an individual's transgender identity without their consent. The Gender Recognition Act allowed people who were diagnosed with gender dysphoria to gain legal recognition by obtaining a gender recognition certificate, which required that a 'gender recognition panel' (including medical and legal experts) had considered that the criteria for issuing a certificate had been met. The criteria specified in the Gender Recognition Act include being at least 18 years old, have been diagnosed with gender dysphoria, that the individual intends to live in their legally obtained gender until death and has lived in their 'acquired' gender for a minimum of 2 years prior to legal recognition being granted.

In 2018 the government began a public consultation intended to be used to reform the Gender Recognition Act introduced in 2004. The proposed reform of the Gender Recognition Act aimed to make it easier for transgender people to achieve legal recognition of their self-declared gender without necessarily having met all of the criteria specified in the 2004 Act. Other countries, such as Ireland and Denmark, have already enacted legislation that treats gender as a self-declared category. Many people found that the current process for obtaining legal recognition is overly intrusive and unnecessarily lengthy and invasive. However, the announcement of the public consultation saw an intensification of online 'debate', which was most commonly framed in relation to 'transgender rights' vs. 'women's rights'. This constructs these rights as two mutually exclusive categories. Conversations around the proposed reform have tended to focus on the perceived implications that this reform will have on the provisions set out in the 2010 Equality Act that allows for the implementation of single-sex spaces and provisions including refuges, toilet facilities and participation in sport. There has been a continued conflation between the two laws and the government consultation has resulted in a narrative being pushed that the reform somehow invalidates the right to single-sex spaces. Conversations have tended to focus on the potential for people, primarily cisgender men, to abuse the system and gain access to 'vulnerable' women and children. However, it important to note that it is not only cisgender men who are positioned as a threat to women's safety, transgender people are also regularly pathologised and constructed as being dangerous (Colliver et al. 2019).

Since the government announcement, a number of high-profile individuals have taken to social media, with many having faced considerable backlash. J.K Rowling has published a number of tweets, of which many were challenged, with claims being made that she is reinforcing harmful, transphobic narratives (Henman 2020). This was followed by the publication of an essay on her personal website in which she set out a number of issues which concerned her, relating to the 'new trans activism'. Many of the claims made in this essay relied on anecdotal evidence. Whilst J.K Rowling appears to have significant support within online communities, her actions have resulted in significant criticism and a number of other high-profile individuals stepping forward to demonstrate their support for transgender communities, including Daniel Radcliffe and Evanna Lynch.

'Concerns' raised by J.K Rowling also included safeguarding issues surrounding children who are transgender. Again, J.K Rowling often drew upon anecdotal evidence of 'de-transitioning' to highlight the risk that the 'new trans activism' posed to children. As such, it is inferred that young people, particularly 'feminine' boys, and 'masculine' girls are being pressured, coerced or 'converted' into being transgender. This narrative has parallels with homophobic rhetorics that have historically claimed that lesbian, gay and bisexual people are a 'danger' to children and may attempt to 'recruit' children into a particular 'lifestyle'. Whilst it is not the aim, nor in the scope of this book, to engage in a full discussion around transgender children, it is important to note that stories and anecdotes of 'de-transition' are often drawn upon to position concerns around transgender children as a 'safeguarding issue'. However, there is no consistent conceptualisation of 'transition', and this term is often interpreted differently for children and adults. When discussing children, 'transition' and 'de-transition' are often used to indicate that a child has disclosed they are transgender, and then at a later date disclosed that they are no longer transgender. In this sense, to 'de-transition' (indicating that a transition has occurred) relies only on self-identification, which is often the most contested area regarding transgender equality. When de-legitimising transgender adults, gender reassignment surgery (or having not gone through this process) is often a key motif used to claim that people are not 'authentic', or have not transitioned. This demonstrates the ways in which narratives are applied inconsistently across populations, depending on the intended outcome of a particular perspective.

The response to the public consultation was delayed significantly. In June 2020, the Sunday Times published a 'leaked document' that outlined government plans for the reform of the Gender Recognition Act (Shipman 2020). The 'leaked document' indicated that the government had dropped any plans to move to a model of 'self-identification' and away from a medical model, whilst also promising to 'protect' single-sex spaces including public toilets and refuges. In September 2020, Liz Truss, Minister for Women and Equalities made an official statement regarding the outcome of the public consultation. It was announced that any plans to move to a model of 'self-identification' had been scrapped, but instead the government would make changes relating to the bureaucratic and financial implications of the current process. These issues would be addressed by moving the application procedure online, opening three new Gender Identity Clinics and reducing the cost to apply for a 'Gender Recognition Certificate'. Whilst these are generally seen as positive movements, the continued reliance on a 'medical model' to obtain legal recognition reinforces the pathologisation of transgender people and contributes to the social 'othering' of transgender people.

The Normalcy of Hate

This book is informed by a wider research project that took place between 2015 and 2018. The research project had a specific focus on transphobic hate crime within the United Kingdom (UK), and whilst there may be some conceptual ideas which traverse geographical boundaries, it is key to highlight that the findings of this research are socially and politically contextual. The focus of this research was to explore transgender people's experiences of 'low-level', or 'mundane' forms of criminal victimisation, incidents that I will later come to describe as 'micro-crimes'. As transphobic hate crime is a relatively understudied area within Criminology in the UK, there exists a significant gap in our understanding of how transphobic hate crime operates and the impact this has on victims.

The wider research project consisted of three primary forms of data collection. Firstly, an online survey was conducted that aimed to explore the prevalence of transphobic hate crime, the nature of crimes experienced, perceptions of policing and experiences of online abuse, among other issues. These issues were selected as they are key in contextualising 'everyday' and 'mundane' hate crime targeting individuals' gender identity. Distributing the survey online meant that participants had complete autonomy over when, where and how they participated in this research project. As a researcher, I was also keen to engage participants who may not publicly disclose their transgender identity, and facilitating the survey online provided an extra layer of anonymity (Potter and Chatwin 2011). A total of 396 transgender people participated in the online survey and were recruited primarily through social media.

Secondly, 31 semi-structured interviews were conducted with transgender people who live in the UK. Interviews were primarily facilitated online, as many participants reported that this was the most convenient and comfortable way for them to participate. The semi-structured interviews aimed to explore some of the trends identified from the online survey and provided a more detailed and contextualised account of transgender people's experiences of victimisation. The focus of the interviews was on participants' experiences of hate crime, with a specific interest in incidents of harassment, verbal abuse, damage to property and online hate speech. The questions centred on participants' understanding and perception of hate crime as a social and legal issue, fear of victimisation and their experiences of victimisation in relation to a number of identity characteristics. Interviews have been utilised by scholars researching hate crime experiences (Awan and Zempi 2017; Gavrielides 2012; Meyer

2010) as Patton (2002: 9) describes the 'simple yet elegant and insightful' nature of qualitative research.

It is the online survey and semi-structured interviews that inform this book. However, the wider research project also consisted of a discourse analysis of YouTube comments posted on videos relating to 'gender neutral toilets' (Colliver et al. 2019; Colliver and Coyle 2020). However, whilst I regularly make reference to this part of the project throughout, the results do not directly inform the claims made throughout. Purposive sampling was used for both the online survey and semi-structured interviews. The only inclusion criteria set was that participants should be transgender, live within the United Kingdom and be aged 16 or over at the time of participation. The age was set at 16 to avoid issues around parental consent needed to participate. It was felt that requiring parental consent could lead to a participant having to disclose their transgender identity to their family, which could place them in significant harm, and therefore 16- and 17-year-old participants were recruited without parental consent. Additionally, bullying within the school setting occurs in an institutionalised context and should be understood 'in terms of the situational dynamics of tension and fear within interactions' (Schott 2014: 205) and therefore the experiences are likely to differ from incidents outside of school. This is not to say that bullying within a school cannot also be considered a hate crime. On the contrary, many actions in school fit within a hate crime framework. However, within school settings it is likely that incidents will be dealt with within the school, using restorative justice. Participants were primarily recruited through social media, which proved to be the most effective method of reaching out to participants, despite having limitations that relate to the representativeness of the sample. However, a diverse sample was obtained in relation to gender identity, ethnicity, religion, age and disability status and was reflective of the broader UK population. In relation to the online survey, 23% of participants identified as male, 38% identified as female and 39% of participants identified as non-binary, gender-queer or gender-fluid. 27% of participants described themselves as heterosexual, whilst 19% were bisexual. 18% of the sample indicated they were pansexual. There was a range of other sexualities that participants identified as that made up smaller percentages of the total sample. Majority of the respondents to the survey were 'white British' (64.4%), which is high but is lower than the last UK census which estimates people who identify as White British make up 86% of the UK population (2011). In the last UK census, people who are 'Black African', 'Black Caribbean' and 'Black British' made up 3.3% of the UK population. However, these categories made up 7% of the sample population for this study. An overwhelming majority (67.4%) of participants identified as not belonging to any religious group. This is much higher than the national average as specified in the UK census (2011), which suggested only 25% of the UK population did not associate with a religious group. Of all religious affiliations described, Christianity was the most common religion (15.9%) selected. Other religions, including Pagan, Wicca, Islam, Hinduism and Sikhism. Despite other religious affiliations making up smaller percentages, it does highlight the diversity of participants. Participants were also asked whether they considered themselves to have a disability. 30.3% of participants considered themselves to have a disability. (See Appendix A for a full breakdown of interview participant demographics.)

The data collected from the online survey were analysed statistically, with a range of statistical tests being performed, looking for different relationships between a number of variables. A range of descriptive statistical tests were used to provide a general overview of the data collected and to evaluate the demographic information of participants. Binary logistic regression was the central statistical test that was conducted, considering the relationship between a number of different variables, and allowed for relationships to be established between experiences of victimisation and different identity characteristics. The semi-structured interviews were transcribed verbatim, and interviews were fully transcribed. The data were analysed thematically, guided by the six steps outlined by Braun and Clarke (2006). An inductive approach was taken to analyse the data as the lack of current research into the 'everyday' and 'mundane' experiences of hate crime targeting transgender people created difficulty in trying to locate pre-existing themes.

Careful consideration was given to the design of the research project, particularly given the inclusion of people aged 16 and 17, and also because of the potentially distressing impact upon participants retelling experiences of victimisation. This research project received a favourable opinion from Kingston University's Ethical Committee. Ample information regarding the nature and purpose of the research project was made available to participants before they agreed to participate. Participants were also offered opportunities to ask questions of the researcher before participating, to clarify any information that was unclear. Additionally, participants were made aware of their right to withdraw from the study throughout their participation, and also for a time after participation had ended. Informed consent was recorded both verbally and electronically.

In recognising the potentially distressing nature of participation, I had established a network of support services that were available to participants to access post-participation. As a researcher, my background is in youth work, facilitating both one-to-one and group support to young, lesbian, gay, bisexual, transgender and queer people. I have spent a significant amount of time supporting young people around issues of hate crime, discrimination, substance misuse, sexual health and mental health. I therefore approached the interviews with extensive experience in discussing sensitive topics, which aided the research process. Care was also taken not to use the word 'victim' excessively; although some argue that the word 'victim' is positive as it has connotations of blamelessness and innocence (Burton 1998), I was cautious not to impose the victim status onto participants who do not consider themselves victims. However, most participants in this study used the word 'victim' to describe themselves when discussing experiences of hate crime, and therefore this is the language that I use throughout this book. Confidentiality and anonymity were guaranteed to safeguard participants from unwanted exposure. Furthermore, confidentiality and anonymity were guaranteed to ensure participants felt comfortable in disclosing information in the knowledge that their opinions and experiences were confidential. To ensure the anonymity of participants throughout this book, all participants have been assigned pseudonyms (which participants were able to choose themselves) when data is reported. Allowing participants to choose their own pseudonyms was one of the ways in which I tried to engage participants throughout the research project, which was particularly important given my identity as a cisgender man.

Cisgender Researcher, Transphobic Hate Crime?

I feel it is important now to outline my motivations for researching this particular area, and also to reflect on how my identity as a cisgender man may have influenced the research project. Before I began this research project, I had worked for a leading 'Equality and Diversity' organisation based in South East London. Part of my role as an LGBTQ[1] Youth Worker included me facilitating youth groups for young LGBTQ people across various London boroughs and also providing one-to-one support for young people. Despite having always had an interest in homophobic, biphobic and transphobic hate crime, it was conversations with young people I worked with which influenced the focus of the research project that informs this book. I would regularly invite speakers along to the youth group to give an overview of services available to victims of hate crime. What struck me, and what also became apparent to the young people I worked with, was a lack of knowledge and understanding about gender identity and transphobic hate crime. It was through these conversations, and through encouragement from young transgender people I worked with, that the focus of this research was shaped.

In engaging in research that explores issues and the victimisation of transgender people, it was key for me to reflect on the research process, my participants, and my own identity throughout. I found that my identity interacted with the research process in three central ways. Firstly, my identity as a member of the LGBTQ community who has experienced discrimination, abuse and hate crime. Secondly, my cisgender identity positioning me as an outsider from transgender communities. Finally, my identity as a white, non-religious researcher and the power and privilege associated with my own identity. These various, and complex, relationships I had with the research process led to decisions being made regarding my interaction and access to participants.

As a cisgender, gay man, I brought my own experiences of oppression and hate crime to the research project. I had pre-existing ideas about how

---

[1] Lesbian, gay, bisexual, transgender and queer.

people understood and reacted to these harmful experiences. However, I was also aware that although both homophobia and transphobia are rooted in cis-normative, heteronormative ideals, the ways in which they manifest and are experienced are not the same. Therefore, whilst I felt a shared sense of experience in relation to exclusion, oppression and discrimination, I was keen to understand the differences and nuances between experiences. Whilst all LGBTQ identities have historically been constructed as deviant, the path to legislative protection and recognition has not been equal. I therefore recognised that the political, cultural and social climate is not equal for lesbian, gay, bisexual and transgender people. Whilst I tried to be 'objective' throughout the research, allowing data to challenge my own assumptions and beliefs, this was a conscious process that required constant reflection (Becker 1998; Hammersley 2000).

Despite feeling a sense of belonging to LGBTQ communities, I was aware that in the context of this research I was very much an outsider, both as a result of my identity as a cisgender person, and also my identity as a researcher. This became most evident to me when looking to recruit participants for the research project, in which I was often met with suspicion and silence. This is unsurprising given that transgender communities have historically had research conducted 'on' them, rather than 'with' or 'for' them, and that research has regularly been used to justify the ill-treatment, discrimination against, and oppression of transgender communities. Despite my position as an outsider, I received encouragement from transgender people that I supported, and their encouragement lead me to embrace Livia's (1996: 34) sentiment that 'we must take on the whole world; we cannot afford "no go areas" of the imagination; we cannot afford to refuse an opinion on any subject'. Despite my decision to maintain a focus on transgender and non-binary identities, I was conscious not to represent myself as a voice, or a representative of the community. As others have argued, 'no one should ever "speak for" or assume another's voice … it becomes a form of colonisation' (Sinister Wisdom Collective 1990). In order to achieve this, I wanted the data and the interpretation to be a collective result. Therefore, I approached participants after I had begun analysing and theming data and asked them to look through. By doing this, I wanted to encourage a collaborative approach to the results and themes that were developed from the data. I wanted to avoid transforming people's experiences into experiences that fitted with my research, or to retell their experiences in my own way.

Despite my outsider position, I acknowledged the privileged position I was in, as a white, cisgender man and how my access to education, resources and a position in which to discuss these issues may be very different to the access afforded to transgender and non-binary individuals (Divan et al. 2016). My work with young transgender and non-binary individuals, whom I have learnt so much from, but have also supported in times of need, left me with an overwhelming sense to use my position to illustrate the unjust ways in which many people are treated. Not only did my own personal identity lead me to be an outsider, it also represented potential power imbalances. My position at the top of most of the oppressive structures could have led to a power imbalance between myself and participants. I did not want my research project to exploit vulnerable people for an academic or research agenda (Arber 2006), which could have been a risk. To minimise this risk, I tried to empower participants through allowing them to make decisions about where and when they wanted to participate in interviews and surveys. I also designed the interviews to be semi-structured, so as to not oppose my own beliefs and assumptions onto the research project. Through re-engaging with participants after data collection was complete, I hope to have been able to portray participants' experiences in an authentic and accurate way.

Structure of Book

In '**Chap**. 2' of this book, I 'set the scene' for the following empirical chapters. In this chapter I address some of the key terms that I use throughout the book. In doing so, I highlight the complex and fluid nature of language and labels, associated with both 'hate crime' as a concept and 'transgender' as an identity category. Although I hope that the conclusions of this book will have international relevance, the empirical data drawn on is situated within the UK. In order to contextualise the experiences described throughout the book, I provide a brief overview of current legislative protections afforded to transgender people in relation to hate crime in the UK. This is key to ensure that the experiences described, which are often 'low-level', can be understood within a legal framework. This chapter also outlines the dominant theoretical and conceptual frameworks that are used within hate crime scholarship, drawing on the work of Perry (2001) and Chakraborti and Garland (2012). These works have been fundamental in an array of research exploring hate crime, often underpinning existing work. I focus specifically on these conceptualisations, as these are the perspectives in which I seek to build on, and expand our interpretation of these concepts throughout the book. It is therefore imperative to engage in a critical discussion at the outset, to build the foundations of claims made later in the book.

'**Chap.** 3' addresses the first contribution I make with this book, introducing and conceptualising participants' experiences of victimisation as 'micro-crimes'. This conceptualisation is key in demonstrating the seemingly 'normal' and 'everyday' nature of much discrimination, prejudice and abuse experienced by participants in this study. This challenges the often-sensationalised depiction of hate crime that relies on extreme cases of physical and sexual violence, overshadowing the often-mundane nature of victimisation. Introducing 'micro-crimes' allows us to engage with experiences which are often overlooked within hate crime scholarship, or subsumed within 'microaggression' literature. In this chapter I critique the complexities and contradictions often present within work exploring microaggressions, which primarily relate to the inconsistencies within the definition of microaggressions. In doing so, I draw upon, and provide a critique of, a commonly used definition provided by Sue et al. (2007, 2008). By addressing and clearly establishing the differences, whilst also acknowledging the connections between microaggressions, micro-crimes and more socially recognisable forms of victimisation I am able to interrogate the relationship that victims have with their experiences of abuse. This reconceptualisation allows for a better understanding and appreciation of all forms of victimisation and better illustrates the matrix of oppression that hate crime victims often face.

The focus of '**Chap.** 4' is deconstructing a range of dominant hierarchies that exist within hate crime scholarship. Utilising empirical data, I interrogate and challenge the existence of hierarchies relating to offence type, protected characteristics and the victim–perpetrator relationship. In this sense, I look at the ways in which notions of the 'ideal victim'

(Christie 1986) are understood to delegitimise transgender people as 'authentic' or 'worthy' victims. The implications this has for victims in relation to the likelihood of reporting transphobic hate crime to the police are explored, and it will be demonstrated that a significant amount of micro-crime victimisation remains unreported and unchallenged. This chapter demonstrates that the social awareness of particular forms of hate crime targeting particular groups of people significantly impact upon victims' perceptions of their own experiences. As such, this chapter deconstructs these hierarchies, highlighting the negative consequences these dominant conceptions of hate crime have for victims in recognising their own victimisation. These negative consequences include a personal lack of recognition of an individual's own victimisation when their experience does not coincide with dominant constructions of 'legitimate' hate.

The focus of '**Chap**. 5' is that of 'space', 'place' and 'identity construction'. I draw upon these concepts as both abstract ideas and as ideas that represent physical spaces. I draw upon my previous work that has explored the ways in which gendered spaces are constructed in an online context and discuss how these online constructs may manifest in the physical world (Colliver et al. 2019; Colliver and Coyle 2020). In particular, I focus on public, sex-segregated toilet facilities and how these spaces can be considered important in the role of identity formation, but also how the ability to access these spaces impacts on some transgender people's social mobility. I also discuss the ways in which identity operates within the context of physical, romantic and/or sexual spaces and relationships. In doing so, I draw upon the notion of 'fragile masculinity', which has previously been used to understand violence against gay men (Kaufman 2007). It is here that I argue that transgender women symbolise a figurative assault on cis-normative, heteronormative masculinities.

I finish this chapter by exploring how transgender people may experience exclusion from seemingly 'inclusive' spaces. I draw on the work of Serano (2007) to demonstrate how trans-misogyny operates to exclude transgender women, and feminine presenting people from LGBTQ 'inclusive' spaces. It is here that I also begin to interrogate how intersectional oppressions operate within these spaces, which tend to be dominated by cisgender, gay, white men. I also interrogate the concept of 'transnormativity' (Vipond 2015). In doing so, I explore how a 'master identity' may be imposed on an individual that does not align with their own sense of self, and how a 'master identity' may be used to exclude transgender people based on a number of factors including religion, race and disability status. Additionally, the exclusion of non-binary people from transgender inclusive spaces is explored, highlighting both personal and political motivations for reinforcing rigid western gender binaries.

In '**Chap.** 6' I revisit the contributions of Perry (2001) and Chakraborti and Garland (2012) and make a contribution to our understanding of how hate crime victimisation operates. I draw upon my previous work to introduce notions of '(in)visibility' and the complicated ways in which varying degrees of (in)visibility interact with the process of victimisation (Colliver and Silvestri 2020). I argue that '(in)visibility is a central feature of hate crime victimisation and that in order to fully understand hate crime we must adopt this lens through which to explore and understand the process of victimisation. I draw upon empirical data to demonstrate the importance of (in)visibility to participants. I extend the work of others who have engaged with the concept of (in)visibility previously (Chakraborti and Zempi 2012; Perry 2015) and extend our understanding of how this operates at both individual and structural levels. By reconceptualising (in)visibility, this concept becomes a useful tool through which we can address the perceived 'public' nature of hate crime and appreciate 'hate' that is experienced within private spheres.

It is here that I also draw on the work of Crenshaw (1989, 1991) to understand how transgender people relate to the (in)visibility of their transgender identity, and how their transgender identity interacts with the (in)visibility associated with other identity characteristics. I therefore emphasise the importance of adopting an intersectional framework when considering hate crime victimisation, as the experiences described by participants in this research are often not motivated by one, individual form of discrimination or prejudice. Through empirical data, I illustrate how (in)visibility is dualistic in nature and can both facilitate victimisation and act as a protective barrier to victimisation.

In '**Chap.** 7' of this book I offer some concluding thoughts. It is here that I seek to highlight how this research; the narratives collected can be used to inform policy and practice. In this chapter I highlight the implications that this research has for those who police incidents of transphobic hate crime, policy makers and prosecutors. I highlight the ways in which the concepts and arguments put forward in this book can be utilised across other studies of hate crime more broadly, studies of identities and also other research that interrogates other forms of victimisation. I achieve this by emphasising the key scholarly contributions I have made through this book.

References

Antjoule, N. (2013). *The hate crime report: Homophobia, biphobia and transphobia in London*. London: GALOP.

Arber, A. (2006). Reflexivity: A challenge for the research as practitioner? *Journal of Research in Nursing, 11*, 147–157.

Awan, I., & Zempi, I. (2017). 'I will blow your face OFF'—Virtual and physical world anti-Muslim hate crime. *British Journal of Criminology, 57*(2), 362–380.

Becker, H. (1998). *Tricks of the trade: How to think about your research while you're doing it Chicago*. Chicago: Chicago University Press.

Braun, V., & Clarke, V. (2006). Using thematic analysis in psychology. *Qualitative Research in Psychology, 3*(2), 77–101.

Burton, N. (1998). Resistance to prevention: Reconsidering feminist anti-violence rhetoric. In S. French, W. Teays, & L. Purdy (Eds.), *Violence against women: Philosophical perspectives* (pp. 182–200). New York: Cornell University Press.

Chakraborti, N., & Garland, J. (2012). Reconceptualizing hate crime victimization through the lens of vulnerability and 'difference'. *Theoretical Criminology, 16*(4), 499–514.

Chakraborti, N., Garland, J., & Hardy, S.-J. (2014). *The Leicester hate crime project: Findings and conclusions*. Leicester: University of Leicester.

Chakraborti, N., & Zempi, I. (2012). The veil under attack: Gendered dimensions of Islamophobic victimization. *International Review of Victimology, 18*(3), 269–284.

Christie, N. (1986). The ideal victim. In E. Fattah (Ed.), *From crime policy to victim policy* (pp. 17–30). London: Macmillan.

Colliver, B., & Coyle, A. (2020). Risk of sexual violence against women and girls' in the construction of 'gender-neutral toilets': A discourse analysis of comments on YouTube videos. *Journal of Gender-Based Violence, 4*(3), 359–376. https://doi.org/10.1332/239868020X15894511554617.

Colliver, B., Coyle, A., & Silvestri, M. (2019). The online 'othering' of transgender people in relation to 'gender neutral toilets'. In K. Lumsden & E. Harmer (Eds.), *Online othering: Exploring digital violence and discrimination on the web* (pp. 215–237). London: Palgrave Macmillan.

Colliver, B., & Silvestri, M. (2020). The role of (in)visibility in hate crime targeting transgender people. *Criminology and Criminal Justice*. [Online First]. https://doi.org/10.1177/1748895820930747.

Crenshaw, K. (1989). Demarginalizing the intersection of race and sex: A Black feminist critique of antidiscrimination doctrine, feminist theory and antiracist politics. *University of Chicago Legal Forum, 140*, 139–167.

Crenshaw, K. (1991). Mapping the margins: Intersectionality, identity politics, and violence against women of color. *Stanford Law Review, 43*(6), 1241–1299.

Divan, V., Cortez, C., Smelyanskaya, M., & Keatley, J. (2016). Transgender social inclusion and equality: A pivotal path to development. *Journal of the International AIDS Society, 19*(2), 79–84.

Gavrielides, T. (2012). Contextualising restorative justice for hate crime. *Journal of Interpersonal Violence, 27*(18), 3624–3643.

Hammersley, M. (2000). *Taking sides in social research: Essays on partisanship and bias*. London: Routledge.

Healy, J. (2020). 'It spreads like a creeping disease': Experiences of victims of disability hate crimes in austerity Britain. *Disability & Society, 35*(2), 176–200.

Henman, E. (2020, June 9). Rowing on Rowling: Jonathan Ross' daughter slams JK Rowling over 'transphobic' tweets just hours after her dad defends them. *The Sun*. Retrieved October 27, 2020, from https://www.thesun.co.uk/tvandshowbiz/11815200/jonathan-ross-daughter-rowling-transphobic-tweets/.

Home Office. (2019). *Hate crime, England and Wales, 2018–2019*. London: Home Office.

Home Office. (2020). *Hate crime, England and Wales, 2019–2020*. London: Home Office.

Jamel, J. (2018). *Transphobic hate crime*. London: Palgrave Macmillan.

James, S., Herman, J., Rankin, S., Keisling, M., Mottet, L., & Anafi, M. (2016). *The report of the 2015 U.S. Transgender Survey*. Washington: National Center for Transgender Equality.

Kaufman, M. (2007). The construction of masculinity and the triad of men's violence. In L. O'Toole, J. Schiffman, M. Kiter-Edwards (Eds.), *Gender violence: Interdisciplinary Perspectives*, 2nd edn, New York: New York University Press.

Livia, A. (1996). Daring to presume. *Feminism and Psychology, 6*(1), 31–41.

Metro Charity. (2014). *Youth chances: Summary of first findings*. London: METRO Charity.

Meyer, D. (2010). Evaluating the severity of hate-motivated violence: Intersectional differences among LGBT hate crime victims. *Sociology, 44*(5), 980–995.

Patton, M. (2002). *Qualitative research and evaluation methods* (3rd ed.). Thousand Oaks, CA: Sage Publications Limited.

Perry, B. (2001). *In the name of hate: Understanding hate crimes*. London: Routledge.

Perry, B. (2015). 'All of a sudden, there are Muslims': Visibilities and Islamophobic violence in Canada. *International Journal for Crime, Justice and Social Democracy, 4*(3), 4–15.

Potter, G., & Chatwin, C. (2011). Researching cannabis markets online: Some lessons from the virtual field. In J. Fountain (Ed.), *Markets, methods and messages: Dynamics in European drug research*. Lengerich: Pabst Science Publishers.

Schott, R. (2014). The life and death of bullying. In R. Schott & D. Sondergaard (Eds.), *School bullying: New theories in context* (pp. 185–206). Cambridge: Cambridge University Press.

Serano, J. (2007). *Whipping girl: A transsexual women on sexism and the scapegoating of femininity*. Emeryville, CA: Seal Press.

Shipman, T. (2020, June 14). Boris Johnson scraps plan to make gender change easier. *The Sunday Times*. Retrieved September 24, 2020, from https://www.thetimes.co.uk/article/boris-johnson-scraps-plan-to-make-gender-change-easier-zs6lqfls0.

Sinister Wisdom Collective. (1990). Editorial. *Sinister Wisdom, 42*(4), 1–6.

Stryker, S. (2006). (De)subjugated knowledges: An introduction to transgender studies. In S. Stryker & S. Whittle (Eds.), *The transgender studies reader* (pp. 1–18). New York: Routledge.

Sue, D. W., Capodilupo, C. M., & Holder, A. M. B. (2008). Racial microaggressions in the life experience of Black Americans. *Professional Psychology: Research and Practice, 39*(3), 329–336.

Sue, D. W., Capodilupo, C. M., Torino, G. C., Bucceri, J. M., Holder, A. M. B., Nadal, K. L., & Esquilin, M. (2007). Racial microaggressions in everyday life: Implications for clinical practice. *American Psychology, 62*(4), 271–286.

Turner, L., Whittle, S., & Combs, R. (2009). *Transphobic hate crime in the European Union*. London: Press for Change.

Vipond, E. (2015). Resisting transnormativity: Challenging the medicalization and regulation of trans bodies. *Theory in Action, 8*(2), 21–44.

2

Defining, Framing and Conceptualising Transphobic Hate Crime

Introduction

In the last chapter, I provided an overview of where this book sits within wider literature. In this chapter, I contextualise the key ideas developed and discussed throughout this book, by providing some acknowledgement of the wider debates within which the topic sits. I begin this chapter by engaging in a discussion around language, highlighting the complexities associated with the language regularly used in hate crime scholarship. In doing so, I provide a comparison of official and academic definitions of hate crime and identify some of the practical issues that may arise when policing incidents of hate crime as a result of definitional ambiguities. This chapter then engages in a discussion around terminology associated with gender identity. The subjective, nuanced and often-fluid nature of language can create significant difficulties when engaging in research around transphobic hate crime and these issues are outlined here. In this section, I highlight the particular definitions relating to key terms that I use throughout this book, as language is often ambiguous and multi-definitional. In defining these key terms, such as, transgender, transphobia and cisnormativity, the reader will be able to understand the content

B. Colliver, *Re-imagining Hate Crime*, Palgrave Hate Studies,
https://doi.org/10.1007/978-3-030-65714-7_2

of the empirical chapters within the particular framing within which this book is written.

I then engage in a discussion around legislation associated with policing hate crime. The discussion begins by exploring the dominant arguments, both for and against the implementation of legislative protection for minoritised, oppressed groups. This section then moves on to provide a brief overview of UK legislation, outlining a short history of legislation associated with hate crime within the UK, before moving on to the specific pieces of legislation that relate to the policing of transphobic hate crime. It will be highlighted that existing legislation is inadequate in appreciating the interlocking systems of oppression that some transgender people face. It is key to discuss existing legislation, as the empirical chapters later in this book speak directly to the material implications of existing legislation in contributing to a hierarchical nature of victimisation.

This chapter concludes by having a critical discussion around existing, dominant theoretical and conceptual frameworks within which hate crime is most often discussed. It is key to begin the book in this way, so that the following empirical chapters are strongly anchored within a wider system of understanding. Whilst the discussions in this chapter are not exhaustive, it is hoped that enough detail is provided to highlight the complexity of writing within this area. I begin by discussing the various ways in which different versions of Strain theories have been utilised to explore and explain hate crime offending. I then provide a discussion of Perry's (2001) concept of 'doing difference', which has gained significant prominence within hate crime scholarship, before engaging with the critiques offered by Chakraborti and Garland (2012). These key concepts underpin the empirical work that is presented throughout this book and the data presented both compliments and extends these notions.

Complex Language, Definitional Issues

The term 'hate crime' gained currency after a series of high-profile media events in the late 1990s with the publication of the Macpherson Report (1999), investigating the racially aggravated murder of Stephen Lawrence in 1993. Defining 'hate crime' is a complex task, compounded by significant differences between government definitions and academic definitions. Government definitions focus on individual incidents of victimisation, thus, reinforcing the media portrayals of hate crime as extreme, singular and public incidents. Legal definitions therefore lack an appreciation of the social, cultural and political contexts within which incidents of hate crime manifest. On the other hand, academic definitions tend to acknowledge the more complex social structures that create a climate in which marginalised and oppressed groups become deemed as legitimate targets for hate crime (Perry 2001). Despite the increased political and social acknowledgment of the concept of hate crime, there is no singular, universally agreed definition of what a hate crime is.

Despite there being no legislative definition of 'hate crime' in the United Kingdom, the term has been defined by The Home Office (2012) as:

> any criminal offence which is perceived, by the victim or any other person, to be motivated by a hostility or prejudice based on a personal characteristic. (2012: 6)

The personal characteristics referred to include race, religion, disability status, sexual orientation and transgender identity (Home Office 2012). However, it should be noted that police forces in England and Wales have the authority to *monitor* hate crimes against other communities, and many have now begun to monitor crime against sex workers, including North Yorkshire Police, and alternative subcultures, including Greater Manchester Police. The problematic nature of definitions of hate crime has been well documented (see, for example, Gerstenfeld 2004; Hall 2005; Jacobs and Potter 1998). The definition provided by the Home Office (2012) is extremely subjective and lacks clarity regarding the parameters of key terms such as 'perceived', 'hostility' and 'prejudice'. The requirement for a crime to only be 'perceived' by the victim, or any other person to be motivated by prejudice or hostility does not provide any objective measures through which this can be assessed. Perception is likely to be highly influenced by an individual's personal identity which may be deeply rooted in cultural and social norms. For some time, there was the added complexity to the policing of hate crimes by the overlap in definition between 'hate crimes' and 'hate incidents'. Hate incidents were originally defined by the Association of Chief Police Officers (2005) as:

> any incident, which may or may not constitute a criminal offence, which is perceived by the victim or any other person, as being motivated by prejudice or hate. (2005: 9)

The clear overlap between the definitions, in which both hate crimes and hate incidents could constitute a criminal offence, may have caused issues when recording and responding to hate crime. If an incident is recorded as such, rather than as a crime, then no criminal prosecution will occur. The definition of a 'hate incident' has since been updated to remove criminal offences and focuses solely on 'non-crime incidents' (Home Office 2018). As noted earlier, academic definitions tend to acknowledge the wider social, political and cultural context within which hate crimes manifest. Despite there being no universally agreed definition of hate crime, I would argue that Perry's (2001) conceptualisation of hate crime has emerged as significantly influential within hate crime scholarship, and she notes that:

> Hate crime … involves acts of violence and intimidation, usually directed towards already stigmatised and marginalised groups. As such, it is a mechanism of power and oppression, intended to reaffirm the precarious hierarchies that characterise a given social order. It attempts to re-create simultaneously the threatened (real or imagined) hegemony of the perpetrator's group and the 'appropriate' subordinate identity of the victim's group. It is a means of marking both the Self and the Other in such a way as to re-establish their 'proper' relative positions, as given and reproduced by broader ideologies and patterns of social and political inequality. (2001: 10)

The conceptualisation of hate crime offered by Perry (2001) clearly provides a more comprehensive account of hate crime, making direct reference to social stigma and oppression. Similar perspectives have also been offered with Hall (2012), suggesting that hate crimes arise from a multifaceted network of events, hierarchies and processes that are interpreted differently according to those involved. However, there are issues with such a detailed definition, in that it may be difficult to apply in a practical sense for those responsible with policing incidents of hate crime. Therefore, whilst there are significant differences between official definitions and academic definitions, it can be argued that they serve different purposes.

However, when considering the language associated with 'hate crime' more generally, commentators have noted the problematic nature of such emotionally charged language (Gerstenfeld 2004; Hall 2005; Sullivan 1999). The word 'hate' is primarily associated with extreme emotion (Hall 2005). It has been noted that not all incidents of hate crime are motivated by 'hate' (Gerstenfeld 2004) and that not all perpetrators are inherently prejudiced, but the incident may result from a specific set of circumstances (Chakraborti and Garland 2012). The problematic nature of language associated with 'hate crime' is key in this book, as in later chapters the concept of 'micro-crime' victimisation will be introduced to better frame the often 'everyday' and 'mundane' nature of hate crime targeting transgender and non-binary individuals. This is in line with the suggestion put forward by Sullivan (1999) that hate crime must be framed in significantly less emotionally charged language, such as bias, prejudice and hostility. Exploring these concepts in relation to hate crime provides a more nuanced understanding of the experiences of victims.

Another key term that is used throughout this book is 'socially recognisable'. This term is used primarily in relation to specific types of victimisation that participants experience. Incidents of victimisation, including harassment and verbal abuse, I often refer to as 'less socially recognisable' forms of victimisation. This term is not to undermine the impact of these forms of victimisation. Rather, as the empirical data presented throughout will demonstrate, these are forms of victimisation that are less socially and personally recognisable as criminal. As such, when making reference to how socially recognisable a particular form of victimisation is, this is specifically in relation to how recognisable the criminality of such victimisation is.

A number of phrases and words are used throughout this book that relate to gender identity and gender expression. Language associated with gender identity and gender expression is consistently changing, and it could be argued that this is representative of the fluid nature of gender identity and expression. Similar to that of hate crime, there is no one universally accepted definition of 'transgender'. Defining this term is a complex, yet necessary task. The term 'transgender' has been defined as denoting:

> a range of gender experiences, subjectivities and presentations that fall across, between or beyond stable categories of 'man' and 'woman'. 'Transgender' includes gender identities that have, more traditionally, been described as 'transsexual', and a diversity of genders that call into question an assumed relationship between gender identity and presentation and the 'sexed' body. (Hines 2010: 1)

This specific definition was utilised within the research project that this book is based on as it acknowledged gender expressions that fall between and beyond the gender binary of 'man' and 'woman'. The Western gender binary is the classification of sex and gender into two distinct, stable categories of 'male' and 'female'. However, it is acknowledged that there is some debate and contention within communities over the use of the term 'transgender', functioning as an 'umbrella' term. Monro (2003) acknowledges the inherently problematic nature of the term, arguing that the inclusion of such a wide range of social groupings leads to the failure to acknowledge their range of needs and interests. As such, throughout this book the term 'transgender', also 'trans' for shorthand, is used when referring to wider transgender communities. Language that is more specific is also used throughout, such as non-binary, to reflect participants' identities where appropriate.

The term 'non-binary' is regularly used throughout this book and refers to individuals whose gender identity falls somewhere between or beyond stable, normative and binary categories of male and/or female (Richards et al. 2016). Non-binary may also function as an umbrella term that may encapsulate gender identities including, but not exclusively, gender-queer, gender fluid and bi-gender (Vijlbrief et al. 2020). Non-binary individuals may experience and express their gender as neither exclusively masculine nor feminine. Their gender identity may vary between masculine and feminine, or there may be a partial or complete rejection of the gender binary (Monro 2019). It is important to note that although non-binary identities are gaining social recognition, there is currently no legal recognition of non-binary identities within England and Wales.

The terms 'transphobia' and 'transphobic' are also drawn upon throughout the empirical chapters that follow. Whilst it is acknowledged that various debates exist regarding the accuracy of these terms, they have been chosen as they are easily recognisable and identifiable within social discourses, and they also reflect the language used by participants. The use of the word 'phobia' to describe a dislike, intolerance or hatred towards trans people may be inaccurate, or misleading, in that it suggests these feelings are irrational. I acknowledge that these feelings can be conceptualised as wholly rational based on a social system that privileges cisgenderism, and therefore these views may not be perceived to be irrational as social systems position trans people as inferior, and 'less than'. In relation to homophobic hate crime, the term 'homophobia' is steadily being replaced by the more accurate term 'heterosexism' (Hill 2016). As such, it could be argued that there is a case to replace the term 'transphobia' with the term 'cisgenderism'. However, it is important that this book accurately reflects the experiences and language used by those who participated in this research study. As such, the term 'transphobia' is used to reflect a hostility towards the deviation of gender norms.

Another identity marker that is used throughout this book is 'cisgender'. This is a term that is used to describe an individual whose gender identity aligns with the sex they were assigned at birth (Stryker 2008). It has been claimed that this term is contentious owing to its potential for use in a pejorative way (Jamel 2018). However, I take the position within this book that these claims do not fully consider the social and political context within which this term is used. Cisgender people are the dominant social group, and therefore identifying them as such does not equate to victimisation. Additionally, as has been argued by Johnson (2015), an overwhelming amount of research around issues affecting trans people allows 'cisgender' to be the unspoken norm, by failing to actively recognise this as an identity marker. In this sense, many studies do not identify participants as 'cisgender', but do identify participants as 'trans'.

Resultantly, cisgender is presented as unremarkable and not requiring definition or specification whilst highlighting the exceptionality of trans people. In choosing to use the term 'cisgender', this book challenges dominant representations of both cisgender and trans people.

As a result of using the term cisgender, I frequently make reference to 'cisnormativity'. Cisnormativity is the belief that all individuals will experience their gender in a stable, fixed way which coincides with the sex they were assigned at birth (Shelton and Dodd 2020). Cisnormativity also reinforces that man and woman are the only legitimate gender identities. The concept of cisnormativity is intrinsically linked to gender essentialism that predicates certain innate, immutable biological or behavioural characteristics tied to an individual's gender. Cisnormative standards are intrinsically engrained within social life and manifest in a number of different ways. Examples of cisnormative practices, which often erase and exclude non-binary people include segregated public toilets, surveys and documentation in which 'male' and 'female' are the only available options and legal recognition of particular genders.

The final term I want to discuss here is the word 'victim'. The word 'victim' is a contested term, primarily relating to its connotations of helplessness, passiveness and vulnerability (Fohring 2018). In response to these negative connotations, there has been a shift towards conceptualising individuals as 'survivors' (Walklate 2014). The victim-survivor dichotomy is not a clear cut one, and neither label provides a value-free conceptualisation of people's experiences. However, despite the negative connotations associated with the term 'victim', I repeatedly refer to participants throughout this book as 'victims' who have been 'victimised'. I am aware of the debates surrounding this label, but I use the language used by participants to describe themselves and their experiences, and do not feel it is appropriate for me to impose a 'survivor' label upon them. Therefore, having considered this, I use both terms when participants specifically describe themselves with this language.

Responding to Hate Crime

Increased legislative protection for minoritised groups against 'hate crime' has developed across most Western countries (Brax 2016). Legislation has primarily been introduced in one of two ways. Firstly, specific aggravated offences have been introduced in which particular forms of victimisation against certain minoritised groups[1], motivated by hate and/or bias or prejudice, are introduced as a new piece of legislation. Secondly, legislation has been introduced which does not create new offences but provides the criminal justice system with the power to enact a 'sentence uplift'. A sentence uplift is primarily in the form of a higher financial penalty or longer period of incarceration. Most legislation associated with hate crime acts as a penalty enhancement, that is, the legislation is drawn upon to provide an additional penalty to the offender. As such, most hate-motivated offences can be prosecuted anyway, as the behaviour that constitutes a hate crime is criminalised already. However, without the specific provision enabled by penalty enhancement, the 'hate' element of an offence may not be considered when a punishment is decided.

The specific type of legislation introduced, and the groups that are deemed 'worthy' of protection, varies globally. This inconsistency also contributes to the difficulties faced when attempting to conceptualise hate crime as a phenomena. Despite this, differing international laws seem to share the purpose of identifying crime where prejudice and bias towards a 'protected characteristic', or presumed protected characteristic, are a fundamental part of the offence (Mason 2014). Additionally, much legislation and guidance around hate crime avoid directly using language associated with 'hate' and opt for a less emotionally charged phrasing such as bias and prejudice. It can therefore be argued that there is an inherent disconnect between the language commonly deployed when discussing 'hate' crime and the language drawn upon to practically police this form of victimisation.

However, the very introduction of these forms of legislation has proven to be a contested topic (Baron 2016; Card 2001; Hurd 2001; Mathis 2018). Many commentators have positioned this tension within the

[1] The minoritised groups which receive protection vary globally.

context of 'liberal societies' (Al-Hakim 2010; Hurd 2001) and some have claimed that hate crime legislation is fundamentally at odds with the values of a liberal society. It has been claimed that the risk of introducing such forms of legislation may lead to punishing an individual for their thoughts (Bruce 2001; Morsch 1991). Criminal law traditionally does not focus on motive when considering the punishment of an offender (Brax 2016). Criminal law within the UK focuses on two key aspects of a criminal offence: the *actus reus* and the *mens rea*. For non-hate offences, the legal system needs to only prove that an individual is guilty of committing a criminal act, and intending to (or acting recklessly or negligently) commit that act. The reason, or motive, for committing that criminal offence is not considered when determining a punishment for an offender, unless it is a mitigating factor (for example, self-defence). Consequently, in non-hate offences the court must only consider what the individual *wanted* to happen, whereas, it is claimed that for hate crimes, the court must also determine *why* an individual committed a certain criminal act (Bakken 2002).

In this sense, the same criminal act may lead to a more severe punishment because of the thoughts of the offender, in which some thoughts are deemed worse than others. This is what critics claim is the fundamental difference between hate crime, and parallel non-hate crime prosecution. Slippery slope arguments have been drawn upon to highlight that, if indeed, the purpose of hate crime legislation is to punish an individual more harshly for their thoughts; it sets a risky precedent which may pave the way to criminalizing any way of thinking that the dominant, majority group within a society reject (Baehr 2003). It is further claimed that regardless of why an individual holds a particularly biased belief, the individual cannot choose to hold a different belief. In this sense, it is questionable whether it is morally acceptable to punish an individual more severely for a belief that may be out of their control (Bakken 2002; Card 2001). However, as Brax (2016: 232) has argued, 'hate crime legislation does not target motives directly, but rather a certain connection between motives and actions. This connection takes the form of a decision—the decision to treat a particular (patently bad) motive as a reason to perform a criminal act'. It can therefore be argued that hate crime legislation does not directly punish individuals more harshly for their 'thoughts', but rather the conscious decision to act upon these thoughts which manifest in hate crimes.

The possibilities of hate crime legislation actually resulting in heightened levels of hate, bias and prejudice have also been explored (Miller 2003). It could be argued that increased legislative protection for minoritised or oppressed groups may heighten hate and bias on the basis that legislative protection is perceived to be special treatment, or even 'reverse discrimination'. Certainly, empirical research has shown that narratives of 'special treatment' are invoked in online discussions around implementing 'gender-neutral' toilets, which are often framed as accommodating the needs of trans people. Various forms of 'affirmative action' have also been negatively received by dominant majority groups who fear that minoritised, oppressed groups will benefit from an unfair advantage (Morgenroth and Ryan 2018). Whilst most research on affirmative action is in the context of education and employment, there are striking parallels between these contexts and the introduction of greater legislative protection for minoritised groups.

On the other hand, increasing legislative protections for minoritised groups has been conceptualised as compatible with liberal values and a positive move towards the recognition of specific harms that these groups face (Al-Hakim 2010; Mason 2014). The symbolic nature of increased legislative protection has been explored and Mason (2014: 75) has argued that the implementation of legislation allows 'liberal democratic states to make a public statement that such crime will not be tolerated'. It has been argued that 'criminal laws plays a fundamental role in furnishing the boundaries of (un)acceptable conduct' (Walters et al. 2018). Effective legislation and criminal prosecution therefore has symbolic value in the messages it sends to the public regarding acceptable and unacceptable behaviour. There is not only symbolic value in hate crime legislation but the introduction of this legislation may also provide a strong form of educational deterrence (Walters et al. 2018).

However, perhaps the most central argument in advocating for hate crime legislation is the conceptualisation of these crimes as 'message crimes' and the resultant community harm that manifests (Perry 2001). It has been argued that hate crimes 'hurt more' than non-hate parallel crimes (Iganski 2008; Iganski and Lagou 2015). As such, advocates for hate crime legislation argue that the enhanced penalty is to reflect the greater harm caused to both the individual, as well as to the minoritised groups the individual belongs to. Craig-Henderson and Sloan (2003: 482) argue that the impact of hate crime motivated by racism are 'qualitatively distinct' from non-hate parallel crimes. Research has consistently shown that victims of hate crime are more likely than non-hate victims to experience sleeping difficulties (Ehrlich 1992), nervousness and higher levels of depression (McDevitt et al. 2001), anger (Herek et al. 1997) and more common thoughts of suicide (McDevitt et al. 2001). Recognising these disproportionate harms that victims of hate crime experience forms the foundation of many arguments for increased legislative protection.

The introduction of these offences was significant as it led to new maximum penalties for specified offences, which was generally seen as a positive move in addressing hate crime, although there has been an exploration of and calls for less punitive measures (Gavrielides 2012; Walters and Hoyle 2010). Restorative justice has received some academic attention in the context of hate crime offences but remains on the periphery of hate crime scholarship. This approach focuses on healing the harms caused by crime and may be used instead of, or in conjunction with, more punitive measures to address the offence. The aim of restorative justice is to engage victims, offenders and communities in meaningful communication about the crime and the subsequent harms experienced. Restorative justice is not widely used in the UK in relation to hate crime, despite Paterson et al. (2018) finding that over half of LGBT and Muslim participants preferred a restorative justice approach compared to an enhanced penalty. The Home Office's (2012) 'hate crime action plan' made a brief mention of investigating the possibility of expanding the offer of restorative justice in cases of hate crime. However, six years later, the Home Office's (2018) action plan still indicated that restorative justice options should be explored further, suggesting that not much progress had been made during this time.

As mentioned earlier, there is inconsistency globally around which characteristics receive 'protected' status. In England and Wales, race, religion, sexual orientation, disability status and transgender identity are protected and monitored annually by the police. Even within the UK, there are varying levels of legislative protection offered to trans people.

Scotland introduced the Offences (Aggravated by Prejudice) Scotland Act in 2009, which gives protected characteristic status to 'transgender identity', including non-binary identities. This is more progressive than legislative protection in England and Wales, which defines transgender identity as having undergone, undergoing or proposing to undergo a process, or part of a process of gender reassignment, therefore excluding many non-binary individuals. At the time of writing, there is currently no specific legal protection for trans people in Northern Ireland. However, an independent review of hate crime legislation in Northern Ireland is currently being undertaken, addressing issues relating to definitions and protected characteristics. Issues of inconsistency become more stark when taking a European or International perspective (see, for example, Jamel 2018 for a more detailed overview of European and International legislation).

Despite there being no legislative recognition of 'hate crime' within England and Wales, there is an array of legislation that polices incidents of crime that are commonly referred to as 'hate crime'. The history of legislation addressing hate crime generally is more extensive than the relatively brief history of legislation concerning transphobic hate crime. This history can be dated back to the introduction of the Race Relations Act (1965) which criminalised discrimination based on race, ethnicity and/or nationality. Some decades after, the Crime and Disorder Act (1998) introduced a number of 'racially aggravated offences'. This Act was amended in 2001 in light of the implementation of the Anti-Terrorism, Crime and Security Act (2001) to include a number of 'religiously aggravated offences'. If an individual is sentenced under the Crime and Disorder Act (1998), they can be subject to a higher maximum penalty. For example, the maximum penalty for common assault is six months' imprisonment, but if found guilty under the Crime and Disorder Act (1998) the maximum penalty is two years' imprisonment. This piece of legislation only creates specific aggravated offences in relation to race and religion and does not create specific aggravated offences related to the other protected characteristics.

In 2003 the Criminal Justice Act was implemented, in which sentencing provisions were introduced in sections 145 and 146. These sections allow courts to increase the sentence imposed on an offender for any offence which is proven to be motivated by hostility or prejudice based on a number of personal characteristics including an individual's actual or perceived race, religion, transgender identity, sexual orientation or disability status. At the initial time of implementation, section 146 of the Criminal Justice Act did not apply to cases where hostility was based on the victim's transgender identity. It was only with the introduction of the Legal Aid, Sentencing and Punishment of Offenders Act (2012) that amended section 146 of the Criminal Justice Act (2003), that transgender identity became a characteristic to be considered as a factor during the sentencing of an offender. Not only did this legislation define transgender identity as an aggravating factor, it further increased the starting punishment from 15 years' imprisonment to 30 years' imprisonment in relation to transphobically aggravated murder. In comparison to the Crime and Disorder Act (1998), offences covered by the sentencing provisions introduced in the Criminal Justice Act are recorded in law as the basic offence, not an aggravated offence.

It should be noted that although there have been significant developments in legislation within England and Wales; the current legislative protections are not without flaws. The current process for considering an aggravating factor does not acknowledge the nuanced intersectional oppressions individuals may face, and consequently, only one aggravating factor can be considered at sentencing. As a result, a perpetrator of a crime which may have been motivated by prejudices of misogyny, transphobia and racism, will only have one characteristic considered at sentencing. This means that the legal recognition of identities is overly simplistic and may reinforce a hierarchy of victimisation; this will be discussed in the next chapter. However, for now, it is important to note that the differing levels of legislative protections offered create a hierarchy of identities, and a symbolic message is conveyed to victim groups about which is most 'worthy' of protection (Garland 2011).

Another piece of legislation that is discussed is not directly related to hate crime legislation; however, it has been key in providing legal recognition to trans peoples' gender identity. In 2004, the Gender Recognition Act (GRA) was introduced which significantly 'improved the protocols … [that] protect the rights of transgender people' (Jamel 2018: 43). However, it should be noted that the GRA simultaneously reinforced the gender binary and did not allow for alternative gender expressions. Resultantly, there is no legal acknowledgement of non-binary genders. It has also been claimed that the current process for obtaining legal recognition is overly bureaucratic, inhumane and invasive (Miles 2018). The act, although progressive, did not extend any legal recognition to those under the age of 18 in relation to their gender identity. On the other hand, the act did place a duty on criminal justice agencies to improve sensitivity when working with transgender communities as this act prohibits the disclosure of an individual's transgender identity without their consent. This was also an important piece of legislation as it did not require an individual to have undergone gender reassignment surgery in order to obtain legal recognition of their gender.

The final piece of legislation that will be discussed is the Equality Act (2010), which, similar to the Gender Recognition Act (2004), does not specifically relate to hate crime. This act makes 'gender reassignment' a protected characteristic, and similar to other pieces of legislation, provides no legal recognition of non-binary identities. However, it does implement a number of regulations and guidelines in relation to education, employment and a range of other public services. These regulations prohibit discrimination in these spheres on the basis of an individual's gender reassignment or perceived gender reassignment. For an individual to possess the protected characteristic of 'gender reassignment', having undergone gender reassignment surgery is not necessary, but they must be proposing to, or undergoing, gender reassignment surgery. Whilst this piece of legislation may be perceived as progressive, and it certainly has symbolic value, it contributes to the reaffirmation of the gender binary.

Understanding Transphobic Hate Crime

This chapter ends with an overview of current theoretical and conceptual explanations of hate crime more generally and then specifically in relation to transphobic hate crime. A number of different perspectives have been utilised within hate crime scholarship, and it is beyond the scope of this book to provide a detailed critique of every perspective. Rather, what follows is an overview of dominant perspectives that the empirical data used within this book directly speaks to. As such, the key theoretical perspectives are outlined to provide a strong grounding for the upcoming empirical chapters. Having an understanding of theoretical perspectives is key in framing the findings of this research project. Additionally, the empirical chapters form the foundation of a considerable critique and extension of current, dominant perspectives.

Despite the complexities found in conceptualising and defining hate crime, two theories have emerged as dominant when seeking to explain the causal factors of hate crime. Various forms of 'strain theory', including Merton's (1968) and Agnew's (1992) perspectives have been drawn upon when exploring hate crime (Kelly 1993; Ray and Smith 2002), whilst more recently Perry's (2001) concept of 'doing difference' has been central in academic theorising. Merton (1968), when theorising around offending more generally, argued that criminal activity is best understood by acknowledging the disequilibrium created by the gap between socially prescribed goals and the legitimate means of achieving those goals. A number of factors such as inequalities in education, housing and other factors that influence an individual's socio-economic status may create barriers to obtaining financial and material goals set by capitalist structures. It is therefore postulated that an individual may resort to criminal activity as a means of obtaining material possessions that are deemed an essential marker of individual success within capitalist societies. As such, the criminal activity serves as a method to alleviate the strain felt by individuals created by the barriers to obtaining societal goals legitimately.

It was later theorised that individuals may experience strain based on a number of different contexts (Agnew 1992). The strains outlined by Agnew are directly caused by another individual and include preventing someone from achieving a positively valued goal, causing the loss of valued stimuli and presenting the individual with negatively valued stimuli. Strain theory has been applied and linked to the cause of racially aggravated hate crime (Gadd et al. 2005; Ray and Smith 2002). The media often sensationalise reports around immigration and housing and employment; as a result, ethnic minority groups are often portrayed as being a strain on the UK's financial economy and also at a more individual level in relation to housing and employment. However, adopting a socio-economic approach when seeking to explore hate crime against transgender people provides only tenuous links. For example, claims made by Pemberton (2018) that the National Health Service (NHS) spends at least two million pounds of 'tax-payer money' on 'sex operations' could be argued to pose a potential socio-economic threat.

Nevertheless, it is much more feasible to adopt a strain perspective when applying the principles outlined by Agnew (1992). The presence of trans people in public domains threatens the cisnormative values of modern society (Bibbings 2004). Persistent media narratives that serve to delegitimise, demonise and other transgender people results in a culture of suspicion, segregation and denigration. Therefore, transgender people's very existence could be conceptualised as noxious stimuli to those who consume such media in an uncritical way. Media narratives often present transgender people by drawing upon harmful stereotypes, emphasising criminality (Hymas 2019), infringing upon cisgender people's rights (Hellen 2019), and being a risk to children. Given the mass consumer population of mainstream media, it would therefore be unsurprising to find that these narratives are consumed and reproduced by large sections of the general population. Indeed, research has shown that similar discourses are drawn upon by people when engaging with issues associated with gender in an online context (Colliver et al. 2019; Colliver and Coyle 2020). The links emphasised between trans communities and crime is likely to constitute that of a negative stimuli. Similarly, the portrayal of trans communities as infringing upon cisgender people's rights is likely to constitute a reasonable expectation of causing the loss of a positively valued stimuli. As such, a strain perspective could certainly be argued to have merit when exploring the motivations of perpetrators who commit transphobic hate crime.

However, Perry's (2001) perspective of 'doing difference' has also been central in understanding the phenomenon of hate crime, as outlined in her definition of 'hate crime' earlier in this chapter: the idea of 'marking both the Self and the Other in such a way' that highlights difference and therefore provides a rationale for ostracising and subordinating groups deemed 'different' (2001: 10). The 'difference' she refers to relates to a number of socially constructed hierarchies pertaining to gender, race, disability and sexuality among other identity markers. As such, hate crime is best understood as an extreme form of discrimination against those who have been identified as 'different'. Through the construction of these hierarchies, a range of dichotomous 'in-groups' and 'out-groups' are constructed and positioned as in direct competition for power and social recognition. Perry (2001) argues that 'difference', in and of itself is a social construct, and those deemed 'different' are constructed and judged in negative relational terms. As the dominant norm, cisgender identities rarely encounter the same level of interrogation that trans identities do. In relation to gender, in the UK, and across large parts of Europe and the West, cisgender identities have been established as the dominant majority, and therefore the social norm. As such, transgender and non-binary people are conceptualised as 'different' and therefore negatively judged by cisgender norms. Therefore, when constructing and expressing individual identity, this should be done within the constraint of the given gender binary, which in turn reinforces societal structural orders. Allport (1954) argued that within social hierarchies, the majority group will always perceive themselves as dominant and this results in other groups being positioned as subordinate. This can also be applied to intra-community power struggles and subordination.

The 'difference' presented by the 'out-group' may lead to feelings of insecurity and fear within the 'in-group' about their dominant place in society. These feelings of anxiety and/or fear may be heightened when the 'subordinate group' gain increasing social and political recognition. This is often accompanied by increasing equality initiatives, which are often conceptualised as infringing on the rights of the dominant group (Colliver et al. 2019). Dominant groups must therefore ensure that the subordinate minority remains subordinate, which functions to maintain the relational power dynamics which Perry (2001: 2) argues 'leave minority members vulnerable to systemic violence'. The power dynamic, which maintains the dominant group's dominance over the subordinate group, is preserved through the social policing of the minority group. This may manifest in a number of ways including animosity, discrimination and violence. Trans and non-binary people may therefore experience transphobic victimisation because of complex, fluctuating social structures and hierarchies. Jauk (2013: 808) suggests that 'violence against trans people is often triggered by gender non-conformity and violence is a form of gender policing'. Transphobic hate crimes are therefore not only personal, but also symbolic. When a transphobic hate crime is committed, a societal message reaffirming the trans communities' subordination to cisgender communities is conveyed, therefore legitimising the continued oppression they experience (Burgess et al. 2013). It can therefore be argued that trans individuals experience hate crime and victimisation as an instrument of 'intimidation and control exercised' by those who need to reaffirm their perceived precarious position in a social hierarchy (Perry 2001: 2). This conceptualisation has been supported by academics who claim that trans individuals who fail to present themselves according to society's accepted beliefs about male and female presentation will be more at risk of experiencing 'regular and extreme levels of physical and verbal abuse' (Johnson et al. 2007: 18; Spalek 2008). Ultimately, Perry (2001) argues that hate crime is a means of subjugating trans and non-binary people for 'doing difference'.

Perry (2009) has also argued that hierarchy, alongside structure and dominance are key in understanding the nature of hate crime. The gender binary that is often rigidly enforced in the UK reflects the levels of discomfort associated with perceiving gender as a spectrum (Hill 2003). Binary gender options are consistently reinforced through popular media, legislation and politics (Knights and Kerfoot 2004). By deviating from the gender binary, trans and non-binary people blur the boundaries of deeply engrained ideas surrounding gender. They also challenge essentialist assumptions about gender. Hall (2005: 78) claims that 'hierarchal structure of power in society is based upon notions of 'difference' with the 'mythical norm' at the top and those who are 'different assigned subordinate positions'. Structural and societal hierarchies therefore feed in to the establishment of transphobia and create insecurities within those at the top of the hierarchy so that their power and privilege are threatened. As a reaction to this fear, dominance is exerted over trans and non-binary people which manifests in the form of 'gender-bashing'. It is therefore argued throughout this book that trans and non-binary people experience victimisation as a result of the perceived threat to the structural order by challenging predetermined gender arrangements.

Whilst it can be argued that through the emotion of fear, strain and difference, the perspectives previously discussed can be conceptualised as complementary, rather than competitive or divergent as explanatory models of hate crime. However, both strain perspectives and notions of 'difference' fail to account for individual difference in the perpetration of hate crime. They do not account for why not everyone in dominant groups commits hate crimes, nor do they account for why particular groups of people may become a bigger target than others. Walters (2011) provides a thoughtful critique of these two dominant perspectives and suggests they illuminate macro-level explanations of hate crime, but they fail to address or acknowledge the individual agency of perpetrators. Walters (2011) advocates for considering another dimension and draws upon self-control theory (Gottfredson and Hirschi 1990) to address the missing facet of hate crime theorisation. Self-control theory proposes that most people are able to control their behaviour, which inhibits their participation in crime. Goode (2008) postulates that the ability to exert self-control over an individual's behaviour is a learnt behaviour accumulated through childhood. A failure to learn self-control can result in impulsive and insensitive behaviour. According to Gottfredson and Hirschi (1990) a lack of self-control is the key influencing factor that causes criminality. As this perspective addresses individual accounts, Walters (2011) suggests that synthesising aspects of self-control theory with strain theory, alongside 'doing difference' provides a more holistic explanation of hate crime. Applying this to the phenomenon of transphobic hate crime, we could therefore suggest that cisgender people may experience fear, which causes feelings of strain as a result of the threat trans people pose to cisnormative societal norms. Individuals with low self-control may therefore react to this fear with impulsive, aggressive and violent behaviour against trans people. Those with higher levels of self-control may be able to rationalise their feelings of fear in less confrontational, aggressive ways.

More recently, Chakraborti and Garland (2012) have offered a further critique of Perry's (2001) theory of 'doing difference' and claim it perpetuates notions of 'stranger danger'. They also claim that this perspective has been embraced by academics in ways that exclude the experiences of a range of marginalised groups. Chakraborti and Garland (2012) draw upon the work of McGhee (2007) to reconceptualise conventional frameworks and highlight the spontaneity of many hate crimes. In doing so, they emphasize that many hate crimes are not the result of any deep-rooted, inherent prejudice or hatred, but result from a specific, individual situation and context. As such, it is argued that not all perpetrators of hate-motivated crimes are prejudiced all of the time, but may act in a prejudicial or hateful way in response to a particular 'trigger event'. In this sense, it can be suggested that a vast array of hate crimes may only be partly motivated by prejudice, therefore contesting the idea that all hate crimes function as a mechanism to oppress the 'other'. In reconceptualising our understanding of hate crime, Chakraborti and Garland (2012) invoke the concept of 'vulnerability'. There are some concerns over the use of the word 'vulnerable' in relation to victimisation, particularly in relation to its connotations of weakness, lack of agency and a need for protection (Roulstone et al. 2011). However, there are less conceptual and more practical implications of adopting 'vulnerability' as a perspective. Perry (2008) claims that this may lead to patronizing attitudes for those responsible for responding to and policing hate crime. As such, this may manifest in an individual's victimisation being miscategorised or victims may be perceived as needing pity and/or compassion.

However, Chakraborti and Garland (2012) address these concerns and suggest that a conceptual focus on 'vulnerability' need not be underpinned by negative connotations, but rather represents offenders' perceptions of victims, rather than suggesting that victims encounter hate crime as an inevitability. In this conceptualisation, they claim that hate crime victimisation cannot be fully understood with an explicit focus on 'difference'. Instead, they argue that it is the victims' perceived vulnerability, which may be intrinsically tied to their 'difference', that makes someone a suitable target for hate crime victimisation. Adopting the perspective of vulnerability to reconceptualise hate crime frameworks allows for a broader recognition of intersectional oppressions that may therefore increase the potentially perceived vulnerability of a victim. As noted earlier in this chapter, hate crime legislation does not currently reflect the complexity of individuals' identity characteristics. Chakraborti and Garland (2012) argue that utilising the lens of vulnerability allows for a greater understanding of the nuances involved and the interplay between recognised minority characteristics, and wider social, class and political marginalisation.

In adopting the perspective of vulnerability, Chakraborti and Garland also seek to draw attention to groups of victims who are often excluded from traditional hate crime frameworks, including, but not exclusively, homeless people (Wacholz 2009) and sex workers (Carter 2010). Utilising the notion of vulnerability allows for a greater recognition of victim groups which do not appear in official discourse. Resultantly, they do not benefit from the legal and social protections that established hate crime victims' experiences. They additionally claim that we should heed caution when discussing a 'community', which is often an empty notion used to describe a diverse and heterogeneous population. As such, the unique experiences and differences within this 'community' are overlooked. This is key when discussing transphobic hate crime, due to the diverse range of gender identities and also differing experiences of victimisation. Existing literature suggests that the likelihood of victimisation is dependent upon a number of factors, including an individual's ability to 'pass' (Jamel 2018) and the gender they present as (Kidd and Witten 2008). Therefore, I refer primarily to 'communities' throughout this book as an acknowledgement of the diversity of trans populations.

Later in this book I draw upon empirical data to offer a critique of the perspectives previously discussed. In doing so, I will suggest that although these perspectives are useful in understanding hate crime victimisation, we must address these perspectives through the lens of '(in)visibility'. As will be demonstrated, (in)visibility is not a dichotomous concept and consists of various functions and manifestations (Colliver and Silvestri 2020). Appreciating the role '(in)visibility' plays in hate crime victimisation allows for a more comprehensive understanding of this phenomenon, at both the individual and structural level.

Conclusion

In this chapter I hope to have provided a relatively brief, yet comprehensive overview of some of the current tensions, issues and debates within hate crime scholarship. Although it is beyond the scope of this book to provide a thorough and detailed critique of all of these issues, I hope to have done justice in outlining these key matters. In this chapter, I have highlighted the various challenges faced by academics, practitioners and lawmakers when attempting to define and conceptualise hate crime. The very subjective nature of hate crime creates practical difficulties in legislating against and policing hate crimes. This is compounded by a lack of clarity associated with the language used in legislation, which is often not defined thoroughly and may therefore lead to inconsistencies in the policing and prosecution of hate crime.

This chapter has also outlined and defined the key terms that are used throughout this book to denote various gender identity markers. As noted, language associated with gender identity is fluid and changes rapidly, perhaps as a strong indication as to the fluid nature of gender. In doing so, I have emphasised the importance of identifying and marking 'cisgender' as an identity label. This conscious decision is to move away from only identifying and interrogating trans identities and leaving cisgender identities unmarked, and uninterrogated. Issues around the use of the term 'phobia' were discussed, highlighting that issues of cisnormativity engrained into social structures may result in intolerance, fear or disgust being rationalised as a legitimate response to transgender people.

The moral and philosophical debates surrounding enhanced punishment were engaged with and framed within the context of a liberal society. Although it was not the purpose of this chapter to put forward an argument either way, to do so would require significantly more space; I have presented they key arguments put forward both for and against penalty enhancement legislation. However, it is important to note that the debate is rather more nuanced and overlapping than simply two opposing sides. In this chapter I have also provided an overview of key pieces of legislation in the UK that relate to hate crime more broadly, and also legislation that provides legal recognition to trans people. In doing so, the current shortfall of legislative protections has been highlighted, including that current legislative provisions reaffirm the gender binary and reinforce a victim hierarchy.

I conclude this chapter by providing an overview of the theoretical perspectives that have dominated hate crime scholarship. It was important to provide this context, as the studies and perspectives drawn upon in this chapter have provided the foundation for this book. It is these works that provided a starting point for the research project that this book is based on. As such, many of the contributions that I hope to make to the field of hate studies with this book are in relation to, and build upon, the work of those outlined in this chapter.

References

Agnew, R. (1992). Foundation for a general strain theory of crime and delinquency. *Criminology, 30*, 47–87.

Al-Hakim, M. (2010). Making room for hate crime legislation in liberal societies. *Criminal Law and Philosophy, 4*(3), 341–358.

Allport, G. (1954). *The nature of prejudice*. Cambridge, MA: Addison-Wesley Publishing Co.

Association of Chief Police Officers. (2005). *Hate crime: Delivering a quality service—Good practice and tactical guidance*. London: Home Office Police Standards Unit.

Baehr, A. (2003). A feminist liberal approach to hate crime legislation. *Journal of Social Philosophy, 34*(1), 134–152.

Bakken, T. (2002). The effects of hate crime legislation: Unproven benefits and unintended consequences. *International Journal of Discrimination and the Law, 5*(4), 231–246.

Baron, M. (2016). Hate crime legislation reconsidered. *Metaphilosophy, 47*(4–5), 504–523.

Bibbings, L. (2004). Heterosexuality as harm: Fitting in. In P. Hillyard, C. Pantazis, S. Tombs, & D. Gordon (Eds.), *Beyond criminology: Taking harm seriously*. London: Pluto.

Brax, D. (2016). Motives, reasons, and responsibility in hate/bias crime legislation. *Criminal Justice Ethics, 35*(3), 230–248.

Bruce, T. (2001). *The new thought police*. New York: Three Rivers Press.

Burgess, A., Regehr, C., & Roberts, A. (2013). *Victimology: Theories and applications* (2nd ed.). Burlington: Jones and Bartlett Learning.

Card, C. (2001). Is penalty enhancement a sound idea? *Law and Philosophy, 20*(2), 195–214.

Carter, H. (2010, December 21). Crossbow cannibal victims' drug habits made them vulnerable to violence. *The Guardian*. Retrieved April 8, 2020, from https://www.theguardian.com/uk/2010/dec/21/crossbow-cannibal-victims-drug-habit.

Chakraborti, N., & Garland, J. (2012). Reconceptualizing hate crime victimization through the lens of vulnerability and 'difference'. *Theoretical Criminology, 16*(4), 499–514.
Colliver, B., & Coyle, A. (2020). Risk of sexual violence against women and girls' in the construction of 'gender-neutral toilets': A discourse analysis of comments on YouTube videos. *Journal of Gender-Based Violence, 4*(3), 359–376. https://doi.org/10.1332/239868020X15894511554617.
Colliver, B., Coyle, A., & Silvestri, M. (2019). The 'online othering' of transgender people in relation to 'gender neutral toilets'. In K. Lumsden & E. Harper (Eds.), *Online othering: Exploring digital violence and discrimination on the web* (pp. 215–238). London: Palgrave Macmillan.
Colliver, B., & Silvestri, M. (2020). The role of (in)visibility in hate crime targeting transgender people. *Criminology and Criminal Justice*. [Online First]. https://doi.org/10.1177/1748895820930747.
Craig-Henderson, K., & Sloan, L. (2003). After the hate: Helping psychologists help victims of racist hate crime. *Clinical Psychology: Science and Practice, 10*, 481–490.
Ehrlich, H. (1992). The ecology of anti-gay violence. In G. Herek & K. Berrill (Eds.), *Hate crimes: Confronting violence against lesbians and gay men* (pp. 105–112). Thousand Oaks, CA: Sage Publications.
Fohring, S. (2018). What's in a word? Victims on 'victim'. *International Review of Victimology, 24*(2), 151–164.
Gadd, D., Dixon, B., & Jefferson, T. (2005). *Why do they do it? Racial harassment in North Staffordshire*. Keele: Centre for Criminological Research, Keele University.
Garland, J. (2011). Difficulties in defining hate crime victimization. *International Review of Victimology, 18*(1), 25–37.
Gavrielides, T. (2012). Contextualizing restorative justice for hate crime. *Journal of Interpersonal Violence, 27*(18), 3624–3643.
Gerstenfeld, P. (2004). *Hate crimes: Causes, controls and controversies*. London: Sage Publications.
Goode, E. (2008). *Out of control: Assessing the general theory of crime*. Stanford: Stanford University Press.
Gottfredson, M., & Hirschi, T. (1990). *A general theory of crime*. Stanford: Stanford University Press.
Hall, N. (2005). *Hate crime*. Cullompton: Willan Publishing.
Hall, N. (2012). Policing hate crime in London and New York City: Some reflections on the factors influencing effective law enforcement, service provi-

sion and public trust and confidence. *International Review of Victimology, 18*(1), 73–87.
Hellen, N. (2019, November 23). Labour 'putting women at risk' with manifesto trans pledge. *The Times*. Retrieved April 6, 2020, from https://www.thetimes.co.uk/article/labour-putting-women-at-risk-with-manifesto-trans-pledge-2njcv8z6g.
Herek, G., Gillis, J., Cogan, J., & Glunt, E. (1997). Psychological sequelae of hate crime victimization among lesbian, gay, and bisexual adults: Prevalence, psychological correlates, and methodological issues. *Journal of Interpersonal Violence, 12*, 195–215.
Hill, D. (2003). Genderism, transphobia, and genderbashing: A framework for interpreting anti-transgender violence. In B. Wallace & R. Carter (Eds.), *Understanding and dealing with violence: A multicultural approach* (pp. 113–136). Thousand Oaks, CA: Sage Publications Ltd.
Hill, D. (2016). Transphobia. In A. Goldberg (Ed.), *The Sage encyclopedia of LGBTQ studies* (pp. 1271–1272). London: Sage Publications Ltd.
Hines, S. (2010). Introduction. In S. Hines & T. Sanger (Eds.), *Transgender identities: Towards a social analysis of gender diversity* (pp. 1–22). New York: Routledge.
Home Office. (2012). *Challenge it, report it, stop it: The government's plan to tackle hate crime*. London: Home Office.
Home Office. (2018). *Action against hate: The UK government's plan for tackling hate crime—'Two years on'*. London: Home Office.
Hurd, H. (2001). Why liberals should hate 'hate crime legislation'. *Law and Philosophy, 20*(2), 215–232.
Hymas, C. (2019, July 9). One in 50 prisoners identifies as transgender amid concerns inmates are attempting to secure prison perks. *The Telegraph*. Retrieved April 6, 2020, from https://www.telegraph.co.uk/news/2019/07/09/one-50-prisoners-identify-transsexual-first-figures-show-amid.
Iganski, P. (2008). *Hate crime and the city*. London: Policy Press.
Iganski, P., & Lagou, S. (2015). Hate crimes hurt some more than others: Implications for the just sentencing of offenders. *Journal of Interpersonal Violence, 30*(10), 1696–1718.
Jacobs, J., & Potter, K. (1998). *Hate crimes: Criminal law and identity politics*. Oxford: Oxford University Press.
Jamel, J. (2018). *Transphobic hate crime*. London: Palgrave Macmillan.
Jauk, D. (2013). Gender violence revisited: Lessons from violent victimization of transgender identified individuals. *Sexualities, 16*(7), 807–825.

Johnson, A. (2015). Beyond inclusion: Thinking toward a transfeminist methodology. In V. Demos & M. Segal (Eds.), *At the center: Feminism, social science and knowledge* (pp. 21–42). Bingley: Emerald Group Publishing Ltd.

Johnson, K., Faulkner, P., Jones, H., & Welsh, E. (2007). *Understanding suicide and promoting survival in LGBT communities.* Brighton: University of Brighton.

Kelly, R. (1993). *Bias crime: American law enforcement and legal responses.* Washington: Office for International Criminal Justice.

Kidd, J., & Witten, T. (2008). Transgender and transsexual identities: The next strange fruit—Hate crimes, violence and genocide against the global trans-communities. *Journal of Hate Studies, 6*(1), 31–63.

Knights, D., & Kerfoot, D. (2004). Between representations and subjectivity: Gender binaries and the politics of organizational transformation. *Gender, Work and Organization, 11*(4), 430–454.

Macpherson, W. (1999). *The Stephen Lawrence inquiry.* [Online]. Retrieved March 3, 2020, from https://www.gov.uk/government/uploads/system/uploads/attachment_data/file/277111/4262.pdf.

Mason, G. (2014). The symbolic purpose of hate crime law: Ideal victims and emotion. *Theoretical criminology, 18*(1), 75–92.

Mathis, S. (2018). Motive, action and confusions in the debate over hate crime legislation. *Criminal Justice Ethics, 37*(1), 1–20.

McDevitt, J., Balboni, J., Garcia, L., & Gu, J. (2001). Consequences for victims: A comparison of bias and non-bias motivated assaults. *American Behavioral Scientist, 45*, 697–713.

McGhee, D. (2007). The challenge of working with racially motivated offenders: An exercise in ambivalence? *Probation Journal, 54*(3), 213–226.

Merton, R. (1968). *Social theory and social structure.* New York: Free Press.

Miles, L. (2018). Updating the gender recognition act: Trans oppression, moral panics and implications for social work. *Critical and Radical Social Work, 6*(1), 93–106.

Miller, A. (2003). Civil rights and hate crimes legislation: Two important asymmetries. *Journal of Social Philosophy, 34*(3), 437–443.

Monro, S. (2003). Transgender politics in the UK. *Critical Social Policy, 23*(4), 433–452.

Monro, S. (2019). Non-binary and genderqueer: An overview of the field. *International Journal of Transgenderism, 20*(2–3), 126–131.

Morgenroth, T., & Ryan, M. (2018). Quotas and affirmative action: Understanding group-based outcomes and attitudes. *Social and Personality Psychology Compass, 12*(3), e12374.

Morsch, J. (1991). The problem of motive in hate crimes: The argument about presumptions of racial motivation. *Journal of Criminal Law and Criminology, 82*, 659–689.

Paterson, J., Walters, M., Brown, R., & Fearn, H. (2018). *The Sussex hate crime project*. Sussex: University of Sussex.

Pemberton, B. (2018, January 15). What is gender reassignment surgery? Does the NHS offer it, what does it cost privately and how does it work? *The Sun*. Retrieved April 6, 2020, from https://www.thesun.co.uk/fabulous/3374474/gender-reassignment-surgery-nhs-cost/.

Perry, B. (2001). *In the name of hate: Understanding hate crimes*. London: Routledge.

Perry, J. (2008). The 'perils' of an identity politics approach to the legal recognition of harm. *Liverpool Law Review, 29*(1), 19–36.

Perry, B. (2009). The Sociology of hate: Theoretical approaches. In B. Levin (eds.), *Hate Crimes, Volume 1: Understanding and Defining Hate Crime* (pp. 55–76). Westport: Praeger.

Ray, L., & Smith, D. (2002). Hate crime, violence and cultures of racism. In P. Iganski (Ed.), *The hate debate: Should hate be punished as a crime?* (pp. 88–102). London: Profile Books.

Richards, C., Bouman, W. P., Seal, L., Barker, M. J., Nieder, T. O., & T'Sjoen, G. (2016). Non-binary or genderqueer genders. *International Review of Psychiatry, 28*(1), 95–102.

Roulstone, A., Thomas, P., & Balderstone, S. (2011). Between hate and vulnerability: Unpacking the British Criminal Justice System's construction of disablist hate crime. *Disability and Society, 26*(3), 351–364.

Shelton, J., & Dodd, S. (2020). Beyond the binary: Addressing cisnormativity in the social work classroom. *Journal of Social Work Education, 56*(1), 179–185.

Spalek, B. (2008). *Communities, identities and crime*. Bristol: The Policy Press.

Stryker, S. (2008). *Transgender history*. Berkley, CA: Seal Press.

Sullivan, A. (1999, September 26). What's so bad about hate? The illogical and illiberalism behind hate crime laws. *New York Times Magazine*.

Vijlbrief, A., Saharso, S., & Ghorashi, H. (2020). Transcending the gender binary: Gender non-binary young adults in Amsterdam. *Journal of LGBT Youth, 17*(1), 89–106.

Wacholz, S. (2009). Pathways through hate: Exploring the victimisation of the homeless. In B. Perry (Ed.), *Hate crimes volume three: The victims of hate crime* (pp. 199–222). Westport: Praeger.

Walklate, S. (2014). Sexual violence against women: Still a controversial issue for victimology? *International Review of Victimology, 20*(1), 71–84.

Walters, M. (2011). A general theories of hate crime? Strain, doing difference and self-control. *Critical Criminology, 19*, 313–330.

Walters, M., & Hoyle, C. (2010). Healing harms and engendering tolerance: The promise of restorative justice for hate crime. In N. Chakraborti (Ed.), *Hate crime: Concepts, policy, future directions* (pp. 228–249). Cullompton: Willan Publishing.

Walters, M., Owusu-Bempah, A., & Wiedlitzka, S. (2018). Hate crime and the 'justice gap': The case for law reform. *Criminal Law Review, 12*, 961–986.

3

Conceptualising 'Micro-Crimes'

Introduction

In the last two chapters, I introduced transphobic hate crime and contextualised this phenomenon with wider systems of understanding. Now, and in the next three chapters of this book, I draw upon the data that was collected that inspired this book. In using data that was collected, I hope that in these chapters I will clearly demonstrate the ways in which we can develop our understanding of transphobic hate crime, and hate crime more broadly. I have chosen to introduce the concept of 'micro-crime' victimisation first, as this will be an inherent feature of all future chapters. Participants' conceptualisation of their experiences of micro-crimes significantly relate to the social consciousness of victimisation and socially recognisable forms of victimisation. Therefore, it is key to give adequate space to defining and conceptualising what I mean when I discuss 'micro-crimes'. It is important to remind ourselves here that when conducting the research that forms the foundation of this book, I was first and foremost interested in exploring people's experiences of what we might call 'low-level' or 'mundane' incidents of hate crime. That is, experiences of

B. Colliver, *Re-imagining Hate Crime*, Palgrave Hate Studies,
https://doi.org/10.1007/978-3-030-65714-7_3

hate crime that do not fit within sensationalised, media depictions of hate crime that centre on physical and sexual violence.

In order to conceptualise and understand 'micro-crimes', I begin this chapter by briefly presenting the ways in which experiences of 'low-level' and 'mundane' victimisation are understood in relation to the 'everyday'. The relationship between victimisation and the 'everyday' is most commonly understood in two dominant ways. Firstly, victimisation is understood as being a *result* of engaging in 'everyday' routines. In this sense, I will demonstrate the ways in which participants in this study encountered incidents of verbal abuse, harassment and threatening behaviour as a consequence of engaging in the 'mundane'. Secondly, victimisation is often perceived to be an *inherent feature* of the 'everyday'. As such, victimisation is often understood to become part of the 'everyday' routine. As one participant Sam described, experiencing micro-crime victimisation 'was just like part of my daily routine, get up, have breakfast, go out, be abused, come home and then start all over again'. The findings from this study highlight the significantly pervasive nature of micro-crimes and hate crimes being perpetrated against trans people. This is contrary to what official statistics suggest (The Home Office 2017, 2018, 2019, 2020), which indicate that recorded incidents of transphobic hate crime account for only 1–2% of all recorded hate crime. Notions of the 'everyday' will be explored in relation to 'Routine Activity' theory (Cohen and Felson 1979) and victimological perspectives of 'victim-precipitation' (Mendelsohn 1963).

I then move to pay particular attention to victimisation that occurs in online spaces. Whilst there is a growing body of research that explores online hate speech, this has trailed significantly behind offline victimisation. Additionally, research into online hate speech has tended to focus on that which targets race, religion and sexuality (Awan 2014; Awan and Zempi 2016; Cmeciu 2016; Weaver 2013). Resultantly, little is known about the online victimisation of trans people, although research is emerging that explores the construction of trans people in online 'debate' (Colliver et al. 2019; Colliver and Coyle 2020). I draw upon the work of scholars who have previously located online victimisation within a 'routine activity' framework, addressing some of the issues presented when trying to apply a theoretical perspective that was developed specifically for victimisation in the 'physical' world (Yar 2015).

After I have outlined the types of victimisation, and in what context participants experienced transphobic hate crime, I offer my own conceptualisation of their experiences in the form of 'micro-crimes'. In doing so, I suggest that acknowledging 'micro-crime' victimisation is key in recognising the criminality of many incidents of victimisation, and therefore challenge dominant understandings of verbal abuse, harassment and threatening behaviour as being non-criminal, and therefore non-reportable. In conceptualising micro-crimes, I draw heavily on the work of Sue et al. (2007) and their work on conceptualising 'microaggressions'. Whilst the conceptualisation of microaggressions has arguably been key in furthering our understanding of the ways in which people experience discrimination, prejudice and hostility, the ways in which microaggressions have been embraced may result in the overshadowing of 'low-level' and 'mundane' criminal victimisation. In this chapter, I will demonstrate the intrinsic relationship between microaggressions, micro-crimes and more socially recognisable forms of victimisation. Throughout this chapter I refer to hate motivated 'micro-crimes', and whilst I offer a detailed conceptualisation of this later in the chapter, it is important to provide a brief definition here. A hate-motivated 'micro-crime' describes any criminal offence that is motivated by discrimination or prejudice in which the criminality of such an offence is less socially recognisable. In this sense, the term relates to offences that are primarily covered by the Public Order Act (1986) including causing harassment, fear or alarm to the victim. Whilst it is not the case that these forms of victimisation are any less visible than physical and sexual violence, or result in a less severe impact for the victim, as will be shown in the next chapter, the criminality of such experiences is often ambiguous.

Hate Crime, Victimisation and the 'Everyday'

The inherently 'everyday' nature is central in understanding particular forms of transphobic victimisation. This primarily relates to incidents of verbal abuse, harassment and threatening, intimidating and aggressive behaviour. Whilst many participants in this research reported experiencing physical and sexual violence, it was often forms of microaggressions and micro-crimes that were reported as occurring most frequently. Most participants reported experiences of misgendering,[1] dead-naming[2] and threatening behaviour. 76% of participants had experienced harassment previously and 32% indicated that verbal abuse occurred 'regularly'. Such incidents of victimisation were commonplace and interacted with the 'everyday' in two dominant ways. I begin the discussion by exploring the ways in which victimisation was perceived to be a consequence of engaging in 'everyday' activities as part of a routine. The 'everyday' nature of hate crime has been explored and Iganski (2008: 6) highlights the opportunistic nature of many incidents of hate crime 'committed by "ordinary" people in the context of their "everyday" lives: not by "extremists" in the pursuit of ideological goals'. This is certainly the case for many participants in this study who conceptualised many instances of victimisation as a result of chance encounters with perpetrators as a result of engaging in their daily routine. This is not to say that all incidents of victimisation occur purely because of chance, or situational factors, as other participants described the pre-meditated nature of some incidents of victimisation. However, participants certainly described their encounters of micro-crimes as committed by 'ordinary' people in the context of the 'everyday'.

Participants reported high levels of transphobic 'micro-crime' victimisation whilst at work, whilst commuting to and from work, whilst commuting to and from appointments and whilst engaging in social opportunities. In this sense, victimisation is contextualised within a daily routine and occurring because of being in a particular place at a particular time. Illustrated best by an experience described by Ryan:

> I was on a bus on my way home [from college], I had this guy come up to me on the bus and he was just harassing me about the way I looked and whether I was a boy or a girl … and like a bloke was like 'do you have a

[1] Misgendering is when an individual is referred to by pronouns that do not reflect their gender identity.

[2] Dead-naming is the use of an individual's birth name, which may not be the name they are legally (or not legally) recognised as.

> cock?' … he wouldn't leave me alone, and kept getting closer to me … If I hadn't been going home at that time, if I hadn't got on that bus, it never would have happened.

In understanding micro-crime victimisation as part of the 'everyday', it becomes clear that blame and responsibility is shifted from the perpetrator to the victim and for their involvement in that specific situational context in which victimisation occurs. This plays a significant role in minimising the criminality of an event, as a blameworthy perpetrator becomes difficult to identify. As part of this incident, there is a clear focus on Ryan's genitals as an indicator of his gender. A reliance on genitals as a key indicator of someone's gender is routinely drawn upon in the attempted de-legitimisation of trans people (Colliver et al. 2019). This may be perpetuated by media narratives of trans people that often focus on physical transition, thereby placing unnecessary emphasis on an individual's genitals, therefore neglecting social and psychological transition (Lea 2016). Notions of self-blame are evident in Ryan's account, in which he attributes blame to his decision-making and role in the incident. The role of the victim in incidents of victimisation was part of the foundations of victimology as a discipline (Rock 2017). The idea of 'victim-precipitation' is commonly recognised as the first victimological theory and explores the relationship and situational relationship between the victim and perpetrator (Rock 2017). Ideas of victim-precipitation can be engaged with in a neutral sense, in which the specific contextual relationship between the victim and perpetrator is interrogated. Douglas and Waksler (1982: 249) have done so in arguing that the 'perpetrator and victim commonly appear to be involved in a social encounter where the acts of each affect those of the other'. However, it can be argued that traditional applications of victim-precipitation theory contribute to victim blaming, in that it was regularly used to imply the victim was the causal reason, or in some way colluded in their own victimisation (Mendelsohn 1963). Whilst it is evident that Ryan attributes some blame to his own decision-making that resulted in him being in that specific space at that time, therefore speaking to the claims of those who advocated for victim-precipitation as a theory, this does minimise the responsibility of the perpetrator.

Commuting to and from work and places of education were highlighted as routines characterised by abuse, often perpetrated by the same person as a result of the repetitive nature of commuting in terms of time and location. The repetitive nature of routines can often lead to an incident of victimisation developing into repetitive, targeted behaviour. Piper describes how she was 'walking to work and was followed by a man who was shouting "why are you dressed like that" and followed me all the way to work harassing me'. Having found safety in her place of work, and anticipating that this incident was an isolated incident, she later described how this 'happened nearly every day for a few weeks'. The repetitive nature of a commuter routine creates a specific context in which targeted and ongoing victimisation can occur. However, whilst some people experience victimisation because of engaging in specific routines, others described the inescapable nature of verbal abuse, harassment and threatening, intimidating and aggressive behaviour. For Bushra, she experiences these forms of victimisation regardless of whether she is 'walking down the street ... going in to the shops to do shopping...going to the doctors ... or using the bus'. In this sense, some trans people perceive victimisation as inevitable, regardless of what 'everyday' routine someone is engaging in. Experiencing micro-crime victimisation therefore becomes a consequence of engaging in daily life. As will be discussed later in this chapter, this has significant consequences for some trans people's ability to participate in everyday life.

In Piper's experience described earlier, in which she identified her workplace as a refuge from the victimisation she experienced on the commute to work, others identified the workplace as a site of risk. The workplace was often understood to be a place of risk from both colleagues and customers or service users. Trans people may therefore experience micro-crime victimisation as a result of participating in paid or voluntary employment. Sometimes, colleagues were the perpetrators of such victimisation and included transphobic verbal abuse, displaying transphobic posters in communal areas and displaying 'pornographic pictures of trans people' on the victim's locker. These experiences are often minimised by higher management who imply that these forms of victimisation are 'just a joke' and show reluctance to pursue disciplinary action against the perpetrators. In cases when an individual's trans identity is 'outed' within the workplace, some trans people felt pressure from management to resign from their position as a way to 'avoid incidents like that happening again'. This demonstrates the ways in which trans people are often held accountable for their own victimisation, minimising the responsibility of the perpetrator and reinforcing social structures that position trans people as legitimate targets of ridicule, abuse and violence.

An alternative conceptualisation of the workplace is one of relative safety, in which colleagues provide a barrier between an individual and perpetrator(s). Star, who is a tattoo artist described an incident of micro-crime victimisation, which had the potential to escalate into physical violence, but was prevented by colleagues who intervened and gave Star a sense of protection. When engaging in their everyday work routine, Star describes an incident in which:

> Four or five boys walked in … I went over and was talking to them about designs and then one of them asked me if I was wearing men's clothes … I was a bit taken aback and my colleague came over and basically told them it was none of their business. They all started laughing and got a bit rowdy and then one of them just flipped out and was like 'I'm not having a fucking tranny touching me, I don't want to catch nothing, this shit ain't normal' and all the usual bollocks and then threw my drawings across the room. The girl I work with pulled me to the back of the shop and the two men I work with like grabbed them and threw them out the shop.

The experience described by Star consists of a number of important issues. Firstly, the very nature of the language used that implies trans people have something that 'can be caught' and the pathologisation of trans identities as 'not normal' are recurrent motifs drawn upon to delegitimise trans people (Colliver et al. 2019). The group of perpetrators were all perceived by Star to be cisgender men, which is consistent with existing research that indicates perpetrators of hate crime are likely to be groups of young, cisgender men (Chakraborti et al. 2014). This incident also highlights the ways in which engaging in a mundane, everyday routine has the potential to rapidly escalate into a situation in which an individual's physical safety is at risk. In this sense, incidents of transphobic abuse are volatile and unpredictable. Finally, Star's experience differs to that of some other people's in that their colleagues were not the perpetrators, but rather provided a 'safety net' and actively challenged transphobic abuse that Star experienced. The routineness of engaging in employment can act as a facilitator of abuse, in that the workplace creates the environment in which the abuse occurs, whilst simultaneously being a space of safety because of colleague support and protection.

Given the 'routine' nature of victimisation presented so far, it seems pertinent to frame these experiences within a relevant theoretical framework. As outlined in the previous chapter, many scholars have theorised hate crime and the motivations that fuel these instances of victimisation (Chakraborti and Garland 2012; Perry 2001; Walters 2011). However, given the 'everyday' and 'routine' nature of such victimisation, it is worthwhile to frame these experiences with a 'routine activity' framework (Cohen and Felson 1979). Routine activity theory, and other perspectives that centre situational contexts as causes of crime, 'have edged toward the mainstream of criminology' (Miller 2013: 391). According to Cohen and Felson (1979: 589), there are three central conditions that must be met for 'direct contact predatory violations' to occur. The conditions they set out include the presence of a motivated offender, the presence of a suitable target(s) and the absence of capable guardian (Cohen and Felson 1979). All three conditions must be present for a violation to occur, and the absence of one element would prevent a crime from occurring. A key claim of this perspective is that 'everyday' routines impact the visibility of victims, and therefore the accessibility to victimise them (Hindelang et al. 1978). It is the routines in everyday life that 'affect the chances of these factors converging in space and time' (Miller 2013: 392). Unlike ideas of 'victim-precipitation' discussed earlier, which are often critiqued for victim-blaming, routine activities theory examines the specific 'situation that results in victimization' (Stacey and Averett 2016).

In applying routine activities theory to the experiences discussed in this chapter, I will first explore how the 'motivated offender' is identified. In the last chapter I outlined some of the key debates that underpin hate crime scholarship, particularly around the language associated with 'hate'. In this sense, it may not be possible to identify all perpetrators as motivated by 'hate'. However, I would argue that there are a number of motivations that underpin transphobic hate crime that are intrinsically linked to western gender norms associated with the gender binary. Previous research has identified that violence against gay men is motivated by anger at non-conformity to expected gender norms that dictate compulsory heterosexuality as the 'norm' (Franklin 1998). This could arguably be applied to the victimisation of trans people, in which their perceived non-conformity to western gender norms is seen as an assault, or rejection of traditional values and norms. In the application of a revised routine activities theory, Waldner and Berg (2008: 271) argue that gender deviance can be seen as a form of 'target antagonism'. In this sense, trans people's existence and presence within public spaces may evoke a strong, negative emotional response such as anger. It is here that we can understand hate crime as a 'message crime', in which the victim themselves become secondary to that which they are perceived to represent (Perry 2001). I would therefore argue that those who identify within the western gender binary, benefit from its existence and have a strong desire to maintain the status quo, are more likely to be 'motivated perpetrators' than those who perceive the western gender binary to be less significant in everyday life.

The second condition that must be met is that of a suitable target (Cohen and Felson 1979). The suitable target can be conceptualised at both the micro- and macro-levels. At the micro-level, a suitable target for transphobic hate crime will be one who is 'visibly' trans. Whilst there is no logical way of knowing who is trans and who is not, a perpetrator's perception is likely to be influenced and entwined with the western gender binary and gendered expectations of presentation. This does mean that cisgender people who do not conform to gendered expectations of physical appearance may also be seen as a 'suitable target' for transphobic hate crime. However, in some instances, a 'suitable target' may consciously choose to be 'visibly' trans for a number of reasons in different situational contexts (Colliver and Silvestri 2020). Indeed, Bennett (1991) has stressed that the visibility of a target significantly affects the likelihood of victimisation. Therefore, the ability to identify someone as trans, either correctly, or incorrectly, is key in identifying a 'suitable target'. At the macro level, stereotypes surrounding trans people may contribute to them being perceived as a 'suitable target'. Stereotypes surrounding trans people, and trans women in particular, often have connotations of weakness and vulnerability (Dirks 2016; Miles-Johnson 2016). This may be due to a historic conflation of trans women with gay men, who are often perceived to be effeminate, and therefore physically weak (Berk 1990; Franklin 1998; Van-der-Meer 2003). In this sense, macro-level stereotypes may contribute to all members of trans communities being perceived as unable to physically defend themselves, and therefore macro-level stereotypes may influence micro-level decisions of who is a 'suitable target'.

The final condition that must be met is the absence of a capable guardian (Cohen and Felson 1979). A capable guardian may take the form of official criminal justice agencies and law enforcement, or may simply be other members of society present at the time. Felson (2008: 87) later claimed that 'it was evident that police and security guards were considerably less important than ordinary citizens for generating supervision of people and things, thus for preventing crime'. I would argue that even in the presence of other citizens, when a motivated offender and suitable target meet, there may be an attempt at victimisation. It is important to reflect here upon the social context provided in the first chapter of this book, in which trans people and trans lives have received increasing visibility and therefore heightened levels of scrutiny. Resultantly, within the United Kingdom, there is currently a hostile climate for trans people perpetuated by government action, media representation and social media. Although not exhaustive, these outlets contribute to the delegitimisation of trans people as worthy and therefore contribute to the construction of trans people as 'less than' others. Indeed, the regular vilification of trans people in popular culture, news and politics leads to a social, political and cultural climate that positions trans people as 'legitimate' targets of victimisation and unworthy of protection. It is within this social climate that the presence of other citizens may not be enough to constitute a 'capable guardian'. There may be the perception from the perpetrator that others will share their views, and therefore not intervene. This was evident in participants' narratives in which they often non-verbally sought help from those around them, only to experience encouragement for the perpetrator, or a disengagement from the situation.

Having now discussed the ways in which victimisation is understood to be as a result of engaging in an 'everyday' routine, I will now discuss how the frequency of such incidents may also be reconceptualised as an *inherent feature* of the 'everyday' routine. As previously illustrated with the experiences of Bushra who described the ways in which she encountered transphobic abuse and hate crime regardless of which routine she was engaging in, she also described how these experiences are transformative and the victimisation she experienced became *part* of her daily routine. Consequently, the repetitive nature of her experiences was transformative in her understanding of how transphobic abuse featured in her life. This was often the case when abuse occurred in, or near the home. Bushra describes that:

> Once I was coming home from visiting my GP and I walked into the flats where I live … I hear someone shouting from behind me. They are shouting at me 'Oi, oi, oi, tranny! Turn around, look it's a tranny!' Then I feel something hit the back of my head. I grab the back of my head and it is wet, then something hits my back and it hurts. It is a hard hit and it feels like a rock. I began to see them waiting for me every time I went out. They would chase me, shouting at me and throwing things at me.

The repetitive nature of victimisation in which trans people often face ongoing, targeted harassment, abuse and victimisation perpetrated by the same individual(s) results in a normalisation of these experiences. This normalisation is most evident in the conceptualisation of victimisation as a *part* of everyday life. Although the first encounter Bushra had with the group was as a result of engaging in her everyday routine of attending the GP, the abuse she faced, which was most commonly verbal harassment and having eggs thrown at her, became normalised as *part* of her routine. This demonstrates that when an individual has been identified as a potential target for transphobic abuse, the abuse often becomes a prolonged and repetitive feature of a routine. In this sense, the notion of 'routine' is transformative, functioning as both a facilitator of abuse and the abuse becoming an essential feature of a routine. Browne et al. (2011) noted that the normalisation of victimisation is evident within wider LGBTQ communities. Transphobic abuse being conceptualised as part of an individual's routine was common across participants' narratives and as one participant explained, they 'rate the successfulness of [their] day by whether [they] get abused or not'. In this sense, experiences of micro-crimes, such as verbal abuse and harassment, are understood to be a core feature of daily routines and are the measuring rod against which the successfulness of a day is measured.

Conceptualising such victimisation as part of the 'everyday', or as part of a 'routine', functions in a 'protective' way. As such, this normalisation and assimilation of abuse into the everyday allows trans people to prepare both emotionally and psychologically in an attempt to minimise the impact of such experiences. This often appeared necessary due to the commonplace nature of these incidents. Participants often described the certainty they had that 'everyday someone will say something … to harass' them or follow them around in public. The level of abuse experienced is inconsistent and ranges from name-calling to physical violence and the inconsistency contributes to the anxiety and uncertainty some trans people face when engaging in public life. Sam, a 31-year-old trans man describes how abuse is 'just like part of [his] daily routine, get up, have breakfast, go out, be abused, come home and then start all over again'. The quote by Sam best illustrates how experiences of transphobic abuse and micro-crimes such as verbal abuse and harassment are understood to be an intrinsic feature of daily life.

Whilst experiencing physical violence was often discussed to be less 'everyday', and in some ways completely juxtaposed and in contradiction to people's understanding of the 'everyday', it was often seen to be as a result of ongoing, repetitive abuse that was left unreported or unchallenged. Micro-crime victimisation was most commonly discussed in relation to the everyday. When describing the nature of 'everyday' victimisation, participants most commonly described incidents of name-calling, threatening behaviour and harassment in public spaces. The nature of verbal abuse was often explicitly transphobic and Monica, a 20-year-old trans woman describes how she 'gets called names all the time … stuff like "tranny", "he-she" and "chick with a dick". In this sense, Monica experiences verbal abuse that draws upon culturally recognisable and harmful configurations of trans people in which a trans identity is often reduced to a focus on the presence of particular genitals (Bailey et al. 2017). The nature and frequency of these experiences are evident in existing literature (Antjoule 2013; METRO 2014) but are often descriptive in nature. Less attention is paid to how these experiences are framed as a pervasive feature of daily life. When participants did discuss physical violence in the context of the 'everyday', it was often reported that this physical violence was 'not extreme' and included incidents of being 'spat at, shoved, pushed, barged or being tripped over'. As is discussed in the next chapter, understandings of hate crime victimisation are often hierarchical in nature and the conceptualisation of physical violence fits within a 'hierarchy of extremity'.

However, when micro-crime victimisation was repetitive, perpetrated by the same individual(s) there was often reports of significant, rapid escalation in which physical violence ensued. The repetitive and targeted victimisation was most commonly discussed in the context of 'coming out' or as a result of changing residential area in which people find themselves surrounded by the 'unknown', and they themselves represent the 'unknown' to those who already occupy that particular space. Trans people representing the 'unknown' was often conceptualised in two different ways. Firstly, when moving house trans people understood themselves to be unknown to existing residents in the surrounding space in the sense that they were a 'new' resident. Secondly, participants often described their identities as being unknown in that their gender was often read by existing residents as ambiguous, or at odds with the 'norm' and the 'known'. Whilst the "home" is often associated with the "known"' (Van-Krieken et al. 2014), participants often described feeling as if existing residents had never seen a trans person before, in the case that their identities were read as trans by existing residents. This was often not the case, and not to the same level of concern for participants who 'passed', or perceived themselves to pass. Sam, a 31-year-old trans man describes an incident that occurred when he moved into a new flat:

> walking back to the flat, there was a group of like teenagers hanging around outside the entrance … one of them said something about being a 'dirty dyke' … They started asking if I was a dyke and I said no and then one of them was like 'oh, she's one of them ones fluid people' and they all started laughing … I tried to get past them to get to the door and I was holding a bag with food in, one of them kicked the bag and it split and our food went everywhere.

The experience described by Sam was on the first day when they had moved into a new area and therefore had to navigate new social spaces with new people. Although this was the first incident, Sam also described how over a period of just weeks, similar incidents occurred that became 'more and more aggressive, more intimidating and more physical'. Despite the repetitive nature of these incidents, Sam only sought police intervention when the harassment culminated in a physical attack in which Sam also had their phone stolen. This demonstrates that when an individual is identified as being 'different', they may then be subject to an ongoing, targeted campaign of victimisation that spirals from micro-crime victimisation, to physical violence. The 'home', and residential area were often discussed in terms of risk. This was primarily as a result of the amount of time spent in this area, and the difficulty associated with changing residential area. Whilst it may be easier to change a daily routine in relation to which shops are visited and which forms of public transport were used, people are often restricted by the inability to change their living situation. Resultantly, when someone has been identified as a potential target for victimisation in a residential area, there are often limited options from which to make adaptations. Therefore, residential areas are often conceptualised as high-risk areas for victimisation.

As briefly discussed earlier, these experiences are often normalised and understood to be a *part* of everyday life. In this sense, people anticipate, rationalise and normalise their experiences of micro-crimes. Certainly, in this research project, processes of normalisation were the most commonly reported responses to micro-crime victimisation. This arguably has an impact on recognising micro-crime victimisation as a legitimate form of criminal victimisation and contributes to the underreporting of such experiences. However, in normalising these experiences, participants felt able to maintain daily functioning which they felt was critical for their mental health.

The concept of socially recognisable forms of victimisation has been explored by Corteen et al. (2016) who describe the institutionalised nature of many forms of discrimination relating to low-level incidents of racial and sexual harassment and the consequence for their recognition as legitimate forms of victimisation. This is evident in participants' accounts of their experiences; it can be argued that trans people conceptualise incidents of transphobic micro-crimes as a 'normal' feature of everyday life, therefore, the criminality and legitimacy of this type of victimisation is rendered inconsequential. This is often framed within the context of minimising the impact of these incidents. Narratives often focused on the inescapable nature of such incidents and a need to 'accept that it won't stop, so the only way to get through life is to accept it will happen'. As Star claims, this form of victimisation is 'just part of life'. Cody elaborates and explains that normalising these incidents is to avoid 'fall[ing] to pieces' as a result of the frequency of such incidents. In this sense, normalisation, rationalising and anticipating victimisation functions to minimise the anticipated impact of experiencing micro-crimes. This is key in order to maintain daily functioning. There appears to be a certain sense of passiveness associated with the need to rationalise, in which a lack of agency is pervasive throughout the narratives. Notions of power and agency are alluded to throughout the narratives in various ways, particularly in relation to being powerless to avoid victimisation. However, this is not to say that trans people who experience victimisation have no agency at all. Although someone may be powerless to escape a particular situation, they may still have agency in the way they respond to these incidents. In this sense, the normalisation and rationalisation of these incidents is an active, conscious choice. As described by Cody, he is aware that he has agency over the choice to normalise these experiences or 'fall to pieces'. As such, power and agency are contextualised relatively, and an individual may feel both powerless and powerful simultaneously.

The process of normalisation was also evident from the results of the online survey, and this was apparent through three key questions. As shown in Figs. 3.1 and 3.2, 97.5% of participants considered harassment to be a hate crime if motivated by transphobia. Additionally, 76% of participants indicated that they had experienced harassment that they perceived to be motivated by transphobia. However, only 64.9% of participants considered themselves to have experienced a hate crime. This is a key finding, as it demonstrates the ways in which victimisation is easier to identify when discussing hate crime in a broader sense, but the criminal nature of such incidents becomes more difficult to identify when considering personal experiences. This may be as a result of the normalisation of such incidents. This was a similar finding across incidents of verbal

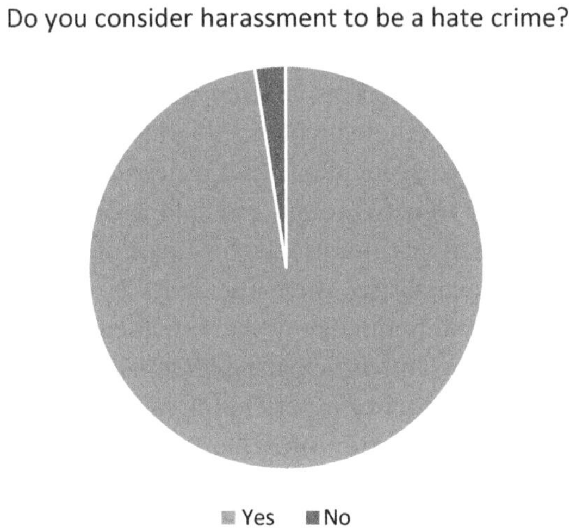

Fig. 3.1 Survey results—do you consider harassment to be a hate crime?

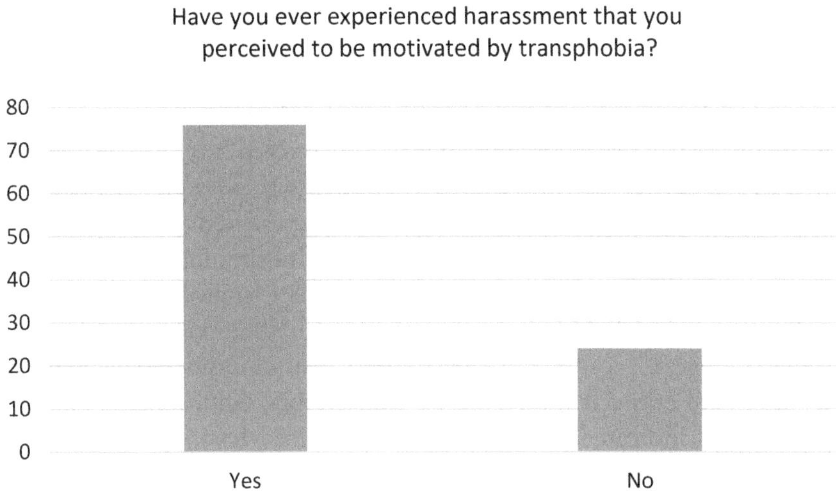

Fig. 3.2 Survey results—have you ever experienced harassment that you perceived to be motivated by transphobia?

abuse reported in the survey and threatening behaviour. In relation to the frequency of micro-crime victimisation, harassment, verbal abuse and online trolling were the only forms of victimisation that more than 10% of participants indicated occurred regularly.

It is important to recognise the normalisation of micro-crime victimisation, as this has implications on recognising the criminality of such incidents and therefore impacts the likelihood of reporting these incidents to the police. Of those who indicated that they had experienced harassment, verbal abuse or threatening behaviour also suggested that they had not reported it to the police because it 'happens too often', of which 74.3% of participants indicated, or because the incidents are 'not serious enough', of which 48.5% of participants indicated. It can therefore be argued that although the normalisation of micro-crime victimisation facilitates continued daily functioning, it also prohibits the formal recognition, and therefore institutional responses to these experiences. The perception that these incidents were not serious enough to be reported, was often perpetuated by interactions with criminal justice agencies when attempting to report. Data from the online survey showed that of all reports made to the police regarding an incident of transphobic hate crime, less than half were officially recorded as a hate crime by the police.

Normalisation of Online Micro-Crime Victimisation

The experiences described by participants in an offline context of persistent, repetitive and targeted harassment, verbal abuse and threatening behaviour were also mirrored within descriptions of online victimisation. In some ways, the normalisation of online victimisation was even more pervasive, due to the conceptualisation of the internet, and social media in particular, as an intrinsic feature of the 'everyday'. It has been argued that social media is an 'extension' of an individual's identity (Belk 2013). Victimisation in an online context is often targeted at this extension of identity and occurs in the context of an 'everyday routine'. Social media was often described as a method of maintaining connections with others, both individuals who are known in the offline world, but also those with whom only an online connection has been established. However, the internet is also a key resource for information and advice about all elements of transition. Participants found the internet particularly useful for 'speak[ing] to people who had already had surgery and see what it was like'. In this sense, the internet operated in two key ways. Firstly, as a resource to access legal and medical advice from key providers such as the NHS website and the Home Office website. Secondly, as a way to access less formal information, from those who have already transitioned, either socially or medically. As Elaine, a 48-year-old trans woman describes:

> I used to use it [the internet] a lot to do research into like surgical options and I follow some like pretty well known YouTubers who are trans, so I can follow their transition.

It is evident that the internet is key in providing both generic, impersonal information, but also providing a sense of the personal through the consumption of other people's transition. In this sense, the internet provides a means for participants to increase their knowledge and awareness in relation to medical, surgical and legal options. As such, the internet provides an opportunity for trans people to access relevant information that may be unavailable, or more difficult to access through mainstream outlets such as educational establishments (METRO 2014). Social media in particular was also seen as initially representing a 'safe space' in which to initially 'come out' or begin to 'socially transition'. Lia, a 17-year-old trans woman explains how social media was where she initially 'presented as female, to see how people would react' to her. Social media was often framed as providing unprecedented and unique opportunities for personal networking and accessing peer support. A reliance on social media for networking and maintaining friendships may be heightened as a result of experiencing continued, targeted victimisation in an offline context. As Bushra explains:

> I use the internet a lot. I never used to use social media as much, but then because I started to go out less, I use the internet a lot now to try and make some friends online.

When individuals become anxious of, or anticipate victimisation in public, this may restrict their ability to socialise and engage in public life. For Bushra, this was certainly the case, and social media provided a lifeline for maintaining some form of social contact with others. Similar experiences were also shared and social media was framed as a platform through which you could combat loneliness and isolation. Being able to locate and network with those perceived to be similar was a key advantage of the internet, particularly for those who felt further marginalised as a result of their disability, race or religion. The availability of networking sites that connect individuals of similar faiths was key for Dilip, a 45-year-old trans man in being able to find networks 'specifically for LGBT people of colour and LGBT people who are Sikh'. Identifying those perceived as similar was key in participants narratives and was understood as being an opportunity uniquely associated with the internet. This was also apparent in the results from the online survey. Bivariate logistical regression was conducted to predict the odds that particular groups of people used the internet to build a network of other trans people, making comparisons across disability status, sexuality, gender, religion and race. Of the conducted tests, disability status produced statistically significant results, and participants who considered themselves to have a disability had 2.520 the predicted odds of using the internet to build a network of trans friends than those who did not consider themselves to have a disability.

The internet has been described as a 'global community' (Ohler 2010) and the ability to connect with others without time, cost or travel implications were detailed by participants in this study. As a result, participants are often able to locate a sense of 'belonging', 'community' or 'family' within online spaces which may be unattainable in the offline world for a multiplicity of reasons. This was often starkly juxtaposed to the sense of 'unfamiliarity' and risk associated with residential areas and 'birth family'. However, it is important to note that the internet does not provide a sense of 'belonging' for all trans people, neither are all trans people necessarily seeking a sense of 'belonging' when engaging online. Whilst the abundance of benefits of the internet were highlighted by all participants, social media was often understood as being dualistic, in the sense that these sites were areas of both support, but also pervasive abuse. The internet as a site of significant risk was also evident in the online survey. 54.8% of people who participated indicated that they felt at risk when engaging with the internet. Additionally, as illustrated in Fig. 3.3, 76.7% of participants highlighted that they had experienced incidents of transphobic abuse online.

In some ways, abuse online is different to that of abuse experienced in the offline world, particularly in relation to the frequency and prevalence of such experiences. Whilst the connectedness associated with the internet is often perceived as a positive feature, it does allow for those who perpetrate abuse to connect, organise and repetitively target individuals. In this sense, online abuse is often perceived to be more sophisticatedly organised and often less random than abuse in the offline world. The quotes from participants below demonstrate the high prevalence of abuse experienced online.

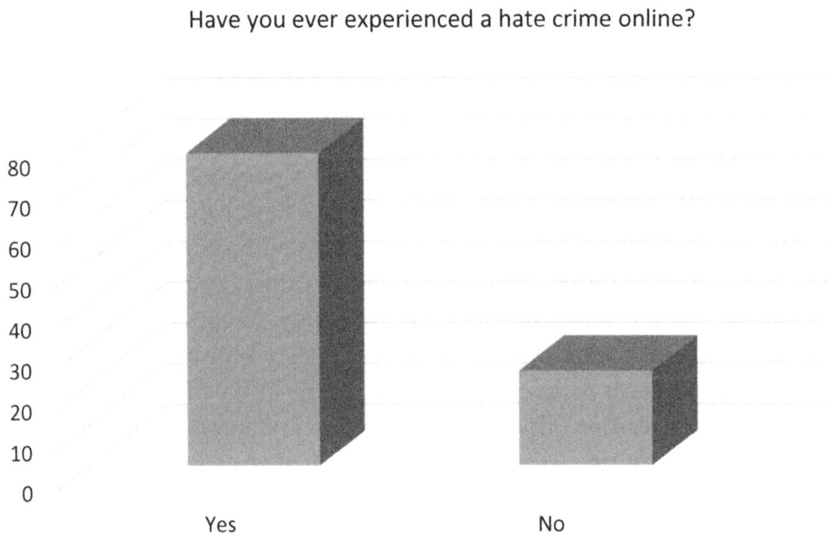

Fig. 3.3 Survey—have participants ever experienced a hate crime online?

> There is much more abuse online than in real life. There are just more opportunities, because the internet is so big and so vast and people from all over the world can see the same thing at the same time and everyone can all respond at once. Like in real life, it would take me months and months to meet every individual that has posted something negative on one of my videos, but online, I meet them all at once in a second. (Ashley, 34, Male)
>
> I think this [online abuse] is the hardest because it normally comes in such huge volumes, like you get involved in a conversation and within twenty-four hours you have received maybe one hundred, two hundred, three hundred inbox messages and comments on your comment. (Isa, 58, Female)

The data presented above demonstrate the difference between online and offline victimisation. It is not only the volume of the abuse experienced, but also the immediacy of such victimisation. The real-time nature of the internet allows for instantaneous victimisation to occur. When discussing victimisation that occurs online, this was often in comparison to offline victimisation. In this sense, abuse that occurs in the offline world is a measuring rod, by which online victimisation is measured against. The very public nature of the internet is perceived to be a causal reason for such high frequencies of abuse. Another element that appeared to be more prevalent within online abuse was the incitement to self-violence. Whilst this did occur in-person, participants reported significantly more experiences in an online context of being encouraged to self-harm or engage in suicidal behaviours. The frequency of this type of abuse is so common that one participant reported not being able to remember how many times they had been told 'to hang [themselves], or take an overdose'. The nature of online abuse that is often more extreme than verbal abuse in-person is attributed to the relative anonymity that the internet provides. This is consistent with existing research that has highlighted the relative anonymity and perceived lack of regulation associated with the internet (Brown 2017; Cohen-Almagor 2011).

A growing body of literature exploring the similarities and differences between prejudicial speech targeting minority groups online and offline is emerging (Banks 2010; Brown 2017; Chetty and Alathur 2018). This is an important area of exploration as the internet has developed as an unregulated site for the expression of discriminatory and prejudicial views and the worldwide scope of the internet permits the spread of dominant, social ideologies (Weaver 2013). The rise in internet-facilitated hate speech may be a result of mainstream published media providing more opportunities for individuals and communities to complain and contest discriminatory media under more stringent regulatory frameworks. For example, the framework set out by The Independent Press Standard Organisation (2016) places a duty on UK newspapers not to publish prejudicial or pejorative references to an individual's race, religion, sexuality and gender identity. There are debates around whether 'hate speech' online should be criminalised, with some arguing that 'although hate speech and other vile utterances can be found in cyberspace, censoring speech in this medium would go against the free, open, anarchic, and global nature of the internet, and severely impede its growth' (Steinhardt 2000: 249). This is not to say that those who advocate for the non-regulation of speech online condone hate speech, but may argue that education is more effective at combatting hate speech than criminalisation. However, the relative anonymity afforded to people by the internet through the use of pseudonyms and ability to create numerous, unidentifiable profiles may create difficulties in implementing educational initiatives. This also creates difficulties in identifying and enforcing existing regulations. A further barrier to addressing hate speech online exists in the lack of a coherent definition, and some have questioned who gets to determine which speech is 'hateful' or 'discriminatory' (Yar 2013). The 'global nature' of the internet can also create difficulties in regulating and policing online hate speech. It may be the case that the victim of hate speech resides in one country, the perpetrator in another, and the servers that host the website in another (Yar 2013). Varying international regulations relating to 'free speech' may compound the difficulty in policing online hate speech given the global community present online.

The scale of the internet, volume and frequency of online hate speech may also create barriers to effectively policing this type of behaviour. It became apparent from participants' narratives that there is also an element of 'copy-cat' behaviour associated with the internet, in which particular phrases of abuse become repetitive and targeted at certain individuals. This appears to be the case for abuse that incites self-violence.

As Ty, who is 21 years old and non-binary explains that 'the messages start … they tell you to kill yourself, they tell you to cut yourself … most of the time people use exactly the same wording. It is almost as if they have just cut and paste the comment from the person who started it. The comments are always freakily similar in the way they are written'. The internet therefore allows for uniquely similar forms of abuse that are not as prevalent within the offline world due to there often being a lack of an audience within offline victimisation. As such, the presence of an engaged audience may exacerbate the online abuse that trans people face. Whilst the incitement to self-violence was more prevalent in online abuse than offline abuse, there were still similarities between the two in relation to the nature of abuse.

Forms of offline victimisation that may be conceptualised as 'micro-crimes' such as name-calling and attempts to delegitimise an individual's gender identity were commonly reported as occurring in an online context. Ruby, a 52-year-old female describes how she frequently experiences name calling and that she is not a 'real woman', often paired with claims that she is 'mentally ill … deranged … or delusional'. Notions of 'mental illness' have been found to be prevalent in the online construction of trans people (Colliver et al. 2019). Other participants described experiencing explicitly transphobic name calling as part of the abuse directed towards them. Names were often based on socially recognisable configurations of trans identities by conflating terms associated with both genders in the gender binary such as 'he-she'. In this sense, name-calling often relies on reinforcing the gender binary and positioning trans people 'in the middle' of the binary. The pervasive nature of transphobic name-calling on social media platforms mirrors the nature of name-calling reported in offline incidents. In this sense, there are evident parallels between both online and offline experiences of victimisation.

The relationship between the online and offline world was key for participants to determine the level of risk and seriousness of an incident. Quite often, the perceived seriousness, or level of risk someone felt, was associated with the physical proximity of the perpetrator. As such, the likelihood of online victimisation manifesting into offline victimisation was central in participants' understanding of their experiences. As Emmet, a 30-year-old male describes:

> If someone was messaging me and being transphobic and threatening to kill me and I thought there was a realistic chance that they could find where I lived or whatever then it would be more serious.

The physical proximity of the perpetrator was most intensely considered in incidents where threats of physical violence had been made in an online context. This was common across participants description of the fear they felt associated with online victimisation. This was also particularly prevalent within geosocial apps such as Grindr,[3] which connect people based on their geographic location. The ability for people to 'hide' their location, and therefore their distance from you heightened the anxiety felt by participants when they received threatening and abusive messages. As Jae, who is 21 years old and non-binary explains, when 'people hide their distance … they could be like in the next room, or in Scotland and you wouldn't know, that is the frightening context'. Being able to assess the likelihood of offline victimisation is key in assessing the seriousness of online victimisation.

The physical distance between a victim and perpetrator was also understood to be a key reason in explaining the frequency of online victimisation. The physical distance between the perpetrator and victim is understood to allow perpetrators to disassociate themselves from the abuse perpetrated. In this sense, the reality of an individual's actions may not be as apparent as in the case of offline victimisation in which the victim and perpetrator are commonly within close physical proximity of each other. As Ashley explained:

> I think because you can abuse someone online, you don't really have to acknowledge the humanity of that person, you don't have to understand the real pain that you cause. I think when it happens in person, they have to acknowledge that you are a real person, because they can see you, they can touch you. Whereas online, you don't necessarily see people as real, you just see online profiles.

[3] Grindr is a geosocial application that is targeted at gay and bisexual men and men that have sex with men. However, it is also used by a number of trans women, and non-binary people.

Participants often believed that perpetrators of online abuse did not consider the real-life implications of their actions, as a result of both physical and symbolic distance between the victim and perpetrator. Therefore, whilst the internet, and social media in particular, is understood to provide unprecedented opportunities for people to connect with others, and indeed, have a positive impact on an individual's journey with their own identity, there is also a dehumanising nature associated with social media. The ability to remain anonymous and often the inability to accurately portray your entire identity in an online interaction may lead to being perceived as just 'another avatar' or 'another profile picture', rather than as an individual.

Despite high levels of online victimisation being described, they were rarely reported. This was also evident in the online survey in which only 23.8% of participants who had experienced online abuse had reported these incidents. Online victimisation was often perceived as 'less serious' than offline victimisation and one participant stated that 'the police have real work to do, they don't need to be bothered by me because someone has threatened me online'. In this sense, the role of the police is to tackle offline crime rather than address online behaviour. When participants did report abuse that occurred online, this was primarily to the platform host and 'no action taken' was a recurrent response reported by participants. When action was taken against perpetrators, this was primarily in the form of a temporary ban in which the perpetrator was allowed to reinstate their social media profile after a designated period of time. However, this was often perceived to be an ineffective means of addressing hate speech online, due to the easy and accessible nature of being able to create a new social media profile immediately. There was a desire for additional police intervention in addressing online hate speech; however, participants were aware of the complicated nature of policing the internet. Currently, social media responses to hate speech seem to be reactionary and the onus is on social media users to report hate speech (De Latour et al. 2017). This was often seen as a barrier to reporting and tackling hate speech online, in which the volume of hate speech encountered was too large to repeatedly report.

Conceptualising 'Micro-Crimes'

Now that I have demonstrated the 'everyday' nature of much victimisation, I will offer a detailed conceptualisation of 'micro-crime' victimisation. In doing so, I will highlight the importance of reconceptualising our understanding of different forms of victimisation. Incidents of verbal abuse, harassment and threatening and intimidating behaviour have largely been overlooked within academic work on transphobic hate crime. As will be explored in more detail in the next chapter, existing literature often reinforces a hierarchical system of victimisation in which different forms of victimisation can be ranked, with physical and sexual violence being considered more severe than other forms of hate crime (Herek et al. 1999; McDevitt et al. 2001). The exclusion of micro-crimes from the social conscience prevents them from being recognised as legitimate forms of criminal victimisation and results in the non-policing of these incidents. This contributes to the subordination of trans people within social hierarchies, therefore positioning trans people as legitimate targets for victimisation. As a result of this, micro-crimes can function as a gateway for more socially recognisable forms of violence and victimisation.

However, work has been done to conceptualise hate crime victimisation as occurring within a 'continuum' (Hollomotz 2012). In conceptualising hate crime in this way, it is claimed that a more nuanced appreciation of the lived reality of hate crime victimisation can be achieved. In acknowledging hate crime victimisation as part of a continuum, greater attention can be paid to offences such as verbal abuse, harassment and property offences. As will be explored in the next chapter, the hierarchical nature of hate crime victimisation has serious implications for victims' understandings of their own experiences as criminal. Hollomotz (2012: 54) argues that by acknowledging a continuum highlights the blurring of boundaries between 'mundane intrusions, derogatory treatment and violence' which can make it difficult for victims to differentiate incidents which are perceived as an 'acceptable', or 'expected' part of everyday life from incidents which are to be understood as criminal. It is important to understand and acknowledge these experiences as literature has highlighted the emotional and psychological impact of experiencing violent hate crime (Ehrlich 1992; McDevitt et al. 2001). However, as will be demonstrated throughout this book, experiencing systematic, 'low-level' abuse can also significantly affect an individual's emotional and psychological well-being.

The prevalence of transphobic hate crime, similar to many other forms of hate crime, is difficult to gauge as it is 'grossly under-reported' (Lombardi et al. 2001: 91). It has been argued that many trans people often experience the 'pervasive and everyday presence of violence' (Moran and Sharpe 2004: 396). Whilst the hierarchical nature of hate crime victimisation has led to significant attention being paid to physical and sexual violence as forms of hate crime, the everyday experiences are often overlooked. Whilst participants described worryingly high levels of physical violence, it was incidents of verbal abuse, harassment and other forms of micro-crimes that were most commonly reported. This was also apparent in the results from the online survey in which verbal abuse and online abuse were the only forms of victimisation that more than 20% of respondents indicated occurred 'regularly'. More recently, a significant amount of research exploring 'microaggressions' has emerged (Conover et al. 2017; Farr et al. 2016; Ong and Burrow 2017; Williams et al. 2016) but has primarily focused on the experiences of religious and ethnic minorities. Research is emerging, albeit to a lesser extent, exploring LGBTQ+ communities' experiences of microaggressions (Mccabe et al. 2012; Roffee and Waling 2016; Swann et al. 2016). Similarly, a small amount of research has been conducted that specifically explores trans people's experiences of microaggressions (Nadal et al. 2014; Pulice-Farrow et al. 2017).

The work of Sue et al. (2007, 2008) has been key in work on microaggressions. When specifically discussing racial microaggressions, Sue et al. (2007: 273) define them as 'brief and commonplace daily verbal, behavioural, and environmental indignities, whether intentional or unintentional, that communicate hostile, derogatory, or negative racial slights and insults to the target person or group'. In this sense, microaggressions can be perpetrated both consciously and unconsciously and function to delegitimise and 'other' an individual, or group of individuals. It is widely acknowledged that the pervasive nature of micro-aggressions can lead to severe consequences for those who are targeted (Brondolo et al. 2008;

Szymanski et al. 2008). Sue et al. (2007) developed a taxonomy of racial microaggressions and differentiated between microassaults, microinsults and microinvalidations. Microassaults are defined as 'explicit racial derogation characterized primarily by a verbal or nonverbal attack meant to hurt the intended victim through name-calling, avoidant behavior, or purposeful discriminatory actions ... they are most likely to be conscious and deliberate' (Sue et al. 2007: 274). The definition of microassaults certainly captures some of the experiences described by participants in this research and accurately reflects some of the experiences of 'low-level', 'everyday' incidents of abuse. Microinsults are defined as 'communications that convey rudeness and insensitivity ... represent subtle snubs, frequently unknown to the perpetrator, but clearly convey a hidden insulting message to the recipient of color'. Whilst this definition is in the context of racial microinsults, as will be explored later in this book, these forms of microaggressions were certainly experienced by participants in this study. These may be in the form of intentional misgendering, and claimed 'accidental' use of the words 'it' and 'that' to describe a trans person.

The final category of microaggressions that Sue et al. (2007) define is microinvalidations. Microinvalidations may also be perpetrated unconsciously and have been defined as 'communications that exclude, negate, or nullify the psychological thoughts, feelings, or experienced reality of a person of color' (Sue et al. 2007: 274). Although this taxonomy was originally developed in relation to racist microaggressions, Sue (2010) later expanded this conceptualisation in relation to other minoritised groups. Forms of microinvalidations that trans people reported experiencing include misgendering and dead-naming. This is also prevalent in online spaces in which trans identities and the authenticity of trans identities are continually delegitimised (Colliver et al. 2019). Research that explores microaggressions has tended to focused on non-criminal incidents, or incidents in which criminality is ambiguous, including anti-social behaviour, name-calling and harassment (Keels et al. 2017; Roffee and Waling 2016). Whilst the acknowledgement of these forms of victimisation is essential in developing our understanding of victimisation as a continuum, as I will argue later, it can also be problematic.

However, Sue (2010) further elaborated on the definition of microaggressions, and specifically in relation to microassaults. In doing so, Sue (2010: 9) defines microaggressions as including 'extreme forms of microassaults' which may include 'teasing and bullying in schools, isolation, physical violence, hate speech, and anti-LGBT legislation'. It is with this definition that I would argue poses a problem to our understanding of hate crime. Two of the forms of microaggressions outlined, microinsults and microinvalidations, seem to fit within the definitional scope of microaggressions, which for the large part focuses on non-criminal incidents. However, the inclusion of physical violence and hate speech within the category of 'microaggressions' seems oxymoronic in nature. I would argue that physical violence and hate speech are not 'brief' encounters which can occur consciously *or* unconsciously. Hate speech and hate-motivated physical violence are intentionally and consciously perpetrated. To conceptualise hate-motivated violence as occurring within the unconscious negates responsibility of the perpetrator and does not acknowledge the often intentional and targeted victimisation of minoritised groups. The prefix 'micro' implies that any action included within this definition should be less 'extreme' than other actions of a comparable nature. Therefore, the inclusion of 'extreme forms' of microaggressions seems somewhat contradictory in nature.

The vast array of actions subsumed within the provided definition of microaggressions appears contradictory to the definition itself. It is therefore unclear which forms of physical violence constitute an 'extreme microassault', and this may prove problematic when researching microaggressions targeting minoritised communities. For example, participants in this study differentiated between 'low-level' physical violence such as pushing, shoving and tripping in comparison to more 'extreme' forms of physical violence including kicking, punching and biting. It is unclear whether all of these forms of physical violence would be subsumed under the label of 'extreme forms of microassaults', or whether this only includes particular forms of physical violence. The inclusion of such acts may exacerbate the hierarchical nature of victimisation, privileging forms of physical violence as more 'severe', or as representing more legitimate forms of victimisation. However, despite the issues associated with this definition, most research exploring microaggressions has tended to focus on non-physically violent, non-criminal incidents (Nadal et al. 2014; Roffee and Waling 2016). As outlined earlier, other research has tended to focus on more physically and sexually violent forms of victimisation (Herek et al. 1999). Therefore, there is a lack of attention on what I would term as 'micro-crimes'.

Micro-crimes are incidents of criminal victimisation, in which the criminality of such incidents is ambiguous, or less socially recognisable as criminal. In considering the term 'micro-crime', this definition extends to offences primarily covered by the Public Order Act (1986), including causing harassment, fear or alarm to the victim but also offences covered by the Malicious Communications Act (1988). Guidance from the Crown Prosecution Service (2011) also suggests that actions including threats of violence, verbal abuse, abusive gestures and unfounded malicious complaints may also constitute a criminal offence. From the interviews conducted as part of this research project, offences covered under these pieces of legislation were often considered part of the 'everyday', and therefore the criminal nature of such acts became difficult to identify. They also do not fit within sensationalised media reports of victimisation (Jewkes 2015) and this may affect an individuals' understanding of their own experiences of victimisation. This undoubtedly has implications for our understanding of the scale and scope of hate crime victimisation in the United Kingdom as a significant amount of victimisation remains unreported to the police as a result of the normalisation of such incidents. I would argue, that in order to fully understand the nature, scale and scope of transphobic hate crime, and hate crime more generally, it is key for us to shift popular understanding of what constitutes a hate crime. Without this shift, we may continue to perpetuate a cycle that overshadows and minimises the severity of micro-crime victimisation.

In this research project, it became clear that participants experienced a range of victimisation ranging from microaggressions to more socially recognisable forms of victimisation such as physical and sexual violence. Quite often, experiences of micro-crime victimisation were conceptualised as part of the 'everyday', fitting with Hollomotz's (2012) description of hate crimes as a continuum. As such, I have identified three distinct, yet interrelated forms of victimisation that trans people experience, which may be similar to that of other minoritised groups. Dominant frameworks of exploring victimisation have often focused on either microaggressions, a category in which micro-crimes are often subsumed, or socially recognisable forms of hate crime, in which micro-crimes are often overshadowed and excluded. Resultantly, the criminality of some experiences of verbal abuse, harassment and other forms of victimisation that fall outside the category of physical or sexual violence are often overshadowed. On the other hand, the inclusion of these experiences within microaggressions studies reinforces the social neglect to recognise these types of victimisation as criminal. It is important to discursively reflect the criminality of many of these incidents, or risk compounding the conceptualisation of these incidents as non-criminal, and therefore, remaining unreported.

Whilst I have conceptualised microaggressions, micro-crimes and more socially recognisable forms of crime as distinct categories of victimisation, they are intrinsically related. This means that they do not happen in isolation of each other. Indeed, participants' narratives attested to the ways in which both microaggressions and micro-crimes were often central features of more socially recognisable forms of victimisation. In this sense, an individual may experience verbal abuse, which could be considered a micro-crime, during an incident of physical violence. In this sense, the different forms of victimisation may occur as distinct forms of victimisation, but may also occur as part of a matrix of victimisation. However, it is important to note that whilst microaggressions may be a feature of an incident of micro-crime victimisation, this is not a reciprocal relationship. As such, micro-crime victimisation is not a feature of microaggressions. Similarly, more socially recognisable forms of victimisation such as physical violence are not a feature of micro-crime victimisation. I would therefore argue that microaggressions are best understood as non-criminal incidents that often occur outside the social conscious, although may still be perpetrated intentionally, and maliciously and that result in the denigration of those they target. Incidents where guidance suggests criminality may be ascertained, such as verbal abuse, harassment, offensive gestures and hate mail are best conceptualised as micro-crimes, to reflect the criminality of these incidents. This is necessary to avoid contributing to the perpetuation of victimisation of this nature as non-criminal. The conceptualisation of these forms of victimisation as non-criminal has

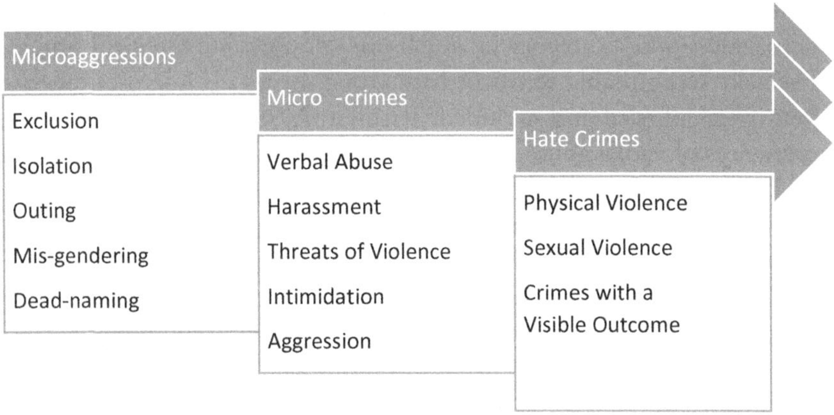

Fig. 3.4 Relationship between microaggressions, micro-crimes and hate crimes

serious implications for people's understanding of their own victimisation as legitimate. Through the narratives explored with participants, I was able to identify an intrinsic relationship between microaggressions, micro-crimes and hate crimes. Figure 3.4 below illustrates the interrelated nature of all three forms of victimisation and how micro-aggressions may appear in all forms of victimisation, and micro-crimes may appear within the perpetration of traditionally recognised hate crimes.

It is important to conceptualise the relationship in this way and not in a hierarchical format to ensure that by highlighting the importance of exploring micro-crimes, other forms of victimisation are not rendered inconsequential. By conceptualising the relationship between microaggressions, micro-crimes and hate crimes as such, the impact of all three forms of victimisation can be considered in relation to trans people's experiences of victimisation in a more holistic way. Therefore, issues that have been raised with previous research exploring hate crime victimisation, such as the overshadowing of micro-crimes based on a hierarchical interpretation of victimisation, can be avoided. I argue that embracing the concept of 'micro-crime' will help to better understand the experiences of trans individuals who experience low-level, mundane incidents of hate crime. Exclusion and isolation may occur both consciously and unconsciously and may not involve direct contact with a victim. 'Outing', or disclosing someone's trans identity, misgendering and dead-naming may also occur consciously or subconsciously, but do not constitute a criminal offence. The exception to this is when these behaviours make up part of an ongoing campaign of harassment. Verbal abuse, harassment, threats of violence and intimidation always occur consciously, and may be considered criminal, whether occurring in the online or offline world. However, the criminality of such incidents was often ambiguous to participants in this study, and it is why I have categorised these actions as 'micro-crimes'. The final category of 'hate crimes' includes all crimes with a visible outcome, and physical and sexual violence. These actions do not need to be qualified with another term, as they are the most socially recognisable forms of victimisation in which criminality is often obvious.

It is important to note that this conceptualisation of victimisation does not necessarily call for more punitive responses to victimisation. Nor does it call for the criminalisation of currently non-criminal acts. Rather, in understanding micro-crime victimisation, we are better able to recognise the already criminal nature of many experiences. Significant work has been done regarding the effectiveness and appropriateness of sentence uplift tariffs (Hall 2012) and there has been work around the issues associated with punitive responses to hate crime offending (Russell 2017). It may therefore be the case that more restorative approaches to micro-crime victimisation could be adopted, which may prove to be more effective at facilitating social change.

Conclusion

In this chapter I have shown that participants in this study experienced a range of victimisation ranging from microaggressions, micro-crimes and physical and sexual violence as an inherent and pervasive part of their everyday lives. The normalcy and everyday nature of transphobic victimisation is clear. As such, 'routine' is not a singular concept, but can be understood in a number of different ways. Firstly, abuse is conceptualised by trans people as a result of engaging *in* their everyday routine. However, transphobic abuse is also understood to be a *part* of trans people's everyday routine in which abuse is to be expected. In this sense, engaging in a daily routine means that trans people consider themselves to be victimised as a result of circumstance, and it can therefore be difficult to identify and recognise the criminality of such events. As such, victimisation is inherently linked to trans people's routine and becomes an indistinguishable feature of daily life.

The normalisation of micro-crimes described by trans people in the semi-structured interviews can also account for some of the contradictory results from the online survey. I argue that there appeared to be a disconnect between participants' perception of hate crime, in which many participants indicated micro-crimes as legitimate forms of victimisation. However, many participants indicated that they had never experienced a hate crime but later indicated that they experienced verbal abuse and harassment on a regular basis. The normalisation described in the interviews is useful in explaining this disconnect in the sense that it is easier to assign criminality to incidents that do not directly involve the victim. When that act becomes directly targeted at the victim, the normalisation of their own personal victimisation prevents them from conceptualising their victimisation as criminal. In this sense, participants' conceptualisation of their victimisation acts as a barrier to reporting these experiences to the police, as they are deemed to be unworthy of police attention, as they are often considered not to meet the threshold of criminality.

I have also discussed the ways in which the internet, and social media in particular, is understood to be part of the 'everyday', and how social media becomes an extension of the self. Extending existing research, this study demonstrates the way in which social media is understood to be a site of significant risk of experiencing transphobic abuse. The experiences of online abuses are often distinct from abuse experienced in the physical world, primarily in relation to frequency and volume of incidents experienced. However, participants also identified that experiencing calls to engage in suicidal behaviour was significantly more prevalent within online spaces, than in the offline world. The extremity of online hate speech and the calls for trans people to engage in self-abusive or self-violent acts was often understood to be as a result of the ability to easily dehumanise someone online. The seriousness of victimisation experienced online was often evaluated in the context of whether this abuse would manifest in the offline world. As such, there appears to be an ability to compartmentalise and disconnect the online from offline worlds, unless it is perceived that these two spheres may collide.

I conclude this chapter by outlining and detailing the concept of 'micro-crimes' more thoroughly. I argue that if we are to fully understand and acknowledge the experiences of people subjected to verbal abuse, harassment and threatening and/or intimidating behaviour, we must conceptualise these experiences in a way that reflects the criminality of such behaviours. In a culture of division and segregation, there is a relationship between microaggressions, micro-crimes and socially recognisable forms of victimisation. In this sense, one form of victimisation may facilitate another. It can be concluded that trans people experience a matrix of victimisation in which micro-aggressions, micro-crimes and more socially recognisable forms of hate crime interconnect and facilitate a culture of othering for trans people. Although each form of victimisation warrants attention, the intrinsic relationship between all microaggressions, micro-crimes and more socially recognisable forms of crime should remain at the forefront of research.

As will be discussed in more depth in the next chapter, the normalisation of these crimes and the inability to perceive them as criminal may be influenced by the hierarchical nature of hate crime victimisation. In the next chapter I begin to deconstruct many hierarchies of hate that influence an individual's ability to recognise their victimisation as criminal. Understanding victimisation in this way fits within the continuum of violence proposed by Hollomotz (2012). Quite often, incidents of hate crime experienced by participants were not understood to be criminal. By recognising the criminality of such incidents, we can begin to tackle one of the issues attributed to the persistent underreporting of hate crime.

References

Antjoule, N. (2013). *The hate crime report: Homophobia, biphobia and transphobia in London*. London: GALOP.

Awan, I. (2014). Islamophobia and twitter: A typology of online hate against Muslims on social media. *Policy and Internet, 6*(2), 133–150.

Awan, I., & Zempi, I. (2016). The affinity between online and offline anti-Muslim hate crime: Dynamics and impact. *Aggression and Violent Behavior, 27*, 1–8.
Bailey, L., McNeil, J., & Ellis, S. (2017). 'I worry that they'll pick on someone I care about': Trans people's perceptions of the British mass media and its impact on their mental health and well-being. In A. Dhoest, L. Szulc, & B. Eeckhout (Eds.), *LGBTQs, media and culture in Europe* (pp. 98–118). London: Routledge.
Banks, J. (2010). Regulating hate speech online. *International Review of Law, Computers and Technology, 24*(3), 233–239.
Belk, R. (2013). Extended self in a digital age. In A. Ruvio & R. Belk (Eds.), *The Routledge companion to identity and consumption* (pp. 83–90). London: Routledge.
Bennett, R. (1991). Routine activities: A cross-national assessment of a criminological perspective. *Social Forces, 70*, 147–163.
Berk, R. (1990). Thinking about hate-motivated crimes. *Journal of Interpersonal Violence, 5*, 334–349.
Brondolo, E., Brady, N., Thompson, S., Tobin, J. N., Cassells, A., & Sweeney, M. (2008). Perceived racism and negative affect: Analyses of trait and state measures of affect in a community sample. *Journal of Social and Clinical Psychology, 27*, 150–173.
Brown, A. (2017). What is so special about online (as compared to offline) hate speech? *Ethnicities, 0*(0), 1–30.
Browne, K., Bakshi, L., & Lim, J. (2011). It's something you just have to ignore: Understanding and addressing contemporary lesbian, gay, bisexual and trans safety beyond hate crime paradigms. *Journal of Social Policy, 40*(4), 739–756.
Chakraborti, N., & Garland, J. (2012). Reconceptualizing hate crime victimization through the lens of vulnerability and 'difference'. *Theoretical Criminology, 16*(4), 499–514.
Chakraborti, N., Garland, J., & Hardy, S.-J. (2014). *The Leicester hate crime project: Findings and conclusions*. Leicester: University of Leicester.
Chetty, N., & Alathur, S. (2018). Hate speech review in the context of online social networks. *Aggression and Violent Behavior, 40*, 108–118.
Cmeciu, C. (2016). Online discursive (de)legitimisation of the Roma community. *Journal of Media Research, 9*(1), 80–98.
Cohen, L., & Felson, M. (1979). Social change and crime rate trend: A routine activity approach. *American Sociological Review, 44*, 588–611.

Cohen-Almagor, R. (2011). Fighting hate and bigotry on the internet. *Policy and Internet, 3*(3), 1–25.

Colliver, B., & Coyle, A. (2020). 'Risk of sexual violence against women and girls' in the construction of 'gender-neutral toilets': A discourse analysis of comments on YouTube videos. *Journal of Gender-Based Violence, 4*(3), 359–376. https://doi.org/10.1332/239868020X15894511554617.

Colliver, B., & Silvestri, M. (2020). The role of (in)visibility in hate crime targeting transgender people. *Criminology and Criminal Justice* [Online First]. https://doi.org/10.1177/1748895820930747.

Colliver, B., Coyle, A., & Silvestri, M. (2019). The 'online othering' of transgender people in relation to 'gender neutral toilets'. In K. Lumsden & E. Harper (Eds.), *Online othering: Exploring digital violence and discrimination on the web* (pp. 215–238). London: Palgrave Macmillan.

Conover, K., Israel, T., & Nylund-Gibson, K. (2017). Development and validation of the ableist microaggressions scale. *The Counselling Psychologist, 45*(4), 570–599.

Corteen, K., Morley, S., Taylor, P., & Turner, J. (2016). *A companion to crime, harm and victimisation*. Bristol: Policy Press.

Crown Prosecution Service. (2011). *Hate crime fact sheet.* Retrieved May 20, 2020, from www.cps.gov.uk/news/fact_sheets/hate_crime/index.html.

De Latour, A., Perger, N., Salaj, R., Tocchi, C., & Oteri, P.-V. (2017). *We can! Taking action against hate speech through counter and alternative narratives.* Strasbourg: Council of Europe.

Dirks, D. A. D. (2016). Transgender people at four big ten campuses: A policy discourse analysis. *The Review of Higher Education, 39*(3), 371–393.

Douglas, J., & Waksler, F. (1982). *The Sociology of Deviance: An Introduction.* Boston: Little, Brown and Co.

Ehrlich, H. (1992). The ecology of anti-gay violence. In G. Herek & K. Berrill (Eds.), *Hate crimes: Confronting violence against lesbians and gay men* (pp. 105–112). Newbury Park: Sage Publications.

Farr, R., Crain, E., Oakley, M. K., Cashen, K., & Garber, K. (2016). Microaggressions, feelings of difference, and resilience among adopted children with sexual minority parents. *Journal of Youth Adolescence, 45*, 85–104.

Felson, M. (2008). The routine activity approach. In R. Wortley & M. Townsley (Eds.), *Environmental criminology and crime analysis* (2nd ed., pp. 87–97). London: Routledge.

Franklin, K. (1998). Unassuming motivations: Contextualizing the narratives of antigay assailants. In G. Herek (Ed.), *Psychological perspectives on lesbian and*

gay issues: vol. 4. Stigma and sexual orientation: Understanding prejudice against lesbians, gay men and bisexuals (pp. 1–23). Thousand Oaks: Sage.
Hall, N. (2012). Policing hate crime in London and New York City: Some reflections on the factors influencing effective law enforcement, service provision and public trust and confidence. *International Review of Victimology, 18*(1), 73–87.
Herek, G., Gillis, J., Cogan, J., & Glunt, E. (1999). Hate crime victimization among lesbian, gay and bisexual adults: Prevalence, psychological correlates and methodological issues. *Journal of Interpersonal Violence, 12*(2), 195–215.
Hindelang, M., Gottfredson, M., & Garofalo, J. (1978). *Victims of personal crime*. Cambridge: Ballinger.
Hollomotz, A. (2012). Disability and the continuum of violence. In A. Roulstone & H. Mason-Bish (Eds.), *Disability, hate crime and violence* (pp. 52–63). London: Routledge.
Home Office. (2017). *Hate crime: England and Wales, 2016/17*. London: Home Office.
Home Office. (2018). *Hate crime: England and Wales, 2017/18*. London: Home Office.
Home Office. (2019). *Hate crime: England and Wales, 2018/19*. London: Home Office.
Home Office. (2020). *Hate crime: England and Wales, 2019/20*. London: Home Office.
Iganski, P. (2008). Criminal law and the routine activity of 'hate crime'. *Liverpool Law Review, 29*(1), 1–17.
Jewkes, Y. (2015). *Media and crime* (3rd ed.). London: Sage Publications Ltd..
Keels, M., Durkee, M., & Hope, E. (2017). The psychological and academic costs of school-based racial and ethnic microaggressions. *American Educational Research Journal, 54*(6), 1316–1344.
Lea, A. (2016). Gender identity and the politics of etiology. *Endeavour, 40*(3), 148–151.
Lombardi, E., Wilchins, R., Priesing, D., & Malouf, D. (2001). Gender violence: Transgender experiences with violence and discrimination. *Journal of Homosexuality, 41*(1), 89–101.
Mccabe, P., Dragowski, E., & Rubinson, F. (2012). What is homophobic bias anyway? Defining and recognizing microaggressions and harassment of LGBTQ youth. *Journal of School Violence, 12*(1), 7–26.
McDevitt, J., Balboni, J., Garcia, L., & Gu, J. (2001). Consequences for victims: A comparison of bias—And non-bias-motivated assaults. *American Behavioral Scientist, 45*(4), 697–713.

Mendelsohn, B. (1963). The origin of the doctrine of victimology. *Excerpta Criminologica, 3*, 239–245.
METRO. (2014). *Youth chances: Summary of first findings*. London: Metro Charity.
Miles-Johnson, T. (2016). Policing diversity: Examining police resistance to training reforms for transgender people in Australia. *Journal of Homosexuality, 63*(1), 103–136.
Miller, J. (2013). Individual offending, routine activities, and activity settings: Revisiting the routine activity theory of general deviance. *Journal of Research in Crime and Delinquency, 50*(3), 390–416.
Moran, L., & Sharpe, A. (2004). Violence, identity and policing: The case of violence against transgender people. *Criminal Justice, 4*(4), 395–417.
Nadal, K., Davidoff, K., Davis, L., Wong, Y., & Gonsiorek, J. (2014). Emotional, behavioural, and cognitive reactions to microaggressions: Transgender perspectives. *Psychology of Sexual Orientation and Gender Diversity, 1*(1), 72–81.
Ohler, J. (2010). *Digital community, digital citizen*. London: Sage Publications Ltd..
Ong, A., & Burrow, A. (2017). Microaggressions and daily experience: Depicting life as it is lived. *Perspectives on Psychological Science, 12*(1), 173–175.
Perry, B. (2001). *In the name of hate: Understanding hate crimes*. London: Routledge.
Pulice-Farrow, L., Brown, T., Galupo, M., & Gonsiorek, J. (2017). Transgender microaggressions in the context of romantic relationships. *Psychology of Sexual Orientation and Gender Diversity, 4*(3), 362–373.
Rock, P. (2017). Theoretical perspectives on victimisation. In S. Walklate (Ed.), *Handbook of victims and victimology* (2nd ed., pp. 30–58). Oxon: Routledge.
Roffee, J., & Waling, A. (2016). Rethinking microaggressions and anti-social behaviour against LGBTIQ+ youth. *Safer Communities, 15*(4), 190–201.
Russell, E. (2017). Queer penalities: The criminal justice paradigm in lesbian and gay anti-violence politics. *Critical Criminology, 25*, 21–35.
Stacey, M., & Averett, P. (2016). Routine activities and perceived homophobia among older lesbians. *Sexuality Research and Social Policy, 13*, 22–34.
Steinhardt, B. (2000). Hate speech. In Y. Akdeniz, C. Walker, & D. Wall (Eds.), *The internet, law and society* (pp. 249–271). Harlow: Longman.
Sue, D. W. (2010). Microaggressions, marginality, and oppression: An introduction. In D. W. Sue (Ed.), *Microaggressions and marginality: Manifestations, dynamics, and impact* (pp. 1–13). New Jersey: John Wiley and Sons.

Sue, D. W., Capodilupo, C. M., Torino, G. C., Bucceri, J. M., Holder, A. M. B., Nadal, K. L., & Esquilin, M. (2007). Racial microaggressions in everyday life: Implications for clinical practice. *American Psychology, 62*(4), 271–286.

Sue, D. W., Capodilupo, C. M., & Holder, A. M. B. (2008). Racial microaggressions in the life experience of Black Americans. *Professional Psychology: Research and Practice, 39*(3), 329–336.

Swann, G., Minshew, R., Newcomb, M., & Mustanski, B. (2016). Validation of the sexual orientation microaggression inventory in two diverse samples of LGBTQ youth. *Archives of Sexual Behavior, 45*(6), 1289–1298.

Szymanski, D. M., Kashubeck-West, S., & Meyer, J. (2008). Internalized heterosexism. *Counselling Psychologist, 36*, 510–524.

The Independent Press Standard Organisation. (2016) *The editors' code of practice*, [Online] Retrieved June 28, 2020, from https://www.ipso.co.uk/editors-code-of-practice/.

Van-der-Meer, T. (2003). Gay bashing—A rite of passage? *Culture, Health and Sexuality, 5*, 153–165.

Van-Krieken, R., Habibis, D., Smith, P., Hutchins, B., Martin, G., & Maton, K. (2014). *Sociology* (5th ed.). New South Wales: Pearson Australia.

Waldner, L., & Berg, J. (2008). Explaining antigay violence using target congruence: An application of revised routine activities theory. *Violence and Victims, 23*(3), 267–287.

Walters, M. (2011). A general theories of hate crime? Strain, doing difference and self-control. *Critical Criminology, 19*, 313–330.

Weaver, S. (2013). A rhetorical discourse analysis of online anti-Muslim and anti-Semetic jokes. *Ethnic and Racial Studies, 36*(3), 483–499.

Williams, A., Oliver, C., Aumer, K., & Meyers, C. (2016). Racial microaggressions and perceptions of internet memes. *Computers in Human Behavior, 63*, 424–432.

Yar, J. (2015). The novelty of 'cybercrime': An assessment in light of routine activity theory. *European Journal of Criminology, 2*(4), 407–427.

Yar, M. (2013). *Cybercrime and society*. London: Sage Publications Ltd..

4

Deconstructing Hierarchies of Hate

Introduction

In the last chapter I explored the idea of 'micro-crimes' to better understand the experiences of trans people and their experiences of victimisation. In this chapter I demonstrate the ways in which a number of hierarchies exist that have contributed to the overshadowing of these forms of victimisation and have a significant impact on the decision-making process as to whether to report an incident or not. As Perry (2001) claims, a number of social hierarchies exist in which individuals organise themselves and identify with. It is therefore unsurprising to find that hierarchical structures permeate individuals' experiences of victimisation and other elements of social life.

In this chapter, I explore the existence of three dominant hierarchies which appeared to be key in people's understanding of their own experiences. Firstly, the apparent hierarchy of protected characteristics will be discussed, in which trans people were acutely aware of the unequal social recognition afforded to different identity characteristics. This is often the result of different levels of legislative protection and different histories in relation to oppression, recognition and protection. The second hierarchy

B. Colliver, *Re-imagining Hate Crime*, Palgrave Hate Studies,
https://doi.org/10.1007/978-3-030-65714-7_4

that I interrogate in this chapter relates to offence type. This discussion aligns with the content discussed in the previous chapter, in which a hierarchy of 'seriousness' is established with physical and sexual violence firmly at the peak. Those who experience victimisation that falls outside of this may either not recognise this as criminal, or may be hesitant to report this out of fear that their report undermines the seriousness of physical or sexual violence. The third and final hierarchy that I discuss relates to the victim–perpetrator relationship. In this hierarchy, notions of 'stranger danger' permeate people's perceptions of whether their experience of victimisation was 'legitimate'. I frame these ideas in relation to Christie's (1986) conceptualisation of the 'ideal victim'. Although discussed in detail further in the chapter, the concept of the 'ideal victim' is one who has no pre-existing relationship with the perpetrator, is considered weak, blameless and engaging in morally appropriate activities at the time of victimisation. As I have previously written about, trans people are often constructed and presented in contradictory ways that are incompatible with the core tenets of the 'ideal victim' (Colliver 2020; Colliver et al. 2019; Colliver and Coyle 2020).

Hierarchies exist on a number of levels, both consciously and subconsciously. All of these hierarchies lead to a greater level of social awareness for particular forms of victimisation, whilst others may be overshadowed. This social awareness appeared to affect both victims and wider society. This has implications as to whether an individual recognises their own victimisation as criminal and therefore affects the likelihood of an incident being reported to the police. Often, an individual's anticipation, prediction and assumptions about how those in power will respond to their victimisation impact the perception of whether an incident is 'worth' reporting. This relates more specifically to the ways in which 'micro-crimes' are understood by victims and are most commonly framed in two ways. Firstly, micro-crimes are often understood to be of no interest to the police and other criminal justice agencies. In this sense, experiences of verbal abuse, harassment and other forms of micro-crimes are perceived to be a 'waste of police time', but also as a waste of the victim's time. Secondly, micro-crime victimisation is conceptualised in comparison to more socially recognisable forms of victimisation such as physical and sexual violence. In this comparison, incidents of micro-crimes are often considered to be trivial, or not serious enough for intervention to be required. The trivialisation of micro-crimes prevents legitimacy being assigned to these forms of victimisation as 'valid'.

Social Hierarchy of Protected Characteristics

There has been significant debate within hate crime scholarship surrounding which social groups receive legislative protection from 'hate' (Hardy and Chakraborti 2020; Hodkinson and Garland 2016). In this sense, the very existence of 'five monitored strands' creates a social and legislative hierarchy as to who is deemed 'worthy' of protection. This also has symbolic value, in that it tells us which groups of people may experience the most harm as a result of hate crime and this may have implications for those who experience victimisation based on an identity marker that is not officially monitored. This means that there will be no legal recourse to have this particular aspect of their victimisation recognised. However, for those who experience victimisation targeting an identity marker that does have some form of legislative protection, the seriousness of the victimisation, or the victim's sense of 'worth' as a 'victim', may be judged in comparison to other officially monitored characteristics.

Trans people who participated in this research project often perceived their own victim status in relation to more socially recognisable minoritised groups. Despite race, religion, sexuality, trans identity and disability status all being formally recognised as hate crime victim groups, it can be argued that the social recognition of these groups is not equal. Overwhelmingly, participants conceptualised race as a privileged characteristic in relation to its protected status and this has been explored by Jamel (2018). This is also evident in research given the overwhelming amount of literature exploring racist, anti-religious and homophobic hate crime (Bleich 2007; Harvey 2012; Zempi and Chakraborti 2015). It can be argued that trans people's perception of their own victim status as 'illegitimate', or 'unworthy' are heavily influenced by a wider historic societal unawareness of trans identities, and as one participant described, trans identities being the 'last taboo'. The feeling that trans identities were the 'last taboo' when discussing identities was recurrent within participants' narratives, and this seemed to influence how participants conceptualised their own victimisation.

A clear hierarchy of protected characteristics exists when people conceptualise their own experiences of victimisation. This hierarchy exists consciously for some and subconsciously for others. Given that all participants were aware that the interviews they participated in were centred around transphobic hate crime, when they were asked to discuss their understanding of hate crime, many discussed other protected characteristics first. It was common for interviewees to list protected characteristics. In some interviews, when participants discussed their understanding of hate crime, gender identity was not discussed at all; rather their discussion focused on race, religion and sexuality. In this sense, participants' responses demonstrate the existence of a hierarchy of characteristics in which race, religion and sexuality are privileged and at the forefront of people's consciousness. As Dilip, a 45-year-old trans man explains, a hate crime is when 'someone assaults you and it's because you are not white'. Or as Star, a 44-year-old non-binary individual, more broadly defines, a hate crime is a crime that is 'viewed by the victim … to have happened because of a protected characteristic … so either like race, sexuality, disability, religion [or] being transgender'.

In these instances, I suggest that this demonstrates the way in which a hierarchy of protected characteristics subconsciously manifests. Race, religion and sexuality were more commonly acknowledged when defining hate crime. Similar to trans identity, disability status was rarely acknowledged by interviewees when discussing hate crime. This is not particularly surprising, given that policy-makers, academics and society have been slow to respond to the needs of trans people and those living with a disability (Colliver and Silvestri 2020; Wilkin 2020). Given that transgender identity was the last characteristic to gain legislative protection under the Criminal Justice Act (2003), it is unsurprising that a hierarchy exists. The slow legislative response to the victimisation of trans people may be reflective of a wider societal acknowledgement of trans communities and the subsequent oppression, discrimination and victimisation they often face. The heightened social awareness of racism, various forms of anti-religious discriminations and homophobia may therefore permeate the social consciousness and the individual consciousness in which other forms of victimisation, that may or may not directly affect an individual, become more recognisable as legitimate forms of victimisation.

However, some participants in this research study were also consciously aware that a hierarchy of protected characteristics exists. Many participants alluded to the idea that transphobia was 'very low on the social agenda'. Sam, a 31-year-old trans man believes that transphobia is much lower on the social agenda 'than … racism, or homophobia'. In this sense, Sam speaks of a social hierarchy in which different forms of prejudice and oppression can be ranked in relation to importance and severity. A wider social awareness of racism, Islamophobia and homophobia underpinned many participants' narratives whilst many participants claimed that society did not perceive 'transphobia as a big deal that needs to be acknowledged'. Notions of (in)visibility are discussed later in this book, but the idea that trans people are often 'invisible victims', in which the victimisation they experience is not acknowledged and addressed underpinned many participants' narratives. In this sense, ideas of (in)visibility directly relate to the notion of the 'social conscious'. The social conscious refers to the wider social recognition of particular issues, in which transphobia is not as widely recognised as other forms of discrimination and oppression.

This may be the result of more socially recognised histories in relation to other forms of oppression, particularly racial oppression and homophobia. In England and Wales, legislative protection against racist discrimination date back to the Race Relations Act (1965). Since then, there have been several high-profile incidents that relate to racism at an individual, institutional and societal level. Incidents such as the racially aggravated murder of Stephen Lawrence (Holdaway 1999), the murder of Mark Duggan (Elliott-Cooper 2018) and the overrepresentation of young Black men in all elements of the Criminal Justice System (Warde 2013), have resulted in issues of race and racism gaining significant societal attention, although not always in a positive or progressive way. As a result, there have been several inquiries into racism permeating various levels of society (Lammy 2017; Macpherson 1999; Scarman 1981). To date there has not been a public inquiry to this scale that explores issues of transphobia.

Similarly, there is a longer history of acknowledgement of the oppressions that sexual minorities face. This is often spoken of in relation to 'LGBT equality', and indeed, the contribution of trans communities to liberation movements has been documented (Denny 2006; Minter 2006). The 1969 Stonewall riot which took place in the Greenwich Village of New York City are often memorialised as the beginning of a worldwide LGBT movement (Armstrong and Crage 2006). The Sexual Offences Act (1967) saw the partial decriminalisation of sex between men in England and Wales; however, the effectiveness of this legislation on equality has been questioned (Ashford 2017). Since the partial decriminalisation there has been various legislative gains for lesbian, gay and bisexual people, including the introduction of the Civil Partnership Act (2004), Marriage (Same Sex Couples) Act (2013) and the Adoption and Children Act (2002). However, there has also been recurrent media representations which demonise and sexualise LGBT communities, primarily relating to the AIDS epidemic and the inclusion of same-sex relationships in the school curriculum (Colliver 2019). Despite many of the legislative introductions being coined as progressive gains for the LGBT community, mainstream representation and social tolerance has tended to benefit cisgender, gay men and women (Richardson and Monro 2012). Research has also seen significantly more attention being paid to issues associated with homophobia, often overshadowing issues of biphobia, transphobia and queerphobia (Colliver and Silvestri 2020; Monro et al. 2017).

Ideas around societal awareness were perceived to permeate those in positions of authority, with responsibility for providing protection and support. As such, reporting hate crime targeting trans identity was often pre-empted to be dismissed. This has implications for trans people who experience victimisation as to whether they seek assistance from the police. As Elaine, a 48-year-old trans woman explains:

> Racism is much higher on the police's agenda. As soon as you mention racism the police are on it because they don't want to sit back and do nothing and then be accused of racism themselves you know? There isn't such a huge public fuss about transphobia, so I don't think the police feel the same pressure they do to do something about it when it's about gender.

In relation to social awareness, Elaine speaks directly about the influence a lack of societal awareness can have on the policing of particular forms of prejudice, discrimination and hate. Therefore, as there is a long history of institutional racism within the police (Macpherson 1999) and a number of high-profile incidents that have called into question the legitimacy and effectiveness of the police in relation to the over-policing of Black, Asian and minority ethnic communities, the police may feel the need to respond more rigorously to particular incidents of racist hate crime. Police responses to racism are therefore framed within a political context in relation to the police's accountability and response to racism. In this sense, the police may be perceived to respond positively and proactively in order to maintain a positive image, rather than as a result of actual care. Elaine further contextualises this perception within her own personal experiences of interactions with the police:

> It [reporting racism] was much better than when I reported the incident about my gender, it was almost like as soon as I said racist the police jumped on it. I think because of the way things are with the police and the Black community, they panic and act straight away so that they can't be accused of being racist. So, they take it more seriously because they have something to prove you know.

The data presented above demonstrates the perceptions that individuals may have after having interacted with the police. It is also important to note that the experience Elaine described above occurred some years before she transitioned, and since transitioning she has also reported incidents of racism to which the police 'did not take it seriously'. Elaine perceives this to be because of her identity as a trans woman. In this sense, the seriousness of her racist victimisation was perceived to be negated by her trans identity. The perception that reports of transphobia may be received by the police with less importance than other forms of discrimination was framed within a wider political and social recognition of particular forms of oppression and hate. Participants alluded to historic and contemporary tensions between the police and Black, Asian and minority ethnic communities and attributed significance to this as a causal reason for more thorough responses to racist hate crime. As a result, racism is firmly positioned at the top of the hierarchy of protected characteristics. This is not to say that institutional racism, racial profiling and the over-policing of Black, Asian and minority ethnic communities is not still a significant social and political problem, as research has documented these issues (Souhami 2012). However, it may be the wider media and political attention paid to these issues that positions race at the top of the hierarchy.

This was a recurrent issue within participants' narratives, in which issues of legitimacy and authenticity of victimisation were drawn upon. This was considered key in whether an incident of victimisation was reported to the police or not. Many participants had a perception that the 'police wouldn't take it seriously unless it … was racist or homophobic … which are always taken seriously'. Trans people appear to evaluate the likelihood of their claim being taken seriously in comparison to other forms of hate. There is a perception that 'verbal abuse that [is] racist would be more likely to be considered as a hate crime by the police than transphobic verbal abuse'. In this sense, race and trans identity are simultaneously positioned at opposite ends of the hierarchy, with trans identity gaining the least social recognition in relation to victimisation. As such, there is a cycle of perpetuation in which a dominant societal framing of authentic and legitimate victimisation creates barriers for trans people to report incidents of transphobic hate crime. The lack of societal awareness of transphobic hate crime is also perpetuated by a reluctance, or hesitancy to report; therefore, transphobic hate crime continually fails to gain social recognition.

Inconsistencies in legislative protections for various minoritised groups also seemed to influence participants' understanding of the seriousness of their victimisation. Whilst there are five 'monitored characteristics', the legislative protections afforded to each 'characteristic' are unequal. As noted earlier in the book, the Crime and Disorder Act (1998) introduced a number of 'racially aggravated offences' and through a later amendment a number of 'religiously aggravated offences'. Not only did this piece of legislation create new, specific offences related to race and religion, it also introduced new maximum penalties for individuals sentenced under this piece of legislation. However, this act does not extend legislative protection to those who experience victimisation targeting their trans identity, and therefore the Criminal Justice Act (2003) is utilised in sentencing those found guilty. Whilst the inclusion of trans identity in the Criminal Justice Act can be seen as a positive step forward in terms of trans equality, the unequal legislative protection afforded to different 'identity characteristics' does have symbolic value (Mason 2005). The Criminal Justice Act (2003) does not introduce specific 'transphobically aggravated offences' and does not introduce new maximum penalties, although an uplift tariff can be applied. Beyond a perceived social hierarchy that exists, the varying legislative protections create a formal, legal hierarchy in which more punitive responses are adopted for the victimisation of some minoritised groups than others. This appeared to have implications for participants in this research and influenced their perception of themselves as 'worthy' victims. Undoubtedly, this has an impact on how confident participants felt in reporting their experiences to the police.

Results from the online survey showed that only 34.9% of trans people felt that the police were 'very aware' or 'slightly aware' of issues facing trans and non-binary communities. This is in comparison to 53.9% of trans people who felt the police were either 'very unaware' or 'slightly unaware' of issues facing trans and non-binary communities. Interviewees highlighted that they felt the police had a much greater awareness of issues affecting lesbian, gay and bisexual communities. Even though the police regularly attend and engage in Pride festivities, this was often perceived as catering to the needs of cisgender, gay men. Indeed, Australian research has shown that police initiatives around LGBT engagement and visibility are rarely tailored to the needs of trans communities (Dwyer and Ball 2020). This was often considered to be at the cost of trans people, and resultantly many experienced a range of microaggressions when interacting with the police which delegitimised their gender identity. The hierarchical nature of protected characteristics contributes to a much wider police awareness of issues pertaining to race, religion and sexuality. This negatively affects trans people's perception of the police and their ability to respond effectively to reports of transphobic hate crime. Star, who is 44 years old and non-binary describes that:

> there needs to be some way of knowing that transphobia is taken as seriously, you know, as crimes that are racist, or homophobic. I think

> transgender is like the last taboo so there is a lack of knowledge around gender identity … Everyone has spent much longer on things like raising awareness for homophobia and racism. This makes it hard for trans people to report to the police, you think they won't understand.

A lack of awareness of issues affecting trans and non-binary communities was perceived to be the underlying cause for instances of misgendering, dead-naming and asking intrusive questions about genitalia when interacting with the police. Although it is important to note that for some participants these incidents were perceived to be deliberate. Experiences like this reflect a lack of police awareness, but also contribute to a level of mistrust between trans communities and the police. Existing research has demonstrated that positive police–community relations and interactions are vital in establishing confidence, trust and enhancing perceptions of police legitimacy (Bradford et al. 2009; Hough et al. 2010). Whilst these incidents fall outside the remit of crime, they still negatively affect trans people's perceptions of the police as 'protectors'. Mandatory gender identity awareness training for police officers may lead to greater levels of confidence in the police and a decrease in trans people's sense of risk of experiencing further discrimination and microaggressions when reporting. The lack of awareness of the issues affecting trans and non-binary people translates into an underreporting of transphobic hate crime. Of those who participated in the online survey, only 39.8% of the people who had experienced a hate crime had reported it to the police. The underreporting of transphobic hate crime is framed within the interviews as often being a direct consequence of the hierarchical nature of hate crime victimisation. The lack of awareness that trans people perceive the police to have in relation to gender identity was also key in the online survey. Of all participants who indicated that they had reported an incident of transphobic hate crime to the police, only 3.4% of participants indicated that they were satisfied the police understood their needs directly relating to their trans identity.

The hierarchical nature of hate crime victimisation also extended to the notion of the 'legitimate victim'. Christie (1986) argues that only certain stereotypical 'victims' are assigned 'legitimate victim' status. A key tenet of the 'ideal victim' relies on the victim being 'free from blame'. In this research, many participants describe experiencing blame from family, friends and criminal justice agencies in relation to their victimisation. This is mostly seen in suggestions made to censor and present a more socially conformative gender presentation in order to avoid further victimisation. In this sense, Christie's notion of 'free from blame' is a significant factor in trans people's self-perception of the legitimacy of their victim status. Indeed, it has been argued 'that being LGB and/or T can provide opportunities, for those who so wish, to ascribe both culpability and agency to any misfortunes that they might experiences' (Donovan and Barnes 2018: 84). The construction of being transgender as a 'choice' is a common trope employed in the delegitimisation of trans identities (Colliver et al. 2019). It became clear through the narratives in this research that other people would not experience the same level of blame directly associated with their identity. In this sense, an individual's race, or disability status for example, are not constructed as a 'choice', and therefore victims of racist or disablist hate crime may be assigned legitimate victim status more readily.

It became clear that interviewees perceived sexuality to be more socially recognisable, and not only did this have implications for their perceptions of how seriously transphobia would be taken, it also influenced the type of verbal abuse they experienced. Many trans people experience abuse as a result of their 'difference', but the nature of the abuse is often homophobic, as a result of perpetrators conflating sexuality and gender identity. As such, a greater social awareness of sexuality, and homophobia in particular resulted in trans people experiencing homophobic hate crime, regardless of whether they were heterosexual or not. Many trans people experience name-calling that draws upon homophobic slurs such as 'faggot', 'dyke' and 'queer'. Trans people's presentations of masculinity and femininity are intrinsically linked to perpetrators' perception of sexuality, rather than gender identity. This may be the result of cisnormative expectations that assume everyone is cisgender and can be neatly categorised as 'male' or 'female' (Sumerau et al. 2018), and therefore deviating from expected gender presentations is more significantly associated with lesbian, gay and bisexual identities. The homophobic nature of verbal abuse may also be related to a wider societal awareness of sexual minorities and derogatory terms associated with this protected characteristic. As such, motifs of abuse targeting a victim's perceived sexuality are more readily accessible within perpetrators' discursive repertoires. Resultantly, there is also a continued invalidation of a victim's gender in which they are not perceived to be trans, but rather, may be seen as lesbian, gay, bisexual or queer.

The historic conflation of gender identity with sexuality (Salamon 2010), which has been dominated by the experiences and exposure of white, gay men (Jones and Newburn 2001) has led to a significantly lower awareness of trans identities and communities. In this sense, a hierarchy of protected characteristics is established that assigns 'legitimate' victim status to particular groups based on their positioning on the hierarchy. It can be argued that transphobic hate crime is positioned at the bottom of the hierarchy, in which legitimate victim status may be ambiguous in trans people's perception of their own victimisation. This is important to interrogate, as the external construction and representation of trans people may therefore be internalised into a lower sense of 'worth' or recognition in relation to their victimisation. This is therefore likely to impact the amount and ways in which transphobic hate crime is recorded. I would therefore argue that the low level of officially recorded hate crimes (Home Office 2020) is partially as a result of a 'cycle of delegitimisation' of trans people as worthy victims. Structural, institutional and legislative policies and cultures have symbolic value that suggest trans people are less worthy as victims, and the internalisation of these beliefs creates barriers to reporting. In order to address the underreporting of transphobic hate crime, it is key to acknowledge and address these wider cultures of delegitimisation.

Social Hierarchy of Offence Types

It is not just 'protected characteristics' that are perceived to be hierarchical in nature. The type of victimisation that trans people experience was also key in their conceptualisation and understanding of their own victimisation. In this sense, a clear hierarchy is established in which physical and sexual violence are privileged as 'legitimate' and 'authentic' forms of victimisation, whereas micro-crime victimisation was often perceived to be 'wasting police time'. This is not a new concept; across the world, crimes are often ranked from those considered to be most serious, which often have the most punitive responses, down to those considered the least serious (Cogan 2002). Verbal abuse, harassment and online abuse were generally not considered worthy of police attention. In some ways, reporting verbal abuse, harassment and online abuse was conceptualised as reducing the legitimacy, authenticity and validity of 'real' victimisation such as physical violence. This is problematic as research shows that a significant amount of victimisation targeting trans people is what might be termed 'low-level', encompassing incidents of verbal abuse, harassment and online victimisation (Chakraborti et al. 2014; METRO Charity 2014). Resultantly, the ordering, ranking and hierarchizing of forms of crime and victimisation has implications for the likelihood of reporting any victimisation experienced to the police.

When defining and discussing the meaning of a hate crime, crimes such as 'assault, ABH and GBH' were drawn on when providing examples of what a hate crime might be, often with participants noting that the most serious manifestation of hate could result in the 'murder of a trans person'. This demonstrates the way in which the hierarchy of offence type permeates social and individual understandings of crime and victimisation and demonstrates that physical violence is at the forefront of people's conscious when discussing hate crime. Physical and sexual violence are therefore more socially recognisable forms of victimisation. This is not to say that verbal abuse, harassment and online abuse are not socially visible, but they are not as easily recognisable as criminal victimisation. This was certainly reflected in the online survey, in which 97% of participants indicated that they would consider physical violence, motivated by prejudice or discrimination to be a hate crime.

This may be perpetuated by the constant media overshadowing of micro-crime victimisation, in place of more extreme forms of victimisation (Iganski 2008). As outlined by Jewkes (2015), there exists a number of different values that are considered when deciding which stories appear in mainstream news outlets. In determining which events will best meet the needs and appetite of the public interest, a number of factors may be considered, including the predictability of an event, and as such, the less predictable, or less commonly occurring an event may be heightens its 'newsworthiness' (Jewkes 2015). Similarly, stories and events associated with violence generally, but specifically sexual violence are deemed to be more newsworthy (Jewkes 2015). As Hall et al. (1978: 70) argue, 'any crime can be lifted into news visibility if violence becomes associated with it … Violence represents a basic violation of the person … It thus represents a fundamental rupture in the social order'. It is therefore unsurprising to find that although the victimisation of trans people is scarcely reported, when it is covered in mainstream media, it primarily focuses on the sexual or physical victimisation of victims. This results in sensationalised headlines such as 'Five sentenced for brutal murder of transgender woman which shocked the world' (PinkNews 2018) and 'Images released after "violent transphobic attack" on Northern line' (Johnson 2020). The absence of media reports on more 'low-level' forms of victimisation may influence trans people's perception of which types of victimisation are 'worthy'.

The overshadowing of 'low-level' and 'mundane' forms of victimisation is also evident within research, in which participants are often required to discuss the 'most serious' incident they have experienced (Rose and Mechanic 2002: 16) or to explain when they have felt most at risk of 'physical danger' (Herek et al. 1999: 201). Resultantly, research perpetuates the privileging of physical and sexual violence as the only forms of 'legitimate' victimisation. Meyer (2010) argues that these methods of research contribute to the hierarchical ranking of incidents in which verbal abuse, which may be persistent, is positioned at the bottom of the hierarchy. This certainly appears to be the case for interviewees who participated in this research and believed that harassment and verbal abuse are 'not serious enough' and may be 'separate from actual hate crime'. This was often reinforced through interactions with the police, in which incidents of verbal abuse in public, harassment and online abuse were regularly recorded as 'hate incidents' rather than as a criminal offence. As Dilip, a 45-year-old man described:

> One time I went to the police to report that someone had been following me down the street calling a 'dirty tranny' and wouldn't leave me alone. The police said it was a hate incident not a crime, so there was nothing they

could do about it. They made a note and stuff, but that was it. So, I don't think verbal abuse like that is a hate crime.

The experience described by Dilip was a common narrative across the interviews; police interactions had a significant impact on individuals' perception of their own victimisation. Despite the dominance of physical violence as the most legitimate form of victimisation, some participants were aware that non-physically violent offences including harassment and verbal abuse were criminal and reportable. In this sense, there is a clear perception of criminality relating to non-violent offences which challenges the established hierarchy of victimisation. However, as discussed in the previous chapter, this is more clearly established in the context of the victimisation of others. Even when incidents of verbal abuse, harassment and online abuse are perceived by the victim to be a criminal offence, police response to this victimisation may lead to victims reconceptualising their victimisation as non-criminal. This means that future incidents of a similar nature are likely to remain unreported. Additionally, this may have implications for an individual's ability to process an experience of victimisation. Someone may experience all of the psychological and emotional impact of victimisation, but be unable to process these feelings as a result of not being able to recognise their own victimisation as 'legitimate'.

One of the most significant cases in England and Wales that demonstrates the tragic consequences of police dismissal is the case of Fiona and Francesca Pilkington. Fiona and Francesca died after Fiona drove them to a secluded area and set the car alight whilst both were still inside (Chakraborti 2010). This occurred after years of targeted abuse against the family which included verbal abuse, criminal damage and physical violence (Sherry 2010). The motivation for this targeted campaign of victimisation is believed to be anti-disability prejudice. Despite making contact with the police at least 33 times, Fiona was often believed to be over-reacting to anti-social behaviour (Ralph et al. 2016). Despite not being transphobic in nature, the experiences of the Pilkingtons epitomise the real-life consequences of a hierarchy of offence type.

Incidents of victimisation are often conceptualised and understood by victims comparatively. As Peter, a 41-year-old trans man claims, he doesn't feel 'the police would take it [harassment] seriously … whereas if a murder was reported they would take it seriously'. In this sense, the hierarchical nature of offence type permeates the ways in which victimisation is understood. Even when incidents in which criminality is a more obvious feature, such as criminal damage, the police did not always respond in the ways people expected. As such, when people report incidents in which criminality is obvious and receive a negative response, they are likely to compare incidents of future victimisation to this experience. Corrina, a 21-year-old trans woman describes how the police did nothing when her stuff was destroyed, so she fails to see 'why they would do anything about verbal abuse'. When people experience physical and sexual violence, it may be 'easier to be seen as a victim' as a result of 'people rallying around' and the sense that people care. This may not be the case when people experience verbal abuse and harassment as the impact of this type of victimisation may not be as visible. This infiltrates people's perception of the police and what is deemed 'worthy' of police attention. Many participants felt that the police had 'more serious issues to deal with' and were 'not likely to take incidents of verbal abuse seriously' as that is 'not what they got the job to do'. As such, more socially recognisable forms of victimisation, characterised by physical and sexual violence, dominate perceptions as to what is reportable. In this sense, wider societal frameworks that assign legitimacy to particular forms of victimisation influence people's understanding of their own victimisation. These perceptions are not unfounded, as existing research has shown that policing interests have historically focused on 'crime fighting' rather than 'helping people' (Charman 2020). Attending to incidents of verbal abuse, harassment or online victimisation may therefore not coincide with police perceptions of what 'real policing is all about' (Bacon 2014: 111). Bowling (1999) refers to the 'hierarchy of police relevance' which indicates a hypothetical set of values that police officers use, sometimes subconsciously, other times consciously, in their response to different incidents. Bowling (1999) refers to 'good crime' as unambiguous criminal offences with a 'good' victim, a 'good' perpetrator and cases that offer the prospect of a 'good' arrest being made that leads to a successful prosecution.

Specifically in the context of offence type, there is a strong perception that victimisation that is not physically, or sexually, violent will not be 'taken seriously' by the police. In this sense, individuals anticipate, predict and pre-empt how their victimisation will be responded to and evaluate whether an incident is 'worthwhile' reporting. This also has implications as to how victims perceive their own responses to hate crime. Ashley, a 34-year-old man explains:

> I thought they would just turn around and be like 'oh, it's only kids messing around, don't take it to heart', so I just didn't bother telling the police, or telling anyone actually.

Even though Ashley experienced significant psychological and emotional turmoil as a consequence of his victimisation, in which he had experienced targeted, and repetitive verbal abuse and having items thrown at him, he pre-empted that people would respond to him in a way that indicates he is overreacting. Fear of being accused of overreacting results in a suppression of feelings in a bid to appear 'rational'. This may have further detrimental consequences as research shows that the suppression of feelings can cause further emotional and psychological trauma (Hooberman et al. 2010). Perceptions of policing priorities were also intrinsic in the decision-making process of whether to report an incident of micro-crime victimisation and the anticipated lack of action that would be taken regarding their victimisation. Even when trans people feel they have experienced hate-motivated criminal victimisation, there is a strong feeling that 'the police wouldn't consider it to be criminal and wouldn't want to waste their time with it'. A fear of 'wasting police time' is common for trans victims of hate crime and this is mirrored alongside a desire to not waste their own time. The process of visiting a police station, making a report, chasing the police for updates was conceptualised as a time-consuming task, which very often led to no outcome. As such, it is easier to just 'deal with it' themselves. The overwhelming consensus is that experiences of micro-crime victimisation will be responded to by the police as non-criminal, and therefore the likelihood of police intervention is minimal. In this sense, more socially recognisable forms of victimisation, such as physical and sexual violence, influence an individual's perception of how worthy their experiences are of being reported.

The hierarchical nature of offence type also impacts trans people's knowledge and understanding of what *can* be reported to the police. There is a strong understanding of the criminality associated with physical and sexual violence, particularly when perpetrated by a stranger, often perpetuated by media representations of victimisation. However, when discussing experiences of micro-crime victimisation, there is a significant gap in knowledge as to what counted as 'criminal' and therefore what could be reported to the police. This is often discussed in the context of legislation and policy guidance being inaccessible for many people. There is a strong need for greater education and social awareness surrounding hate crime, with clear guidance and examples 'of what can be reported and how it should be reported'. The lack of accessibility in relation to legislation and policy significantly impacts the decision-making process in relation to reporting incidents of hate crime. As Ty, who is non-binary explains:

> If I read an official document that said I could report if someone threatened me and called me transphobic names, then I would. I would take that document with me, so I could be confident I would be listened to. So, I think people need to be told very clearly on what is reportable and what isn't.

There is a clear lack of clarity surrounding what is a reportable offence and what isn't. The lack of clarity primarily relates to incidents that would be policed under the Public Order Act (1986), which criminalises behaviours such as threatening behaviour and intentionally causing harassment, alarm or distress. A desire for clarification as to what forms of victimisation 'will be taken seriously' underpinned many discussions around the reporting of micro-crime victimisation. The complexity and nuance of legislative regulations and official policies that police incidents of hate crime allude to a power imbalance between those who create, maintain and enforce the law, and those who are policed and protected by it. Legislation and official polices become characterised by complexity and therefore deemed inaccessible for many trans people, and the wider population more generally. As such, there is a need for simple, clear guidance that offers examples to better equip victims of hate crimes with the knowledge of what is reportable.

Although there was a clearly established hierarchy of offence types, it was the forms of victimisation that were considered the 'least serious' that were most commonly experienced. Data from the online survey showed that 95% of participants who had experienced a hate crime indicated that this was verbal abuse. A range of other types of victimisation were also reported and 63% of participants indicated they had experienced physical violence, 28.7% had experienced damage to their property and 27.1% indicated they had experienced sexual violence. Although high levels of victimisation across all forms of crime were reported, verbal abuse was the most commonly experienced, although was also the least often reported.

Despite a general narrative underpinning participants' perceptions as to what counted as a hate crime, these were also dependent upon people's gender, sexuality, religion, race and disability status. However, race was the most significant characteristic in the analysis. I now draw upon data that was collected as part of the online survey. As part of the online survey, participants were asked to indicate whether they considered a range of behaviours to be a 'hate crime', if motivated by prejudice, discrimination or hostility. Of all the behaviours considered, physical and sexual abuse were the only behaviours that produced non-statistically significant results. This suggests that physical and sexual abuse are always identifiable as criminal, regardless of an individual's gender, sexuality, religion, race or disability status. As shown in Table 4.1, regression analysis indicated that Black, Asian and minority ethnic participants had 0.434 the predicted odds of perceiving hate mail to be criminal in comparison to participants who identified as white British. Similarly, Black, Asian and minority

Table 4.1 Predicted odds of perceiving hate mail to be criminal

		B	S.E.	Wald	df	Sig.	Exp(B)
Step 1[a]	Ethnicity	−0.835	0.373	5.004	1	0.025	0.434
	Religion	−0.237	0.383	0.383	1	0.536	0.789
	Gender	0.190	0.432	0.194	1	0.660	1.210
	Sexuality	−0.801	0.486	2.717	1	0.099	0.449
	Disability	0.044	0.405	0.012	1	0.913	1.045
	Constant	−1.687	0.515	10.706	1	0.001	0.185

ethnic participants had 0.263 the predicted odds of perceiving intimidation to be criminal in comparison to white British participants.

Perceptions of verbal abuse also produced statistically significant results when participants' race was considered. As shown in Table 4.2, Black, Asian and minority ethnic participants had 0.309 the predicted odds of considering verbal abuse to be criminal in comparison to white British participants. These results indicate that white British people are more likely to assign criminality to incidents such as verbal abuse, intimidation and hate mail. This is consistent with other research which has utilised an intersectional framework (Meyer 2010).

Research by Meyer (2010) indicates that white, middle-class individuals were more likely to perceive their experiences to be 'severe' than Black, Asian and minority ethnic individuals. This may be explained by the fact that trans people who may experience multiple, intersecting oppressions are likely to experience higher levels of discrimination, prejudice and abuse. Therefore, a process of rationalisation and normalisation may occur in order to maintain daily functioning. This may result in white trans people perceiving verbal abuse, harassment and intimidation to be more severe, as a result of less experiences of individual, social and structural oppression. Additionally, in considering Christie's (1986) ideas of the 'ideal victim', it could be argued that such forms of victimisation and the harms caused by these types of victimisation are not recognised in the social consciousness (Fohring 2018). This may be as a result of various representations of crime and what appeals to the public interest. As such, those who experience this type of victimisation may not consider it to be 'legitimate', due to a lack of social acknowledgement.

Table 4.2 Predicted odds of considering verbal abuse to be criminal

		B	S.E.	Wald	df	Sig.	Exp(B)
Step 1[a]	Ethnicity	−1.175	0.410	8.214	1	0.004	0.309
	Religion	−0.121	0.415	0.085	1	0.771	0.886
	Gender	0.099	0.490	0.041	1	0.840	1.104
	Sexuality	0.209	0.442	0.224	1	0.636	1.233
	Disability	−0.126	0.431	0.086	1	0.769	0.881
	Constant	−1.858	0.561	10.984	1	0.001	0.156

Hierarchical Nature of the Victim-Perpetrator Relationship

A core tenet of Christie's (1986) conceptualisation of the 'ideal victim' centres on the relationship between the victim and perpetrator. The final attribute of the 'ideal victim' is that there is no pre-existing relationship between the victim and perpetrator (Christie 1986). Despite notions of the 'ideal victim' relating primarily to an individual's ability to receive the 'victim' label from external parties, I would argue that the victim–perpetrator relationship is also key in our internal understanding of our victimhood. This is often perpetuated by media narratives which reinforce notions of 'stranger danger'. Victimisation that is deemed 'newsworthy' often relies on the existence of an 'unknown perpetrator', overshadowing the experiences of those who encounter victimisation in private spaces, committed by those perceived to be closest to them, including family, partners, friends and colleagues. Indeed, existing research has shown that the victim–perpetrator relationship has a significant impact upon the likelihood and extent of news coverage that particular crimes receive (Wong and Lee 2018).

Christie's (1986) 'ideal victim' typology relating to the notion of 'stranger danger' is also a key tenet in participants' perceptions of their own victim status. When trans people experience victimisation that is perpetrated by friends and family, their conceptualisation of 'victimhood' becomes ambiguous. This has been explored in literature relating to familial and domestic violence and abuse (Corteen et al. 2016) in which an existing visible relationship causes the invisibility of perpetrator status being assigned, in turn negating the existence of 'victim' status. In this sense, Christie's idea of the ideal victim being one who has no existing relationship with the perpetrator permeates participants' accounts of their victimisation in relation to a known offender. Therefore, it can be argued that transphobic victimisation within a familial or domestic setting is likely to be significantly underreported as a consequence of the ambiguity of 'legitimate victim' status in these cases.

Media narratives that perpetuate notions of 'stranger danger' were certainly evident in participants' narratives and perspectives of risk. As

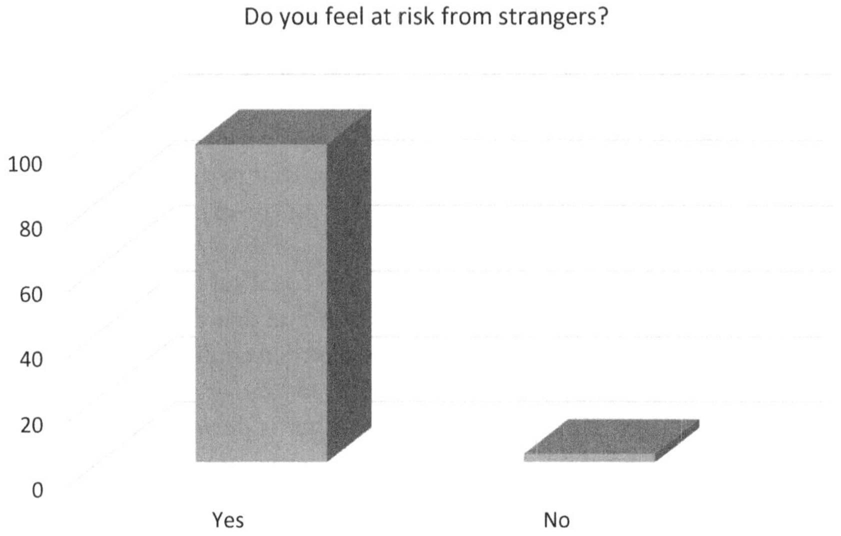

Fig. 4.1 Do you feel at risk of experiencing a hate crime from strangers?

shown in Fig. 4.1, results from the online survey showed that 'strangers' were perceived to present the highest level of risk, with 97.4% of participants indicating that they felt strangers were a risk to their safety. Although strangers were identified as posing the biggest risk, healthcare professionals, criminal justice officials and co-workers were also highlighted as presenting a risk to an individual's safety. The risk that both immediate and extended family present was acknowledged, but only one in five people highlighted family as posing a potential risk. This is significantly less than those who indicated strangers as presenting a risk. Fear of strangers is a key theme in interviewees' reports on perceptions of risk. This is despite many participants recounting abuse perpetrated by family, friends and other 'known' perpetrators. As such, 'stranger danger' is an intrinsic feature in perceiving and evaluating risk and has tangible outcomes for the ways in which everyday life is engaged with. Rose, a 67-year-old trans woman explains that the fear of strangers is rooted in the mystery of how strangers 'will react' to trans people. Resultantly, Rose avoids places like big supermarkets and travels further to find smaller, independent shops that tend to have a smaller clientele. There is a clear implication for how often and how confidently some trans people can engage in public spaces and may take measures to minimise their interaction in public. In this sense, adapting an everyday routine functions as a 'risk-reduction' strategy. This was reiterated by Sam, a 31-year-old trans man who reflected on the 'power of the unknown' and the risk associated with the 'unknown'. Despite Sam recounting incidents of extreme physical abuse perpetrated by family members, perceptions of risk were still predominantly conceptualised in relation to the 'unknown'. This highlights the sheer significance of 'stranger danger' and the way in which it is so intrinsically woven into society's understanding of criminal victimisation. As such, victimisation is most feared from 'socially recognisable perpetrators', rather than those who may have perpetrated violence, but are less socially recognised and acknowledged as perpetrators, such as family and friends.

Despite the image of the 'stranger' being primarily associated with the public sphere, the role of the 'stranger' as a symbolic figure of fear also impacts the ways in which people engage with 'risk-reduction' in private. Ruby, a 52-year-old trans woman explains that:

> I don't feel comfortable around them [strangers]. I think they present the biggest risk to me, but not just strangers you see on the street, strangers that come in to your space, gas men, delivery drivers, postmen.

There are a number of times in which we may find the 'unknown' and 'known' merging, and this has the potential to transform a perceived 'safe space' into a space of perceived risk. Ruby also describes a number of 'risk-reduction' strategies she uses in situations when a stranger must enter her home, such as 'staying in the kitchen' so she is able to access items to protect herself with if needed. Fear of strangers is so prominent that there were no statistically significant results when participants' gender, sexuality, race, religion and disability status were accounted for, demonstrating the inherent risk assigned to the 'stranger'. This is also mirrored in participants' accounts of where they feel most at risk of experiencing abuse, in which the 'home' was one of the least commonly selected answers, mirroring low levels of perceived risk from family and friends. Participants' local area was the most commonly selected answer, reflecting the public nature of victimisation that feeds in to notions of stranger danger.

This is not to say that these fears are unfounded as strangers were often perpetrators of hate crime. However, the overwhelming focus on 'stranger danger' may be misleading and therefore influence people's understanding of their own experiences of abuse as criminal. Even when immediate and extended family members are perceived as presenting a risk to an individual's safety, hate crimes committed by those known to the victim were often conceptualised as non-criminal. After having experienced physical violence perpetrated by her father, Deena, 34 years old, explains how she 'didn't really consider it to be a hate crime, or any crime, because they were family'. Deena frames this understanding within the context of love, respect and a desire not to disappoint her family any further. Often, values such as love, loyalty and respect are central in victims' understanding of their own victimisation. Victimisation that is perpetrated by family is often difficult to conceptualise as 'hate crime', even when the criminality of an act is recognised. This is because 'hate' was in direct opposition with the core values most commonly prescribed to notions of 'family' by participants. This is not to say that family units always offer a safe or 'loving' environment, but even when this is not the case, they are often conceptualised by dominant understandings of what 'family' is. As Bushra, a 29-year-old woman explains:

> No, I did not [consider it to be a hate crime]. I know that it was a crime. I know it is illegal to hurt people, but I did not think it was a hate crime. It was my family, my family I know they loved me, but I brought shame and disgrace to them.

For Bushra, the violence that she experienced when she disclosed her trans identity to her family was perpetrated by her father and brothers. When participants recounted experiences of abuse perpetrated by family members and friends, notions of self-blame are often drawn upon. In this sense, self-blame contributes to the conceptualisation of abuse as non-hate motivated. Bushra is explicitly aware that her victimisation was criminal, yet even so, her feelings of self-blame override the identification of family members as perpetrators of crime. It is also important to note that the role and status of the 'family' were heavily contextualised within religious and cultural frameworks. Participants reflected a diverse range of faiths and beliefs including Buddhist, Christian, Muslim and Sikh alongside a number of people who had no religious affiliation. The role of the 'family' was not as prominent in participants' accounts who identified as having no religion. Religion appeared to be a key characteristic in the analysis of the online survey. Participants who considered themselves religious has 2.995 times the predicted odds of feeling at risk of experiencing a hate crime from a member of their immediate family. Furthermore, those who considered themselves religious has 3.627 times the predicted odds of feeling at risk of experiencing a hate crime from a member of their extended family (Table 4.3).

Given the historic tension between particular religious communities and wider LGBTQ communities (Law 2016; Paul 2017), it can be argued that trans people from religious families and communities are more likely to fear rejection, discrimination and abuse as a result of their trans identity than trans people who are non-religious. Religious responses to gender and sexual non-conformity have included conversion therapy (Clucas 2017) and honour-based violence (Khan et al. 2017). This may also therefore play a part in religious trans people's fear of victimisation from religious communities and family members. It is also likely that trans people who are also religious may face multiple oppressions relating to their gender identity from both non-religious cisgender people and a heightened sense of fear and oppression from religious communities. This is not to say that all religious communities persecute gender and sexual minorities, nor do I claim that all non-religious communities are accepting of gender and sexual minorities. However, the role of religion

Table 4.3 Predicted odds of feeling at risk of experiencing a hate crime from a member of extended family

		B	S.E.	Wald	df	Sig.	Exp(B)
Step 1[a]	Ethnicity	1.203	0.279	18.567	1	0.000	3.331
	Religion	1.288	0.283	20.711	1	0.000	3.627
	Gender	0.326	0.327	0.996	1	0.318	1.386
	Sexuality	−0.024	0.330	0.005	1	0.943	0.977
	Disability	−0.263	0.300	0.769	1	0.380	0.768
	Constant	−0.682	0.383	3.170	1	0.075	0.506

and culture are certainly important factors when trans people consider the level of risk they face.

Organista et al. (2010) claim that 'homosexuality' is primarily conceptualised as an exclusively western identity, and that this may amount to a perceived cultural and ethnic rejection by lesbian and gay people from ethnic minority backgrounds. This is a similar notion that participants describe, in which their experiences of victimisation perpetrated by family members is conceptualised within cultural norms in which self-blame is described as a result of bringing shame to the family through the rejection of cultural expectations. At other times, ideas of self-blame combined with a lack of awareness of what hate crime is contribute to the understanding of victimisation. Some participants who felt blame for their own victimisation also felt 'uneducated on what a hate crime was' and felt that it was 'just family dealing with it in the way that they know how to deal with it'. In this sense, a perpetrator's identity as a family member may become their 'master status' in which it becomes difficult to identify a family member as a perpetrator, as a result of a pre-existing relationship. It is key to recognise the difficulties in identifying a family member as a perpetrator, as this has implications for whether incidents are reported to the police. Deena, who did not report her experience, reflects on whether this would have been different if a stranger had been the perpetrator:

> If it was a stranger, or someone I didn't know, or a random person on the street, I definitely would have reported it. So my family being family, that is a definite reasons why I didn't do anything about it.

The role of the 'family' is central in how victims understand their experiences and whether they seek criminal justice in response. However, it was not just a desire to not bring further 'trouble' to the family that influences whether an incident is reported. For some, the status of the perpetrator as a family member resulted in the perception that the police would not perceive an incident to be criminal. The role of the 'family' in the perpetration of hate crime transformed their victimisation into a 'domestic situation', which would be outside the realms of police intervention. The conceptualisation of hate crime as a domestic incident minimises the severity, in which criminality is no longer a feature. Even when criminality is an obvious feature, 'family values' and loyalty to the family unit often override the desire for justice in the form of police intervention. Sam, a 31-year-old man who was physically attacked, with weapons, by his family, refused to speak with police when they visited him in hospital. In this sense, individual family norms relating to 'grassing', 'trusting the police' and 'turning on your family' may be prominent in the decision-making process as to whether to report a crime or not.

When considering the core tenets of Christie's (1986) concept of the 'ideal victim' in which certain conditions must be met for an individual to be assigned the 'victim' label, it is likely that trans people experience a significant amount of victimisation that is not recognised as 'legitimate'. Existing research has shown that trans communities are more likely to experience rejection from the family home, relationship breakdown and discrimination and abuse within employment than cisgender people (Durso and Gates 2012; METRO Charity 2014). It is likely that whilst all of these may not be abusive in and of themselves, there is a significant likelihood that abuse and victimisation occur alongside these events. Given that being excluded from the family home, relationship breakdowns and discrimination and abuse within employment are all likely to include a perpetrator with whom the victim already has a relationship, victimisation is less likely to be perceived as 'legitimate'. It is important to find practical solutions to addressing these barriers to identifying victimisation as legitimate, as this is likely to have a profound impact on the reporting behaviours of victims and therefore contributing to underreporting of transphobic hate crime.

Impact of Micro-Crime Victimisation and Hierarchies of Hate

Throughout this chapter, and the previous chapter I have alluded to the impact that both micro-crimes and hierarchies have on victims of transphobic hate crime. The impact of hate crime has been explored extensively within hate crime scholarship (Chakraborti and Garland 2015;

Iganski 2001; Perry 2009). However, I hope to build upon existing literature that specifically explores the impact and responses to transphobic hate crime. Given that not all victims of hate crime hold the same social positions, I argue that there is not one homogeneous experience, or resultant impact of hate crime. As a significant amount of existing research has focused on physically violent incidents of hate crime, less is known about the impact of micro-crime victimisation. I argue that it is difficult to identify the 'impact' of a singular experience of micro-crime victimisation. Rather, the 'everyday' nature of these experiences creates a matrix of victimisation, in which it may not be possible to identify the impact from one single incident.

Iganski and Lagou (2015) argue that hate crimes impact victims more than non-hate motivated offences. Previous research has shown that experiencing hate crime can result in high levels of psychological trauma including increased levels of anxiety, depression, nervousness, loss of confidence and an increased fear of further victimisation (Ehrlich 1992; McDevitt et al. 2001; Meyer 2010). Additionally, Williams and Tregidga (2013) found that approximately half of victims of transphobic hate crime disclosed feelings of suicidal thoughts. When specifically exploring the impact of micro-crimes, Chakraborti et al. (2014) found that participants who had experienced verbal abuse, harassment and cyberbullying experienced emotional reactions including anger, anxiety and fear. As outlined in the previous chapter, the normalisation of these experiences was common. Other responses to this victimisation included self-censorship, in which they attempt to make their trans identity less visible by conforming to a more gender normative presentation, avoiding particular areas associated with victimisation and avoiding being in public at certain points of the day. This also fits within wider feminist discourse around women's fear and normalisation of crime. Stanko (1985) describes survival strategies employed by women that include monitoring footsteps behind them and sexualised comments in case the situation escalates into victimisation. However, there is a conceptual difference between the experiences Stanko describes and the experiences of trans people. In discussing the normalisation of women's fear of violence and the resultant survival strategies employed by women to avoid victimisation, it is framed within a discourse of resisting gender norms that relate to the subordination of women and male ownership of female bodies. However, in trans people's conceptualisation of their survival strategies, they may employ methods that heighten their conformity to gender norms, rather than resist them. This can also have negative effects on an individual's mental health, who may feel that they are unable to live authentically.

To explore the impact on participants who had experienced a hate crime, *the Impact of Events Scale—Revised* utilised by Weiss and Marmar (1996) was used. The scale has 22 self-identifiable responses to events which participants were asked to rate themselves on. Scores on this scale were collated and 61.9% of participants who had experienced a hate crime rated with a final score of 37 or more, which Weiss and Marmar signify as an experience of post-traumatic stress disorder severe enough to impact the effectiveness of the immune system. This is reflected in participants' responses when asked to report a word or phrase that best described how they felt after experiencing a hate crime. Many different responses were recorded but the most commonly reported feelings included being angry, isolated, vulnerable, broken, depressed, anxious, lonely and fearful. However, participants also commented on the short- and longer-term impacts of micro-crime victimisation. Isa, a 58-year-old trans woman explains:

> Quite often, when it first happens you feel really emotional, and you think it will subside over time, but before you have a chance to get over it and move on, something else has happened. When I think about how I feel, I can never pinpoint how I feel about a particular time, because it all just seems to blur in to one. I don't know what time I'm angry about or upset about anymore.

The extract above illustrates the way in which it becomes difficult to identify a single incident to which to attribute emotional distress. This highlights the importance of recognising hate crime victimisation as an ongoing process, rather than as single, isolated incidents in which 'impact' can be observed. Participants also noted the practical impacts of experiencing micro-crime victimisation, alongside the emotional impact. Continued, repetitive victimisation often had serious, practical implications for participants, who often withdrew from various aspects of social life. Star, a 44-year-old non-binary individual recalls having to:

> Take time off of work, which is huge for me because I am self-employed, so I ended up losing money, being short on rent, not being able to afford food and gas and stuff, so I ended up being cold in the middle of winter.

Missing work and education was a common experience reported by participants, who felt the need to disengage in order to avoid continued, repetitive victimisation. Melody, a 17-year-old non-binary participant described how they had attended six different places of education and had then dropped out of education completely. The continued verbal abuse and harassment they experienced prevented them from engaging in education when they initially disclosed their non-binary identity. However, after some time, Melody returned to education and was able to cope with the harassment they experienced as a result of normalising these experiences over time. In the online survey, participants were also asked about ways in which they changed their way of living after experiencing a hate crime. Common responses included going out less (43.9%), avoiding being out at night (41.7%), avoiding the area the incident occurred in (58.3%), avoiding being out alone (52.8%) and moderating the way they act, dress or speak (41.3%). It is clear then, that there are various strategies utilised by participants in order to avoid repetitive victimisation, and some of these strategies may have knock-on effects to other areas of an individual's life.

It is also important to consider the impact of victimisation through an intersectional lens. Despite the multiple oppression that some trans individuals experience based on class, gender and race, among other things, Meyer (2010) discovered that white, middle-class individuals were more likely than low-income, Black and minority ethnic respondents to recognise their experience as severe. Yet Herek and Berrill (1992) summarised existing research and concluded that Black and minority ethnic individuals who identified as LGBT experienced more incidents of hate crime than non-minority ethnic individuals. Given the different experiences of the trans community based on social positioning, it is important to recognise the non-homogeneous nature of the community and respond accordingly, exploring the experiences through an intersectional lens. It can be argued that experiences of oppression, subordination and hate violence are likely to be interpreted differently depending upon the individuals' social positioning. As a result, responses to these experiences are also likely to differ depending upon the victims' social positioning and resources available for them to access. Victim's multiple, minoritised identity characteristics may prevent them from being able to 'be less visible' and their economic and social positioning may prevent them from being able to relocate. These are two key coping mechanisms identified by Burgess et al. (2013). This argument coincides with Meyer's (2010) findings and provides some illumination for the potential reasoning of his claims that victims from low-income Black and minority ethnic backgrounds perceive their victimisation to be less severe. He claims that this is due to them experiencing more oppression due to their multiple minoritised identity characteristics and as a result normalise their experiences as the only viable option to them. On the other hand, middle-class, gay, white men may not have experienced oppression to the same extent given their other dominant identity characteristics. This highlights the need for hate crime victimisation to be conceptualised through an intersectional lens in order to develop a more nuanced understanding of the diverse experiences of trans communities.

Conclusion

In this chapter I have identified three central hierarchies that exist both consciously and subconsciously and that relate to hate crime victimisation. These hierarchies function to privilege particular forms of victimisation as 'legitimate' in which the criminality of the incident, the perpetrator and the victim are clearly identifiable. However, the privileging of such incidents contributes to the overshadowing of various other forms of victimisation in which the criminality of the incident, the victim, or the perpetrator is not so readily identifiable (Bowling 1999). Resultantly, many participants in this research study considered their experiences of victimisation to fall at the bottom of one or more of the three hierarchies. The most common outcome of the positioning within these hierarchies was the non-reporting of transphobic victimisation. This speaks to the unreliability of Home Office (2020) statistics regarding the prevalence of transphobic hate crime. In order to address the underreporting of transphobic hate crime, it is key to deconstruct and further interrogate the structural conditions that produce and maintain these hierarchies. I would further argue that victims do not simply exist, rather they are produced in specific social, cultural and political contexts which assigns legitimacy to particular groups of people as 'victims'.

Transphobic hate crime was most commonly seen as the least recognised form of victimisation, and this may be due to longer, publicly acknowledged histories of oppression and discrimination around race, religion and sexuality. In this sense, there was often concern that reporting transphobic hate crime would not be taken seriously. This was generally perceived to be due to a lack of awareness of the issues that many trans people face from those responsible for enforcing the law. Indeed, when attempting to report crime, many participants experienced re-victimisation and a range of microaggressions from those they attempted to report to. The microaggressions experienced were often perceived to be symbolic of a wider institutional disregard for trans lives.

One of the key themes that was developed from participants' interviews is 'socially conscious and recognisable victimisation' and the way this impacts on trans people's perception of their own victimisation. This is intrinsically linked to the hierarchical nature of hate crime victimisation. It can therefore be concluded that transphobic micro-crimes are less socially recognisable forms of victimisation than dominant conceptualisations of hate crime and legitimate victim status is therefore difficult to establish. This may be as a result of less 'extreme' forms of victimisation not capturing the public imagination and not being able to meet public expectations of news reports on crime. This has significant implications for trans people's perception of their own victimisation and whether this is perceived by the victim as a legitimate form of victimisation worthy of police attention.

The hierarchical nature of hate crime victimisation has also been explored, in which trans people conceptualise the legitimacy of their victimisation based on their positioning within a number of hierarchies. Participants described a range of experiences of victimisation that were committed by their family, friends and community and, as such this research contributes to the literature that challenges dominant notions of 'stranger danger' in relation to hate crime victimisation (Mason 2005; Mason-Bish 2010; Meyer 2014). However, this is not to say that strangers were not perceived as posing a risk to trans people or were not responsible for some of their victimisation, but it challenges notions that the victim is always interchangeable and there is no existing relationship between the victim and offender. What can be seen is how notions of 'stranger danger' impact on trans people's decision to report incidents of hate crime. In this sense, those who experience victimisation at the hands of family, friends and colleagues are less likely to perceive their victimisation to be criminal, even when the victimisation is physically or sexually violent.

References

Armstrong, E., & Crage, S. (2006). Movements and memory: The making of the Stonewall myth. *Americal Sociological Review, 71*(5), 724–751.

Ashford, C. (2017, July 24). Buggery, bribery and a committee: The story of how gay sex was decriminalised in Britain. *The Conversation, UK*. Retrieved August 15, 2020, from http://theconversation.com/buggery-bribery-and-a-committee-the-story-of-how-gay-sex-was-decriminalised-in-britain-79597.

Bacon, M. (2014). Police culture and the new policing context. In J. Brown (Ed.), *The future of policing* (pp. 103–119). New York: Routledge.

Bleich, E. (2007). Hate crime policy in Western Europe: Responding to racist violence in Britain, Germany and France. *American Behavioral Scientist, 51*(2), 149–165.

Bowling, B. (1999). *Violent racism: Victimisation, policing and social context*. Oxford: Oxford University Press.

Bradford, B., Jackson, J., & Stanko, E. (2009). Contact and confidence: Revisiting the impact of public encounters with the police. *Policing and Society, 19*(1), 20–46.

Burgess, A., Regehr, C., & Roberts, A. (2013). *Victimology: Theories and applications* (2nd ed.). Burlington: Jones and Bartlett Learning.

Chakraborti, N. (2010). Future developments for hate crime thinking: Who, what and why? In N. Chakraborti (Ed.), *Hate crime: Concepts, policy, future directions* (pp. 1–16). Cullompton: Willan.
Chakraborti, N., & Garland, J. (2015). *Hate crime: Impact, causes and responses* (2nd ed.). Los Angeles: Sage Publications Ltd..
Chakraborti, N., Garland, J., & Hardy, S. (2014). *The Leicester hate crime project: Findings and conclusions*. Leicester: University of Leicester.
Charman, S. (2020). Making sense of policing identities: The 'deserving' and the 'undeserving' in policing accounts of victimisation. *Policing and Society, 30*(1), 81–97.
Christie, N. (1986). The ideal victim. In E. Fattah (Ed.), *From crime policy to victim policy* (pp. 17–30). London: Macmillan.
Clucas, R. (2017). Sexual orientation change efforts, conservative christianity and resistance to sexual justice. *Social Sciences, 6*(2), 54–103.
Cogan, J. (2002). Hate crime as a crime category worthy of policy attention. *American Behavioral Scientist, 46*(1), 173–185.
Colliver, B. (2019, March 21). *Removing 'No Outsiders' School Lessons is Adding to LGBT* people being targets for hate speech and violence, warns social scientist. Birmingham City University [Blog]. Retrieved August 15, 2020, from https://www.bcu.ac.uk/news-events/news/removing-no-outsider-school-lessons-is-adding-to-lgbt-people-being-targets-for-hate-speech-and-violence-warns-social-scientist.
Colliver, B. (2020). Representations of LGBTQ communities in the Grand Theft Auto series. In C. Kelly, A. Lynes, & K. Hoffin (Eds.), *Video games, crime and next-gen deviance: Reorienting the debate* (pp. 131–150). Bingley, UK: Emerald Publishing.
Colliver, B., & Coyle, A. (2020). 'Risk of sexual violence against women and girls' in the construction of 'gender-neutral toilets': A discourse analysis of comments on YouTube videos. *Journal of Gender-Based Violence, 4*(3), 359–376. https://doi.org/10.1332/239868020X15894511554617.
Colliver, B., Coyle, A., & Silvestri, M. (2019). The 'online othering' of transgender people in relation to 'gender neutral toilets'. In K. Lumsden & E. Harper (Eds.), *Online othering: Exploring digital violence and discrimination on the web* (pp. 215–238). London: Palgrave Macmillan.
Colliver, B., & Silvestri, M. (2020). The role of (in)visibility in hate crime targeting transgender people. *Criminology and Criminal Justice* [Online First]. https://doi.org/10.1177/1748895820930747.

Corteen, K., Morley, S., Taylor, P., & Turner, J. (2016). *A companion to crime, harm and victimisation*. Bristol: Policy Press.

Denny, D. (2006). Transgender communities of the United States in the late Twentieth Century. In C. Paisley, R. Juang, & S. Minter (Eds.), *Transgender rights* (pp. 171–191). Minneapolis: University of Minnesota Press.

Donovan, C., & Barnes, R. (2018). Being 'ideal' or falling short? The legitimacy of lesbian, gay, bisexual and/or transgender victims of domestic violence and hate crime. In M. Duggan (Ed.), *Revisiting the ideal victim': Developments in critical victimology* (pp. 83–102). Bristol: Policy Press.

Durso, L., & Gates, G. (2012). *Serving our youth: Findings from a national survey of services providers working with lesbian, gay, bisexual and transgender youth who are homeless or at risk of becoming homeless*. Los Angeles: The Williams Institute.

Dwyer, A., & Ball, M. (2020). 'You'd just cop flak from every other dickhead under the sun': Navigating the tensions of (in)visibility and hypervisibility in LGBTI police liaison programs in three Australian states. *Journal of Contemporary Criminal Justice, 36*(2), 274–292.

Ehrlich, H. (1992). The ecology of anti-gay violence. In G. M. Herek & K. T. Berrill (Eds.), *Hate crimes: Confronting violence against lesbians and gay men* (pp. 105–112). Newbury Park: Sage Publications Ltd..

Elliott-Cooper, A. (2018). The struggle that cannot be named: Violence, space and the re-articulation of anti-racism in post-Duggan Britain. *Ethnic and Racial Studies, 41*(14), 2445–2463.

Fohring, S. (2018). Revisiting the non-ideal victim. In M. Duggan (Ed.), *Revisiting the 'Ideal Victim': Developments in critical victimology* (pp. 195–210). Bristol: Policy Press.

Hall, S., Critcher, C., Jefferson, T., Clarke, J., & Roberts, B. (1978). *Policing the crisis: Mugging, the state and law and order*. London: Macmillan.

Hardy, S.-J., & Chakraborti, N. (2020). *Blood, threats and fears: The hidden worlds of hate crime victims*. London: Palgrave Macmillan.

Harvey, A. (2012). Regulating homophobic hate speech: Back to basics about language and politics? *Sexualities, 15*(2), 191–206.

Herek, G., & Berrill, K. (1992). *Hate crimes: Confronting violence against lesbians and gay men*. Thousand Oaks, CA: Sage Publications Ltd..

Herek, G., Gillis, J., Cogan, J., & Glunt, E. (1999). Hate crime victimization among lesbian, gay and bisexual adults: Prevalence, psychological correlates and methodological issues. *Journal of Interpersonal Violence, 12*(2), 195–215.

Hodkinson, P., & Garland, J. (2016). Targeted harassment, subcultural identity and the embrace of difference: A case study. *The British Journal of Sociology, 67*(3), 541–561.

Holdaway, S. (1999). Understanding the police investigation of the murder of Stephen Lawrence: A 'mundane sociological analysis'. *Sociological Research Online, 4*(1), 1–8.

Home Office. (2020). *Hate crime, England and Wales, 2019 to 2020*. London: Home Office.

Hooberman, J., Rosenfeld, B., Rasmussen, A., & Keller, A. (2010). Resilience in trauma-exposed refugees: The moderating effect of coping style on resilience variables. *American Journal of Orthopsychiatry, 80*, 557–563.

Hough, M., Jackson, J., Bradford, B., Myhill, A., & Quinton, P. (2010). Procedural justice, trust, and institutional legitimacy. *Policing: A Journal of Policy and Practice, 4*(3), 203–210.

Iganski, P. (2001). Hate crimes hurt more. *American Behavioral Scientist, 45*(4), 626–638.

Iganski, P. (2008). Criminal law and the routine activity of 'hate crime. *The Liverpool Law Review, 29*(1), 1–17.

Iganski, P., & Lagou, S. (2015). Hate crimes hurt some more than others: Implications for the just sentencing of offenders. *Journal of Interpersonal Violence, 30*(10), 1696–1718.

Jamel, J. (2018). *Transphobic hate crime*. London: Palgrave Macmillan.

Jewkes, Y. (2015). *Media and crime* (3rd ed.). London: Sage Publications Ltd..

Johnson, K. (2020, April 30). Images released after 'violent transphobic attack' on Northern Line. *Southwark News*. Retrieved August 13, 2020, from https://www.southwarknews.co.uk/news/images-released-after-violent-transphobic-attack-on-northern-line/.

Jones, T., & Newburn, T. (2001). *Widening access: Improving police relationships with 'Hard-to-Reach' groups*. London: Home Office.

Khan, R., Hall, B., & Lowe, M. (2017). *Honour abuse: The experiences of South Asians who identify as LGBT in North West England: Summary report prepared for Lancashire constabulary*. Lancashire: HARM: Honour Abuse Research Matrix.

Lammy, D. (2017). *The Lammy review: An independent review into the treatment of, and outcomes for, black, Asian and minority ethnic individuals in the criminal justice system*. London: Home Office.

Law, S. (2016). Gay rights versus religious rights. In T. Shah, T. Farr, & J. Friedman (Eds.), *Religious freedom and gay rights: Emerging conflicts in North America and Europe* (pp. 41–57). Oxford: Oxford University Press.

Macpherson, W. (1999). *The Stephen Lawrence inquiry*. London: Home Office.
Mason, G. (2005). Hate crime and the image of the stranger. *British Journal of Criminology, 45*(6), 837–859.
Mason-Bish, H. (2010). Future challenges for hate crime policy: Lessons from the past. In N. Chakraborti (Eds.), *Hate Crime: Concepts, Policy, Future Directions* (pp. 58–77). Cullompton: Willan.
McDevitt, J., Balboni, J., Garcia, L., & Gu, J. (2001). Consequences for victims: A comparison of bias—And non-bias-motivated assaults. *American Behavioral Scientist, 45*(4), 697–713.
METRO Charity. (2014). *Youth chances: Summary of first findings*. London: METRO Charity.
Meyer, D. (2010). Evaluating the severity of hate-motivated violence: Intersectional differences among LGBT hate crime victims. *Sociology, 44*(5), 980–995.
Meyer, D. (2014). Resisting hate crime discourse: Queer and intersectional challenges to neoliberal hate crime laws. *Critical Criminology, 22*, 113–125.
Minter, S. (2006). Do transsexuals dream of gay rights? Getting real about transgender inclusion. In C. Paisley, R. Juang, & S. Minter (Eds.), *Transgender rights* (pp. 141–170). Minneapolis: University of Minnesota Press.
Monro, S., Hines, S., & Osborne, A. (2017). Is bisexuality invisible? A review of sexualities scholarship 1970–2015. *The Sociological Review, 65*(4), 663–681.
Organista, P., Marin, G., & Chun, K. (2010). *The psychology of ethnic groups in the United States*. London: Sage Publications Ltd..
Paul, J. (2017). The varieties of religious responses to homosexuality: A content and tonal analysis of articles in Pastoral Psychology from 1950–2015 regarding sexual minorities. *Pastoral Psychology, 66*(1), 79–101.
Perry, B. (2001). *In the name of hate: Understanding hate crimes*. London: Routledge.
Perry, B. (2009). 'Theres just places ya' don't wanna go': The segregating impact of hate crime against Native Americans. *Contemporary Justice Review, 12*(4), 401–418.
PinkNews. (2018, April 6). *Five sentenced for brutal murder of transgender woman which shocked the world*. Retrieved August 15, 2020, from https://www.pinknews.co.uk/2018/04/06/five-sentenced-for-brutal-murder-of-transgender-woman-which-shocked-the-world/.
Ralph, S., Capewell, C., & Bonnett, E. (2016). Disability hate crime: Persecuted for difference. *British Journal of Special Education, 43*(3), 215–232.

Richardson, D., & Monro, S. (2012). *Sexuality, diversity and equality.* Basingstoke: Palgrave Macmillan.
Rose, S., & Mechanic, M. (2002). Psychological distress, crime features and help-seeking behaviors related to homophobic bias incidents. *American Behavioral Scientist, 46*(1), 14–26.
Salamon, G. (2010). *Assuming a body*. Columbia: Columbia University Press.
Scarman, J. (1981). *The Brixton disorders, 10–12th April (1981).* London: Home Office.
Sherry, M. (2010). *Disability hate crimes: Does anyone really hate disabled people?* Farnham: Ashgate.
Souhami, A. (2012). Institutional racism and police reform: An empirical critique. *Policing and Society, 24*(1), 1–21.
Stanko, E. (1985). *Intimate intrusions: Women's experience of male violence.* London: Routledge and Kegan Paul.
Sumerau, J., Mathers, L., & Cragun, R. (2018). Incorporating transgender experience toward a more inclusive gender lens in the sociology of religion. *Sociology of Religion, 79*(4), 425–448.
Warde, B. (2013). Black male disproportionality in the Criminal Justice Systems of the USA, Canada and England: A comparative analysis of incarceration. *Journal of African American Studies, 17*(4), 461–479.
Weiss, D. S., & Marmar, C. R. (1996). The impact of event scale—Revised. In J. Wilson & T. M. Keane (Eds.), *Assessing psychological trauma and PTSD* (pp. 399–411). New York: Guilford Press.
Wilkin, D. (2020). *Disability hate crime: Experiences of everyday hostility on public transport.* London: Palgrave Macmillan.
Williams, M., & Tregidga, J. (2013). *All wales hate crime research project.* Cardiff: University of Cardiff.
Wong, J., & Lee, C. (2018). Extra! Extra! The importance of victim-offender relationship in homicide newsworthiness. *Journal of Interpersonal Violence,* 1–21. https://doi.org/10.1177%2F0886260518789142.
Zempi, I., & Chakraborti, N. (2015). 'They make us feel like we're a virus': The multiple impacts of Islamophobic hostility towards veiled Muslim women. *International Journal for Crime, Justice and Social Democracy, 4*(3), 44–56.

5

Space, Place and Exclusion

Introduction

In the last two chapters, I have dedicated space to exploring the experiences of trans participants in this research study, particularly the specific forms of transphobia they have experienced, and framed this within the hierarchical nature of hate crime. Having covered the types of victimisation participants experienced and deconstructing hierarchies related to perpetrators and protected characteristics, I now move on to explore ideas around 'space' and 'place'. In this chapter I use the terms 'space' and 'place' in a dualistic way. I explore the role of 'space' and 'place' in relation to the spatial implications of navigating the physical world and which physical spaces trans people may experience exclusion from. However, I also use the terms 'space' and 'place' to represent the more abstract concept of 'belonging', in which trans people may feel 'out of place', or unable to access a 'safe space'.

I begin this chapter by discussing the experiences of participants when navigating 'sex-segregated' spaces. In particular, this discussion focuses on public toilets, which may be one of the most commonly used public, sex-segregated spaces. Although I have previously written on how public

B. Colliver, *Re-imagining Hate Crime*, Palgrave Hate Studies,
https://doi.org/10.1007/978-3-030-65714-7_5

toilets are discursively constructed (Colliver and Coyle 2020), in this chapter I seek to highlight the lived reality for some trans people when negotiating and accessing these spaces. In doing so, I emphasise that particular sex-segregated spaces are conceptualised as significant spaces of risk. I frame this discussion in relation to the 'public-private' divide and argue that this distinction is not a clear-cut concept and the boundaries between public and private may become blurred in particular spaces (Davidoff 2003).

The second part of this chapter focuses on a sense of 'belonging' within romantic and/or sexual 'spaces' or relationships. In this discussion, I highlight the intrinsic link between gender and sexuality and the ways in which both homophobia and transphobia operate simultaneously in particular circumstances. In doing so, I also contextualise violence against trans women in relation to cisnormative, heteronormative ideals and the impact that this has on cisgender men's own understanding and relationship with their sexuality. This draws upon ideas of 'internalised homophobia' and also heterosexual men's fear of socially being perceived as homosexual. Furthermore, I frame violence against trans women in the context of 'fragile masculinity' (Kaufman 2007), and explore the ways in which violence against trans women functions to bolster and reaffirm the perpetrators' sense of masculinity. I end this section of the chapter with a discussion on the exclusion of trans people from same-sex relationships, particularly when navigating online spaces including dating apps. As discussed earlier, many trans people experience transphobia within an online context, and dating and/or 'hook-up apps' specifically targeted towards minoritised sexualities are no exception.

I then move on to discuss ideas of inclusion and exclusion within wider, offline LGBTQ spaces, primarily the night-time economy. I frame the exclusion of trans women in particular from these spaces within the context of 'trans-misogyny', highlighting the complex, and often-tense relationship that lesbian, gay and bisexual communities may have with femininity. However, it is not only trans women who may experience exclusion from these spaces; I also discuss the exclusion, discrimination and oppression that trans men may face in these spaces.

I close this chapter with a discussion around the problematic nature of uncritically discussing the needs or experiences of a 'trans community'.

This is problematic, as it locates issues of exclusion and oppression solely outside of trans communities and overshadows the experiences of those who may be excluded from 'within'. This discussion focuses more on the implications for trans people occupying an ever-increasingly politicised identity, in which their authenticity as a trans person may be called into question. This focuses on a number of issues, including the exclusion of non-binary people from 'trans-inclusive' spaces and also the 'othering' of trans people who may choose not to, or may be unable to undergo gender reassignment surgery. Furthermore, I draw upon the work of Crenshaw (1989, 1991) to highlight the experiences of trans people who may occupy multiple, marginalised social positions. As such, I explore the concept of how a 'master identity' may be assigned to an individual, based on another's perception of their identity and how this may lead to the exclusion of trans people from multiple spaces.

Sex-Segregated Spaces

Sex-segregated spaces, or rather, access to these spaces, have been a central feature of public and online 'debate' regarding trans rights. This has garnered increasing attention since the public consultation was launched that sought public opinion on reforming the Gender Recognition Act (2004). Discussions around sex-segregated and 'gender-neutral' spaces have primarily focused on the risk of sexual violence against cisgender women and children, particularly from cisgender men (Colliver and Coyle 2020). Within these 'debates', very little attention is paid to the risks that trans people may face when accessing sex-segregated spaces. A leaked government document indicated that plans to reform the Gender Recognition Act (2004) would be scrapped, and instead, would focus on protecting 'sex-segregated' spaces, and who can access them (Milton 2020). Similar steps have been taken in the United States of America, as in 2017 President Donald Trump rescinded instructions issued in 2016 by then-President Barack Obama that instructed schools to allow students to access toilets in line with how they identified in terms of gender. In 2015, the city of Houston put forward the 'Houston Equal Rights Ordinance' which aimed to protect individuals from discrimination based on a number of identity markers including race, sexuality, age and religion. However, this legislative effort was unsuccessful after the opposition campaign centred on public toilets and transgender women's access to these spaces (Sanders and Stryker 2016).

I focus heavily on public toilets in this section as participants identified them as important spaces and existing research has shown that these spaces are sites of significant risk, anxiety and policing for some trans people (Browne 2004; Doan 2010; Faktor 2011; Namaste 2000). Doan (2010: 635) has argued that trans people experience a 'special kind of tyranny—the tyranny of gender—that arises when people dare to challenge the hegemonic expectations for appropriately gendered behavior in Western society'. Public toilets are one of the most commonly used sex-segregated spaces in Western society and represent the ultimate sex-segregated spaces (Doan 2010; Greed 2019). Resultantly, they are often spaces that participants identified as being spaces of 'extreme gender policing'. Although public toilets may be considered to be 'sex-segregated', in that assumptions are often made about the secondary sex characteristics (genitals) that people in these spaces have, the spaces are most commonly policed through the enforcement of heteronormative, cisnormative constructed expectations relating to gender presentation. Public toilets in particular are differentiated by constructions of the biological distinction between men and women, and Browne (2004: 332–333) describes them as 'sites where individuals' bodies are continually policed and (re)placed within sex categories'.

Public toilets are also architecturally designed to facilitate surveillance of others and the spatial structure of these spaces allows an individual to fall under the 'gaze' of others (Bender-Baird 2016; Cavanagh 2010). In this sense, public toilets are spaces that may blur the boundaries between the public–private divide. Within the space of a single cubicle, an individual may feel that they are in a 'private' space, but the wider washroom area may represent a more quasi-private space. In this sense, the entire space may be considered 'private', but this is only in relation to particular groups of people, and they do not represent total, individual privacy. The spatial structure of public toilets, alongside the quasi-private nature of these spaces can lead to a heightened sense of gender policing. Namaste (2000) argues that this can contribute to and legitimise abuse against trans and gender non-conforming people, who may be perceived to 'contest the "natural" connections between sexed embodiments and sexed lives' (Browne 2004: 333). It may therefore be the discontinuity between an individual's gender identity and how others read their gender presentation that results in abuse and violence against trans people in these spaces, which are so vigilantly policed. This discontinuity has been described by Browne (2004: 332) as 'genderism', that is, 'hostile readings of gender ambiguous bodies'. As will be discussed later in this book, the fear of, and anxiety attached to hostile readings of an individual's gender presentation has profound implications for how participants navigate the physical world.

The heightened awareness of gender policing in these spaces directly fed in to participants' understanding of risk. This was primarily framed within the Western gender binary and how this impacts others' perception of which spaces participants should access. As Ruby, a 52-year-old trans woman explains:

> I feel like the women inside [public toilets] act like security guards, and if you don't fit in to what they think a woman should look like, which I don't, then they think you must be a man. There are only two options for toilets, male and female, so if they don't think you belong in the female toilet, then they instantly assume you belong in the male toilet ... Either as soon as I walk in, or after when I'm at the sinks, women have come up to me and caused a big fuss about me being in there and then it is just embarrassing because it doesn't stay in the toilet, they come out and start telling all their friends and their family and then I feel like everyone in the place is staring at me ... it just makes me feel so anxious and unsafe.

The account given by Ruby speaks to a number of issues that I have already outlined. In this account, it becomes clear that Ruby experiences 'genderism', in that she perceives her gender identity to be interpreted differently, in a way that does not coincide with her internal sense of self, her gender identity. This is clearly perceived by her to be the reason that other women in public toilets approach her and cause 'a big fuss' about her occupying that space. In this sense, Ruby very clearly experiences a form of 'gender policing', in which cisnormative, heteronormative assumptions about gender are used to make judgements about who should be in particular spaces. It is important to note that this form of gender policing also has implications for cisgender people, who may be gender non-conforming. Gender policing is not specifically reserved to be carried out against trans people, and therefore gender non-conforming cisgender people may also experience harassment and abuse in these spaces for failing to conform to expected gender norms (Davidson 2019; Robertson 2016). Furthermore, her experience highlights the fluid nature of the 'public gaze'. Ruby does not recount experiencing gender policing in the wider space of the venue and her trans identity had not fallen under the public gaze. However, when being subject to this gaze in the toilet space, in which people's vigilance around gender presentation may be heightened, and being identified as trans, this gaze then also becomes significantly more heightened in the wider space of the venue. In this sense, being subject to the public gaze is spatially dependent and is also transferable between spaces.

The transferable and fluid nature of the 'public gaze' was also discussed by other participants, but was understood to be transferable to a wider space than just that of the immediate surroundings of the public toilet. This was often discussed in relation to the internet, and social media in particular. The rise of social media has led to the public gaze moving from the physical world, to simultaneously being ever-present in online spaces. Often, these two spaces interact and an incident in either of those spaces can lead to a heightened sense of experiencing the public gaze. As Joby, who is 17 years old and non-binary, describes:

> When I first started college I used the women's toilet and then someone realised I wasn't born female and posted it all over Facebook through like school Facebook groups and writing my name on there. They were posting that there had been a boy in the girls toilet and then everyone was commenting on it saying that I must be sick and I must be a pervert and stuff like that and it was horrible. It's weird, because nowhere else in the college did anyone ever mention my gender or ask me about my gender. If I hadn't gone to the toilet then people might not have been so aware. After that, I try to avoid all toilets in public.

Not only does Joby refer to the heightened sense of gender policing in public toilets, in comparison to other spaces they occupy in daily life, but they also demonstrate the relationship between the online and offline worlds. The role of social media in this example illustrates the fluidity of the 'public gaze' and the reciprocal relationship between the online and offline worlds in which being visible in one, can lead to heightened visibility in another. In this sense, it is key to acknowledge and understand the 'public' nature of the internet, and how an individual may become subject to the 'public gaze' on various platforms, without their consent or knowledge. As such, the internet, and social media platforms in particular, provide unprecedented opportunities for individuals to fall under the public gaze.

Despite the risks associated with public toilets, the heightened sense of gender policing in these spaces also acts as a form of validation for some participants who actively sought to 'pass'. When some participants accessed public toilets without experiencing discrimination or abuse, they often understood this to be an affirmation that they were 'doing gender' successfully. In this sense, how well an individual passes, or how well they 'do their gender' is measured through their acceptance and assimilation into sex-segregated spaces. As Isa, a 58-year-old trans woman, describes:

> The female toilet is almost like the pinnacle area of feminism and sisterhood and I am happy when I use the toilet and I don't get questioned. For me, that is like a total sign that I am being seen and accepted as a woman.

Given the heightened sense of vigilance and gender policing in these spaces, it is unsurprising that accessing these spaces without experiencing judgement acts as an indicator for how well an individual passes. As Madee, a 24 year-old trans woman explains, the 'toilet [is] the ultimate goal'. Although accessing sex-segregated spaces may become a measuring rod for some people in which the authenticity and validity of their identity is measured, it is important to note that this will not be the case for all trans people. Additionally, despite a general awareness of the social policing that is associated with sex-segregated public spaces, the fear of being policed, or falling under the public gaze, is dependent on how successfully an individual 'passes' and how successfully their gender identity and presentation is read by others as cisgender. For participants who felt that they did pass, the risk of experiencing backlash for accessing a particular sex-segregated space was often significantly lower, or non-existent in comparison to participants who felt unable, or did not want to pass. Interestingly, there also appeared to be a gender divide in these experiences, with non-binary people and trans women expressing greater sentiments of fear and anxiety associated with these spaces. Male participants were often less cautious of accessing these spaces, particularly when they felt they passed. As Dilip, a 45-year-old male explains regarding his comfort of using male public toilets:

> I don't mind public toilets too much, I have been on hormones for years and years, I have lots of facial hair and I pass as a man. I have never really had any trouble in toilets because I am trans, because I don't really stick out.

As Dilip perceives himself to assimilate into Western, cisnormative expectations of gender presentation, his concern of being policed within public toilets is minimal. Peter, a 41-year-old male also claims that due to his testosterone levels he 'just looks like a regular guy'. When discussing the idea of gender policing in sex-segregated spaces, Simon, a 47-year-old explains that 'men don't pay enough attention to other people's gender in the toilet to realise I am trans, like at first glance I appear masculine, like a man'. Dilip, Peter and Simon all feel relatively at ease when accessing these spaces due to conforming to a stereotypically masculine aesthetic, which they characterise as being identified by physical build and facial hair. In this sense, it appears there is a particular privilege associated with 'passing' in that an individual may not constantly and consciously consider their safety in sex-segregated spaces. However, it is also key to highlight that men are characterised as paying less attention to the gender of others in sex-segregated spaces, whereas the women in this study often acknowledged the heightened sense of policing.

The heightened sense of policing in women's public toilets may be associated with women's experiences and fears about victimisation in public spaces (Greed 2019). The fear of physical and sexual violence that women experience in public spaces, which are characterised as male-dominated, is well documented (Pain 1997; Stanko 1985; Vera-Gray and Kelly 2020). However, it has also been noted that the gendered nature of crime is paradoxical, in that women experience higher levels of fear of victimisation than men do but experience lower levels of actual victimisation (Hale 1996). This claim has been contested due to experiences of sexual harassment being routinely excluded from victimisation surveys (Vera Gray and Kelly 2020). As such, sexual and physical violence, abuse and harassment are conceptualised as a means of informal social control by which women's access and movement in public spaces are controlled (Kelly 1988). It is within this context that we may understand heightened levels of gender policing within women's public toilets.

This is not to say that it is only women's toilets that are conceptualised as unsafe. Many male participants felt anxiety and fear in men's public toilets, but this was often explained to be as a result of the hyper-masculine nature of men's toilets, rather than as a direct consequence of their trans identity. Rather, men's toilets were conceptualised as spaces of competition, in which men compete to assert their masculinity. Whilst Simon earlier described how men do not pay significant attention to other people's gender presentation in public toilets, he does note:

> It's like all 'men only' spaces just turn men in to these animals, like it's all misogynistic, locker-room chat. I don't know why, but men, when they are all together, particularly cisgender, straight men, it's like they need to out-do each other on who is the most masculine.

As outlined by Simon, even though men may not pay attention to other's gender in public toilets, they are spaces in which men may consciously engage with, enact and bolster their own gender and masculinity. This may be achieved through enacting or discussing traits and characteristics associated with hegemonic masculinity (Connell 1995). This is most commonly associated with wealth, aggression and violence, and sexual virility. These cultural framings of masculinity permeate participants' evaluation of their own safety in men's public toilets. In this sense, the significance of masculinity as a cultural, structural and social concept regulates and polices who is able to access men's public toilets safely and without fear. Masculinity is policed within male toilets in a variety of ways including whether an individual uses a urinal or cubicle, in which the latter may be considered a display of femininity (Cavanagh 2010). As such, the urinal becomes the pinnacle area of male toilets to enact hyper-masculinity. Therefore, if trans men do not use the urinal, which may be impractical for a number of reasons, their masculinity may be called into question. Notions of masculinity were also a significant theme within participants' accounts of fear and victimisation outside of public toilets. Masculinity was understood to be in direct conflict with trans identities, particularly feminine identities, and was central to understanding violence and abuse directed at trans women.

Men, Masculinity and Romance

The victimisation of trans women in public spaces was often associated with the perpetrator attempting to establish or bolster their sense of masculinity, particularly in front of other men. Perpetrating transphobic abuse, particularly against transgender women, becomes a way of establishing a masculine identity. This was also perceived to be the case when men perpetrated transphobic abuse in front of other cisgender women. As Rachel, an 18-year-old female claims:

> I feel like they start abusing me to show off and make themselves look big in front of whatever girl they are trying to impress. It's like by attacking a trans woman is their way of flexing their muscles.

Rachel understands the abuse she experiences within the context of heterosexual relationships and romantic culture in which cisgender men are required to 'impress' cisgender women. In this sense, perpetrating transphobic abuse becomes a mechanism through which an individual's masculinity becomes established and affirmed. This very public display of 'masculinity' comes at the expense of trans people. As such, the 'public gaze' in this sense operates in a dualistic manner, in which a trans person's gender identity may fall under public scrutiny, but the gender performance of the perpetrator is also under the 'public gaze' which may intensify an individual's desire to exert and express masculinity. However, participants also understood transphobic hate crime and abuse, perpetrated by cisgender men against transgender women, as being motivated by a deep-rooted insecurity surrounding the perpetrator's own relationship with masculinity. Rose, a 67-year-old woman believes that 'trans women are a huge slap in the face to masculinity … they have to show off their masculinity to prove that they are not like us … they see us as completely un-masculine so they have to show off just how super masculine they are so they don't get associated with us'. Rose understands transphobic hate crime and abuse perpetrated by cisgender men to be performative in nature, particularly when perpetrated in front of the perpetrators friends, family or associates.

This was reiterated by other participants who felt that masculinity was performative, and that perpetrating transphobic hate crime and abuse, particularly against trans women, was a way for cisgender men to perform masculinity and disassociate themselves with the feminine. Ideas of 'fragile masculinity' have been explored in relation to violence-targeting gay men (Kaufman 2007; Murphy 2001) and more recently in relation to violence-targeting trans women (Kehrli 2016) in which it is conceived that the existence of trans women is a figurative assault on cisgender, heterosexual masculinity. As such, transphobic abuse perpetrated by cisgender men was considered to be a largely gendered crime in which transgender women were the main targets, alongside those who identified between or outside of the gender binary, but may be perceived to be more feminine. Callum, who is 19 years old and non-binary claims that:

> Trans women definitely get a worse time off [of] men than trans men do. I think it has to do with masculinity and how men perceive themselves and how they think others will see them. It's like, if a man knows that a woman is trans, if they don't abuse them, then other men will think that they agree with it, then that somehow takes away from their status as a man. By abusing trans women, men don't lose that status, and their status as a man actually increases.

For Callum, it is certainly cisgender men's complex relationship with masculinity that is understood to fuel transphobic abuse against transgender women. Masculinity can therefore be considered an ongoing negotiation, achieved and maintained through interactions and the performance of masculinity in relation to others. An individual may therefore assert their own masculinity through the perpetration of either symbolic or physical violence against trans women. Trans women, and non-binary people who are perceived as feminine, may therefore become a 'suitable target' for this violence as they come to symbolise a rejection of dominant gender norms and their identity may be interpreted as a symbolic assault on traditional, culturally situated configurations of masculinity. A masculine identity can therefore be affirmed through the symbolic or physical subordination of those deemed to be deviating from expected gender norms.

However, the conceptualisation of masculinity as performative, in conjunction with others, speaks directly to those very public acts of hate and violence. As discussed earlier, whilst mainstream media narratives may perpetuate ideas of 'stranger danger', a significant amount of transphobic hate crime occurs within private spheres (Stotzer 2009). In order to avoid overshadowing the experiences of participants in this study who experienced victimisation in private, I now turn my attention to victimisation that occurs in the context of romantic and/or sexual relationships, in private. In understanding these experiences of abuse and violence, it was often understood to be because of a complex relationship between masculinity, transphobia and homophobia. Violence-targeting trans women in these contexts was often in response to the disclosure of their trans identity, although, this would also occur even when a partner was aware of someone's trans identity prior to entering into some form of relationship with them. Elaine, a 48-year-old woman describes a situation in which she disclosed her trans identity to a former sexual partner:

> All of a sudden Kian just jumped up and pushed me. He didn't hit me, but he was holding my neck. He spat in my face … Basically, he attacked me because I gave him head and he enjoyed it. Now, he suddenly feels like less of a man, because I am a trans woman. He was so worried about everyone thinking he was gay and his masculinity was challenged.

The experience described by Elaine demonstrates the material, real-life consequences of hetero- and cis-normative social structures which position trans people as legitimate targets for violence. The concept of 'trans panic' has been explored academically (Jamel 2018; Noble 2012) and may be the result of an internal struggle with sexual identity within a perpetrator. This may be because the attraction to transgender women challenges deeply engrained hetero- and cis-normative notions of sexuality. In hierarchies of masculinity, homosexuality is a barrier for individuals striving to achieve hegemonic masculinity (Connell 1995). This can be seen in Elaine's account, in which the perpetrator becomes concerned over other's perception of him as homosexual, thereby lowering his position in the hierarchy of masculinity. However, given that 'trans panic' is a legal defence across a number of states in America, it may also be used to justify violence and aggressions against trans people. Blaming Elaine for 'deception' allows her to be held responsible for her victimisation and removes blame from the perpetrator. It has been argued that the harmful stereotype of deception 'has been perhaps the most historically consistent and successful idiom through which transgender rights are abrogated and transgender lives are pathologized, demeaned, or cut short' (Fischel 2019: 99). This is often used as a means to justify violence against transgender people, transgender women in particular. In exploring media coverage of over seven thousand news stories relating to murders of transgender and gender non-conforming people, Schilt and Westbrook (2009) found that the dominant media framework positioned the violence and murder of trans people as a response to the perceived deception that the perpetrator felt. The stereotype that trans people are in some way 'deceptive' is also perpetuated through various media representations of trans people (Colliver 2020).

Although Elaine experienced violence after disclosing her trans identity, other participants provided accounts of entering sexual relationships with cisgender men who were aware of their trans identity, but continued to perpetrate violence after the sexual encounter had finished. Madee, a 24 year-old woman, who is also a sex-worker, described various incidents of violence perpetrated by men who had paid for some form of sexual activity. Despite openly advertising as a transgender sex-worker, and with many men requesting to either perform oral sex on her, or requesting penetrative anal sex, she would often experience an amalgamation of transphobia and homophobia. After engaging in either oral and/or anal sex with cisgender men, she described regularly experiencing verbal abuse that was homophobic in nature, including being called 'a faggot and a queer'. Additionally, she regularly experienced damage to her property, with men reacting violently towards her or her possessions. In this sense, there appears to be a conflation between gender identity and sexuality, and this may be the result of perpetrators not seeing trans women as 'real women'. Resultantly, perpetrators of transphobic and/or homophobic abuse who have engaged in a sexual relationship with a trans women may understand their encounter to be homosexual in nature, rather than heterosexual, particularly when the perpetrator has requested to be anally penetrated. Some existing research has identified that trans female sex workers may be at a higher risk of experiencing violence than their cisgender counterparts (Fletcher 2013). In a society which places value in heterosexuality, and subordinates those who deviate from this expected norm, it may be the case that some cisgender men experience feelings of shame and guilt after engaging in sexual activity with trans women, particularly if they conceive this relationship to be homosexual in nature. Abuse and violence directed at trans women in this context therefore functions as a coping mechanism for internal feelings of guilt and shame, and also reaffirms the perpetrators' own sense of masculinity.

Trans people's experiences of victimisation, violence and abuse within the context of romantic and sexual relationships has not garnered significant academic attention. However, in framing transphobic abuse and hate crime in the context of masculinity, it has been argued that masculinity is precarious because of its performative, rather than biological nature (Stotzer and Shih 2012). Furthermore, it has also been claimed that men are significantly more conscious about their gender role than women and are significantly more likely to engage in behaviours that attempt to 'prove' or 'evidence' their masculinity (Whitley and Kite 1995). Coinciding with the experiences described above, Vandello et al. (2008) argue that men display higher levels of anxiety than women do when their gender role is threatened or questioned and are more likely to enact physical violence and aggression. This can certainly be seen in the experiences of participants in this study, in which the nature of verbal abuse perpetrated by cisgender men was homophobic in nature, which indicates it is the perpetrator's own sexuality which is the motivation for violence. In this sense, perpetrators of transphobic abuse and violence are re-establishing their sense of masculinity and heterosexuality by distancing themselves from, and actively subordinating those who they have come to associate with femininity and/or homosexuality. In subordinating those who they associate with characteristics in direct opposition to masculinity, their own sense of internal identity can be rebalanced and re-established.

Trans Exclusion, 'Gay Culture' and Masculinity

Notions of masculinity also permeated participants' accounts of exclusion they experienced from wider 'LGBTQ spaces', and I will focus on two key areas. Firstly, the exclusion of trans men from dating apps and spaces targeting gay and bisexual men was prevalent. Secondly, I will discuss the concept of 'trans-misogyny' and the exclusion of trans women and feminine non-binary people from these spaces. Trans men in this study often reported being able to access physical spaces which are dominated by cisgender gay and bisexual men without significant issues. However, issues often arose when cisgender men perceived the participant to be attempting to engage them in a sexual or romantic relationship. Simon, a 47-year-old male describes how:

> I used to go to the scene all the time, I never really had any problems just going in there and having a chat and having a good time. I had loads of mates who were gay guys. I only ever really had bad experiences when I was like getting on with a guy, and things were going well and I thought it might be more than friendship, and then if they found out I was trans. Gays can be so bitchy, and so vicious with their mouths. I always tried to just walk away, but then sometimes their friends would get involved, they would always call you typical names, you know, he-she, tranny and all that shit. It's like, I have probably got a bigger cock than them, but they are worried that sleeping with me takes away from them being gay.

The experience described by Simon was recurrent throughout participants' narratives, in that trans men were often welcomed into wider

LGBTQ spaces, but occupying this space was conditional. In this sense, trans men experience a process of desexualisation in spaces dominated by cisgender, gay men. This reinforces how sexual relationships between men are framed through a cisnormative lens. Trans men may therefore be able to access these spaces safely, until the dominant group feel that their own sense of identity is in some way compromised. This kind of rhetoric was also evident when participants accessed online spaces occupied predominantly by gay and bisexual men. As Dilip, a 45-year-old male explained:

> I have experienced a lot of abuse from within the LGBT community, mainly gay men on dating sites. I would get messages all the time on my dating profiles saying 'Sorry, don't date trannies' or 'Only interested in real men' and stuff like 'Don't want a vagina to have sex with'. It was horrible, these are people who are supposed to be part of a community, who are meant to stick together and all they do is persecute people who aren't the same as them.

Both Simon and Dilip describe their experiences within spaces targeting the commercialisation of gay and bisexual, cisgender men. Dilip described their experiences on dating apps for gay men, in which he experienced a sense of exclusion from gay communities. This is not restricted to just dating spaces, mainstream spaces for the wider LGB community in which cisgender gay men act as gatekeepers, determining those who meet expected standards to authentically inhabit gay spaces, were also discussed. The common thread that runs through participants' account denotes notions of legitimacy and 'belonging' relating to those seen as legitimately LGB and those who are not. Others' perception of legitimacy polices and regulates those who are able to access spaces deemed exclusive for LGB people. It was not only trans men that experienced exclusion from wider LGBTQ spaces, trans women often reported experiencing trans-misogyny within these spaces.

Cisgender gay men's relation with femininity, misogyny and space has been well documented (Hale and Ojeda 2018). However, these issues have tended to focus on issues of 'femmephobia' that cisgender, gay men may experience, whilst the experiences of transgender women in LGBTQ spaces has remained largely overlooked (Hoskins 2019; Richardson 2009). Although these spaces are primarily referred to as 'LGBTQ spaces', they are often designed to meet the needs of, and dominated by, cisgender, white, gay men, and therefore they may not be 'safe spaces' for the broader spectrum of sexual and gender minorities (Casey 2004; Nash 2013). It has been claimed that gay male communities have complex and unstable relationships with expressions and performances of masculinity and femininity (Sánchez and Vilain 2012). In this sense, an individual's gender presentation may be central in establishing and maintaining a sexual identity. It has been argued that femininity is often rejected and 'othered' from 'gay spaces', with 'straight acting', masculine identities being constructed as the most desirable identity. As such, masculinity becomes the measuring rod in which all of forms of gender identity and presentation are judged. Masculinity thereby becomes a key indicator of desirability and attractiveness (Bailey et al. 1997; Phua 2007).

The rejection of femininity and the construction of masculinity as desirable was evident in some participants' narratives. Serano (2007: 14–15) claims that trans women 'become the victims of a specific form of discrimination: *trans-misogyny*'. In this sense, trans women experience both transphobia and misogyny simultaneously, that results from deviating away from expected gender norms and also being perceived as embodying 'femininity'. In patriarchal societies that devalue women, and thereby femininity as 'less than', the perceived 'choice' to embody femininity presents a unique set of challenges for trans women and feminine-presenting non-binary people. Deena, a 34-year-old female described an encounter in an LGBTQ venue:

> So I was in the smoking area chatting with my friend, a really hot gay guy, he gets loads of attention … He is like, the perfect gay boyfriend, he is masculine, ripped, facial hair, beautiful eyes … These guys come over, both muscle guys, and I realise I used to see them a lot before I transitioned … Anyway, I decided to come out to them, so I reminded them who they would previously have known me as. The first guys response was 'why would you choose to do that? You were so hot and manly before'. The second guy chipped in and agreed and then really annoyed me. He was like

> 'OH MY GOD, yes! I remember you, you were the beautiful black guy that we all wanted to fuck!'

There are a number of issues identified by Deena that warrant interrogation. Firstly, despite Deena no longer identifying with a masculine gender identity or presentation, her description of her friend, which highlights physical characteristics associated with masculinity, contributes to the narrative around masculinity being desirable. This is further reinforced by the way Deena is described as 'hot and manly before', in which manly signifies them as being masculine. As such, Deena is constructed as previously desirable, and therefore currently undesirable for her move away from masculine ideals. The comments made in this incident also drawn upon socially recognisable motifs of trans people 'choosing' a gender identity. The construction of trans people 'choosing' to engage in a particular 'lifestyle' is a key rhetoric in justifying transphobic discourse (Colliver et al. 2019).

On top of the trans-misogyny that Deena experiences, in which she is chastised for 'rejecting' her masculinity, she also experiences the racist, fetishisation of Black men (McKeown et al. 2010). This adds a further layer of complexity to gay communities' relationships with masculinity, which may also be situated and framed within racialised expectations and the hyper-sexualisation of Black men. It is important to note at this point that social configurations and expectations of gender presentation may be culturally situated in which gendered expectations are not universal. Therefore, Deena is constructed as not only deviating from her gendered expectation of masculinity, but for also disappointing those who may 'gaze' upon particular formations of masculinity.

What also became clear through the narratives provided by participants in this study was a feeling of relative acceptance of femininity in LGBTQ spaces, providing these expressions of femininity were in the context of entertainment that was deemed consumable for some cisgender, gay men. Piper, a 42-year-old woman describes an encounter she experienced in her local 'gay venue':

> I was in my local gay pub … Sunday is always cabaret [at the pub]. I am standing at the bar, talking to two guys … They were happily chatting away

> and then they asked me what time I would be performing. I must have instantly look confused as the other one instantly asked 'oh, sorry, are you not the drag queen?' I was quite taken aback, I know my make-up was a bit messy, but I didn't think I looked like a drag queen. So I confirmed that I wasn't the drag queen, trying to be as polite as possible. Then one of them turns around and just bluntly says 'ooooh, you're a tranny'. It was said in a way that was posed as a question. I replied and told them I was a woman and one of them just laughed. The one standing next to me just turned his back on me. It was clear that conversation was over.

The example provided by Piper is a clear example of how complex cisgender, gay men's relationship with femininity is, and how in particular contexts, expressions of femininity may be deemed 'acceptable' and even desirable. When Piper is initially understood to be a 'performer', or drag queen, the interaction is understood to be friendly, with the patrons of the pub consuming this form of 'acceptable femininity'. This aligns with Perry's (2001) claim that there are appropriate and acceptable ways to 'do difference'. Therefore, 'performative femininity', which is often rooted within comedic values, is somewhat socially accepted within cisgender, gay male culture; however, this is conditional on the basis that a social distance is maintained between the performer and the audience (Berkowitz et al. 2007). However, the patrons' reaction to Piper when she discloses her identity as female illustrates the harsh juxtaposition of femininity within 'gay spaces'. The temporary 'crossover' to femininity, which is perceived to be comedic, performative or satirical in nature is deemed 'consumable entertainment' and an appropriate way to 'do difference'. Whereas, to be perceived as permanently crossing the 'gender binary' is met with hostility.

Femininity may therefore be acceptable 'on stage' and in performance areas. However, this is significantly different to the experiences of some trans women when they try to authentically occupy social space designed for LGBTQ+ people, which tend to be dominated by cisgender, gay men (Pritchard et al. 2002). Trans women may therefore experience trans-misogyny when attempting to access and occupy 'inclusive' spaces, which are regulated and policed by cisgender men. The use of the word 'tranny', which in itself signifies contempt or hostility towards trans people, is also highly gendered and is commonly used to denigrate trans women. The use of language provides a more explicit example of trans-misogyny that some participants faced. Whilst there may be benefits to acknowledging 'LGBTQ' communities and spaces, these experiences highlight the heterogeneity of these communities which may represent different, and sometimes conflicting, needs and desires. However, it is not only within wider 'LGBTQ' spaces and communities that these issues arise. I now move on to provide an analysis of the ways in which some trans people experience exclusion and discrimination within 'trans inclusive' spaces.

'Not Trans Enough'—Inclusion and Exclusion from 'Inclusive' Spaces

I have referred throughout this book to trans 'communities', as a plural. This is a conscious, and intentional decision to acknowledge and reflect that there is no singular, cohesive and homogeneous community of trans people. I therefore consider that trans communities do not exist as a singular group and are diverse in needs and desires (Jamel 2018). Therefore, when discussing issues of transphobia, discrimination and prejudice, referring to a singular trans community locates the problem of oppression firmly outside of trans communities. This is not to say that cisgender communities are not the main perpetrators of oppression, and that cisnormative, heteronormative social structures allow for individual discrimination to occur. However, focusing solely on this overlooks the experiences of trans people who experience discrimination, prejudice and exclusion from other trans people. Moran and Sharpe (2004: 400) claim that academia often overlooks 'the differences, the heterogeneity, within what are assumed to be homogeneous identity categories and groups'. In doing this, the lived reality of hate crime experiences may be blurred. It is therefore key to acknowledge here that identities are multiple and fluid, and that our own understanding of identity may not coincide with others' perceptions of our identities (Wetherell 2009).

It is also important to acknowledge that trans people do not all experience hate crime, oppression and exclusion in the same ways, and that these experiences are likely to be compounded by other factors such as sexism, classicism and racism. Roen (2001) highlights that the diversity of trans communities and their differing experiences continue to be overlooked. This is supported by Jamel (2018), who claims that an overwhelming amount of research into trans lives is white. I therefore argue that the role of intersectional oppressions are often overlooked and research into hate crime victimisation is commonly conceptualised along a single identity axis. It became clear throughout this research that the role of religion, race, gender, disability status and sexuality were all influencing factors in the experiences of participants.

The work of Crenshaw (1989, 1991) and her theorising around 'intersectionality' are therefore central in understanding the diverse range of experiences described by participants. Crenshaw (1989) introduced the term 'intersectionality' when theorising that issues of race and gender were predominantly treated as mutually exclusive categories that are perpetuated by single-axis frameworks. Crenshaw claimed that the sole focus on either race, or gender, and never both at the same time, led to the erasure of Black women's experiences of discrimination. Similar claims can be made about research into transphobic hate crime, which has tended to centre the experiences of white, trans men and women. Essentially, intersectionality refers to the overlapping of an individual's membership and assigned place in various social hierarchies that interact and create unique experiences of oppression, discrimination and exclusion. Despite Crenshaw writing in 1989, issues of lack of representation still permeate research today; Hines (2010: 12) argues that 'much work … has lacked such an intersectional analysis with the effect that "trans people" are often represented as only that—as only trans'. It is key to address this, as Meyer (2010, 2012), who conducted an intersectional analysis of the impact of anti-queer violence, found that participants' class, race and gender all interacted in unique ways and impacted victims' evaluation of their experiences.

Ideas of privilege, oppressions and victimisation have been discussed widely by those concerned with intersectionality (Collins 2004; Crenshaw 1991; McCall 2005; Nash 2008). The key arguments offered are that the intersections of different marginalised identity markers form a matrix of oppression, and it may therefore become difficult to separate these intersecting systems of oppression. Given the wider acknowledgement of the importance of recognising intersectional oppressions within wider hate crime studies (Burnap and Williams 2016; Meyer 2010; Perry 2009), in this chapter I hope to extend our understanding of how intersectional oppressions impact the lives of trans people. Issues of intersectional oppression were certainly evident within participants' narratives, in which issues of racism, sexism, islamophobia and ableism were entangled with their experiences of transphobia. Whilst I address this in Chap. 6 of this book, in this chapter I address issues of discrimination, oppression and othering from so-called inclusive spaces, in which marginalisation is perpetuated by other trans people. I explore these issues with a particular focus on how a 'master identity' is assigned to people, particularly in relation to race and religion. I then move on to discuss non-binary exclusion from trans space and finish this chapter with a discussion on the role of 'coming out' for political reasoning or activism. Resultantly, I argue that a hierarchy of trans identity becomes established, in which some trans people are considered to be authentic, and others are subordinated as 'not trans enough'.

Participants who also identified with other minoritised groups relating to religion and race reported experiences of being othered and discriminated against by other trans people. The 'competition' felt by some participants can best be summarised by Laura, a 57-year-old female:

> Some of the most hateful things that are said are from one transgender person to another … The intersectional rivalry just appals me and there is so much insecurity in our community, so much need to be right for want of a better word and the presumption that everybody is against us that the first reaction is to attack and that happens so much and its disproportionate in the trans support groups that it gets to another level.

In Laura's account of diversity, competition and intersectionality within trans communities, she describes the nature of rivalry between different intersecting groups of trans communities. Laura refers to the overwhelming nature of othering within and between trans communities as a mechanism of defence, normalised as a reaction to continual discrimination. In this sense, Laura conceptualises these tensions as resulting from a fear of experiencing discrimination, and thereby ostracising anyone deemed 'different'. This translated to a number of participants who were also religious and experiencing exclusion from a number of apparent 'inclusive' spaces. Simon, a 47-year-old male, describes how when he discusses his faith with other trans people, he is responded to with suspicion about his motivations for being in a trans-inclusive space, and his religious identity overshadows his identity as a trans man. In this sense, a 'master identity' is imposed on Simon, in which his 'difference' becomes a more significant identity marker than the similarities he shares with other trans people. This was also reiterated by Isa, a 58-year-old female, who experiences:

> Comments like 'oh, who invited the God squad along'. It's like there is a stereotype about Christians all being these crazy preacher people who want to force religion in others' faces.

Similar to Simon, when accessing social spaces facilitated by, and organised for, other trans people, Isa often experiences her religious identity being imposed on her by others as her 'master identity'. In this sense, she is seen as religious first, and as trans second. Resultantly, she has experienced exclusion from trans-inclusive spaces as a result of her 'difference' to other trans people who are non-religious. It may be the case that historic tensions between minoritised genders and sexualities and certain religious sectors permeate trans people of faiths experiences when accessing social spaces. Participants' narratives indicate that their religious affiliation is often perceived as their defining characteristic and is therefore used as a means to 'other' them for not conforming to a particular trans identity. As such, exclusivity is key in understanding these experiences, in which one must exclusively belong to either a trans community, or a religious community, but not both simultaneously. Therefore, for trans people who are also of faith or with a religious affiliation encounter a social dilemma in which they must choose one identifying characteristic to represent their identity. This may result in them suppressing particular parts of their identity in order to 'fit in', within particular spaces.

Additionally, there were also more explicit examples of racism provided by participants that were beyond feelings of exclusion. Some of these experiences were in social spaces for trans people, and some were experienced within wider LGBTQ spaces. Sam, a 31-year-old male explained that some of the worst racism they had experienced had 'come from white, gay men. They seem to think they hold all the rights to discrimination and they have had it worse when they have probably had it easiest. Mainstream queer culture is very white, there isn't a space for people of colour and that is very much felt'. Similarly, this was also emphasised by Deena, a 34-year-old female who was:

> Surprised at how much racism and Islamophobia I receive from other trans people, not just outsiders of that community. It shocked me, I feel very isolated because I feel like I don't fit in to any particular community or group.

Deena speaks to her experiences of racism and Islamophobia that has been perpetrated by white, non-religious trans people. This demonstrates one of the many ways in which trans people's experiences of oppression, discrimination and hate are different and unique to the individual. For Deena, it is not only transphobia she experiences, but also racism and Islamophobia within spaces she accesses to feel safe as a trans person. In this sense, some trans-inclusive spaces are not safe or accessible for all trans people. Sam also alludes to this and highlights the whiteness of 'queer spaces', in which trans and queer people of colour are othered for their very existence as trans people who are also situated in oppressed positions within dominant societal racial hierarchies. In this sense, racial hierarchies that dominate mainstream society are applied within trans communities, assigning privilege and power to trans people who identify at the top of racial hierarchies and further marginalising trans people of colour. What occurs is a marginalisation of those already marginalised, furthering the silencing and othering of trans people of colour.

However, one of the most pervasive forms of exclusion that was reported, particularly by participants who identified between or outside the western gender binary, was associated with non-binary identities. This form of exclusion was most often conceptualised within two dominant frameworks: exclusion as a result of unawareness and exclusion as a result of identity politics. Joby, a 17-year-old gender-fluid individual describes how they experience exclusion from other trans people:

> Like not even all trans people know and understand non-binary people and so like they just exclude you. Like there has been times I have been in like LGBT spaces and seen other trans people, and like they will talk to you, and as soon as you say you are non-binary you kind of get excluded, it's almost like they don't want to be offensive so would rather just exclude you than risk saying the wrong thing.

In participants' accounts above, a lack of understanding is conceptualised to be the core reason non-binary individuals experience exclusion from wider trans communities. This is a common rhetoric that can be found through all non-binary participants' accounts of their sense of otherness. A lack of awareness is conceptualised as the causal reason for the otherness of all trans people from dominant cisgender communities, but also as the reason for a sense of otherness felt by non-binary people from dominant trans communities. In this sense, those who are perceived to be different experience policing by dominant communities in order to maintain a hierarchical structure. This was also emphasised by Joe, a 28-year-old gender-queer individual who described how 'people don't understand' their gender, and because of this Joe feels that they 'get written off by everyone, including other trans people'. This is not to say that all trans people who identify within the gender binary lack an understanding of non-binary identities. Sam, a 31-year-old man describes how:

> Quite often, trans people who are white, they are much more dominant than any other trans people, particularly trans men and women who identify within the binary. I think people who identify as non-binary or identify somewhere outside of the binary are also further kind of oppressed because there is even less understanding of gender identities that don't conform.

Sam, who isn't non-binary acknowledges the further marginalisation that non-binary people and individuals who identify with a gender outside of the western gender binary face. However, this is also contextualised within a wider discussion around the dominance of white trans people. As such, there are various hierarchies of dominance that exist within trans communities in which power and privilege may be assigned. Indeed, this has been identified before with Stryker (2009: 89) arguing for a greater acknowledgement of the ways 'in which "transgender whiteness" functions in (post)colonial contexts'. Resultantly, colonial constructions of gender which are intrinsically binary may privilege those who identify exclusively with either male or female and further marginalise those who do not fit within this model of gender.

However, the exclusion of non-binary individuals was also conceptualised as being a result of broader social and political contexts. As such, notions of identity politics and activism permeated some participant's accounts of exclusion. In this sense, the subordination of those deemed different functions to uplift the social status of more dominant communities. Quite often, the advancement of political recognition was given as a direct reason for the exclusion non-binary participants faced, Melody, a 17-year-old non-binary individual describes their general experiences of exclusion:

> I think within trans communities, there is like an attitude of exclusion for non-binary people because they think that we have the luxury of choosing which gender to present as and we will never undergo surgery and so our experiences must be so much easier than theirs. I have been told by trans women that they have enough trouble getting people to understand and accept trans people who were male or female, and people like me were making things even harder by not choosing a gender to identify with.

The experience described by Melody is clearly situated within a tense political climate in which trans rights and issues affecting trans communities have garnered significant political and social attention. For some trans people, acceptance or assimilation may be a key goal as this may be associated with reduced risk of violence, discrimination and oppression. Due to the inherently binary nature of western society, trans people who are not exclusively male or female may be perceived as a barrier to acceptance or assimilation into a cis-normative society. This was emphasised by Ty, a 21-year-old non-binary individual who claims that if you don't 'fit in with that [binary] image of trans and don't identify as male or female … you just [aren't] welcome'. This was also a feature of online experiences, and reinforces the political context in which identities are shaped. Star, a

44-year-old non-binary individual describes a situation in which they become involved in an online debate concerning trans rights:

> Trans people were telling me I shouldn't speak on their behalf because apparently I am not trans … The trans women were debating with cis women, and started excluding me, they were telling cis women not to listen to what I said, that I wasn't a voice for trans people because I wasn't even trans. Basically saying that trans people just want to live life and fit in and not change anything and it was radical people like me that cis people needed to be wary of because apparently I personally want to eradicate all gender systems and labels and want everyone to not have a gender.

In Star's experience, their identity is constructed as radical and in direct opposition with cis-normative expectations and standards. Resultantly, Star experiences 'othering' from predominantly trans women for failing to conform to binary gendered expectations. The nature of the messages Star received also highlight the politicised nature of trans identities, in which strives towards legal and political recognition and protections are perceived as being hindered by associating non-binary, gender-fluid and gender-queer people within the 'trans' umbrella. For non-binary, gender-fluid and gender-queer participants in this study, there appeared to be a perception that trans people who identified exclusively as male or female understood their identities to be 'superior' to non-binary individuals. Star also describes a social situation they were in, when they were asked to leave as a result of disclosing their non-binary identity:

> I was attending a social event for trans people … the organiser of the event came over and asked that I leave, apparently the event was only for trans people and I didn't quite meet the criteria of being trans because I didn't plan on having surgery and didn't identify definitively as male or female … But you know, that is a similar kind of experience I have had whenever I try to access trans only spaces, I get made to feel like I am not trans enough.

In all of the accounts provided above, non-binary, gender-fluid and gender-queer identities are perceived to be in direct conflict with cis-normative gender expectations, but additionally as in conflict with 'trans progression' as a political movement. In this sense, trans identities become politicised and trans identities are conceptualised as a political force, characterised by the motivation of progression. Non-binary people are perceived to be a threat to the stability of trans identities and consequently a barrier to their progression within a mainstream political and social climate. As can be seen in the exclusion of trans people from wider LGB communities, notions of authenticity and legitimacy are drawn upon to police trans identities within trans communities. Participants' report notions of failing to meet gendered expectations associated with dominant trans identities and are policed for not being 'trans enough' through their failure to conform to medical and surgical interventions. In this sense, notions of 'transnormativity' permeate participants' accounts of othering in which a hierarchy of 'transness' is established and those who do not identify within dominant gendered binary systems are positioned at the bottom of the hierarchy (Vipond 2015). Gendered binary systems are therefore used to gatekeep access to those who can and cannot claim 'transness'. In this sense, a 'right way' to transition is established and becomes the marker by which trans people are judged. Similar notions of agency and choice in relation to gender identity that are often used to de-legitimise trans people who identify within gendered binary structures are also drawn upon to de-legitimise those who identify outside or between stable categories of man and woman (Colliver et al. 2019). The reliance on the gender binary serves as a way to police access to trans inclusive spaces and exclude those who do not fit within the gender binary from accessing particular spaces such as youth groups and social spaces for trans individuals.

In what participants can articulate and express, the role of language is used as a means of policing and 'othering' those who fall outside of dominant norms relating to 'transness'. However, the language and terminology available to trans people is the result of unobservable structures relating to the gender binary. As Pearce (2018) argues, the use of the terms 'trans' and 'cis' create a notion of exclusivity in which an individual must identify as *either* trans *or* cis. In doing so, the gender binary is reinforced, leaving little scope for those whose identity is more fluid. In this sense, one is exclusively always 'trans' or always 'cis', which also further marginalises individuals who no longer identify as trans, but simply as male or female. Gender identity and presentation can be a complex issue and the politicisation of language has significant impact on who 'trans' as an identity marker is available to and contributes to the exclusion of non-binary people and others who identify between or outside of the gender binary.

Conclusion

In this chapter, space, place and belonging have been explored in relation to trans people's conceptualisation of risk and othering. It is argued that trans people's experiences of victimisation differ according to their positioning on several different social hierarchies. In this sense their level of visibility as 'different' is fluid in relation to the spaces they occupy. Public, sex-segregated toilets clearly represent spaces of concern for some trans people. This has been explored by Faktor (2011) who claims that toilets represent a significant space of fear, anxiety and victimisation for trans people. However, as becomes clear, trans people in this study who 'pass' are less likely to fear victimisation in sex-segregated spaces. Furthermore, accessing these spaces often becomes a signifier of acceptance. For trans people who identify outside the binary and have a visibly gender-incongruent presentation, risk of abuse is conceptualised within both male and female toilets. As a result of this, coping mechanisms are often employed that reduce the frequency that trans people use the toilet. Access to public toilets significantly impacts on trans people's ability to engage in 'everyday' life and relatively mundane activities may require significant planning and consideration to ensure safe spaces are accessible.

Masculinity has also been discussed in terms of its fragility, in which perpetrator's masculinity becomes unstable in the context of sexual, emotional or romantic relationships with trans women. I therefore claim that transphobic abuse acts as a facilitator for the re-establishment of masculinity. Trans women therefore experience violence, hate crime and oppression as a mechanism of establishing identity. This is often in the context of perpetrators negotiating their own identity, in which the conflation between gender and sexuality is intrinsic to cisgender men's understanding of their own sexualities. This was particularly the case for participants who experienced violence and abuse after engaging in penetrative sex with cisgender men, and therefore it is key to interrogate both the victim and perpetrator's sense of identity when exploring violence in this context.

I further considered notions of masculinity in relation to trans-misogyny, particularly within broader LGBTQ spaces and cultures. Participants' experiences within this study highlight the complex, and often harmful, relationship that exists between femininity and some cisgender, gay men. This is key, in acknowledging harmful attitudes, actions and practices that exist within LGBTQ communities, often overlooked as a result of locating issues of transphobia and trans-misogyny solely outside of LGBTQ communities. For participants in this study, issues of trans-misogyny were highly associated with male perpetrators, whilst this is not to say that women do not engage in these behaviours; in the context of LGBTQ spaces it was perceived to be a gendered issue. This highlights the often uncomfortable relationship cisgender, gay men have with femininity, and trans women may therefore experience trans-misogyny because of this discomfort, particularly when it is presented in an authentically, embodied manner.

The multiple marginalisation experienced by participants who identify with multiple minoritised social groups that relate to race and religion has also been discussed. In doing so, the exclusion that trans people who do not identify as heterosexual, atheist and White British was explored. As such, trans culture is characterised by whiteness, in that those who identify as white British are significantly privileged. In addressing some of these issues, I hope to have contributed to literature that seeks to challenge the 'whiteness' of much trans research (Jamel 2018). In doing so, I have explored how individuals may be assigned a 'master identity', which may, or may not coincide with the individual's own interpretation and understanding of their identity. This raises interesting questions around power distribution within trans communities and who is able to assign a 'master identity' to another. Throughout this research, it became clear that this was typically white, atheist trans people who identified as either exclusively male or female and in some way conformed to the gender binary.

Notions of 'transnormativity' are also explored which assigns legitimacy to particular presentations of 'trans' and excludes those who do not conform to these expectations. A 'right way' to transition, and to be trans, was clearly evident in some participants' experiences of exclusion and othering. Trans people who identify with a gender identity outside of the traditional gender binary face significant levels of othering from both cisgender populations and trans populations. As Garrison (2018: 624) argues, 'the desire to bring one's body "into alignment" with one's identified gender is essential to legitimating trans identity'. In this sense, it is essential for trans people to follow a pre-prescribed journey in which the end goal is medical transition to align with the traditional gender binary. Garrison (2018) further argues that when people perform gender in ways that are unrecognisable to others, their gender may be challenged. However, an increasing social visibility of binary trans identities has challenged mainstream ideas of pre-existing gender systems that correlate gender with biological sex. As a result of this, those who identify outside of the binary have been excluded (Shuster 2017). I therefore argue that trans people who identify outside of the gender binary disrupt societal understandings and conceptualisations of 'trans' as a category. Transnormativity is therefore employed as a method of policing gender boundaries, reinforcing the gender binary and regulating the inclusion of trans people. Trans people are therefore held accountable to these standards of gender presentation which are specific to trans people. Those who do not meet these standards may therefore be excluded from trans spaces.

Perry (2001) claims that minority-on-minority violence can also be conceptualised in relation to 'doing difference'. Minority 'othering' is still the result of hierarchical conflict and is the result of identity politics in which particular groups seek legitimisation and validation; this is often thought to be achieved through the subordination of other minorities. In relation to the 'othering' of non-binary, gender-fluid and gender-queer peoples' experience of victimisation, they may experience double-discrimination. In this sense, they experience victimisation from cisgender people for violating dominant gender norms and challenging the gender binary. At the same time, they may experience exclusion and discrimination from trans people who identify within the gender binary, as male or female. This became clear in participants' accounts of trans people's claims that non-binary people do not represent the trans community and this is often presented within the notion that non-binary identities may pose as a barrier to trans progressive movements because of their gender non-conformity.

References

Bailey, J. M., Kim, P. Y., Hills, A., & Linsenmeier, J. A. W. (1997). Butch, femme, or straight acting? Partner preferences of gay men and lesbians. *Journal of Personality and Social Psychology, 73*, 960–973.

Bender-Baird, K. (2016). Peeing under surveillance: Bathrooms, gender policing, and hate violence. *Gender, Place & Culture, 23*(7), 983–988.

Berkowitz, D., Belgrave, L., & Halberstein, R. (2007). The interaction of drag queens and gay men in public and private spaces. *Journal of Homosexuality, 52*(3–4), 11–32.

Browne, K. (2004). Genderism and the bathroom problem: (Re)materialising sexed sites, (re)creating sexed bodies. *Gender, Place & Culture, 11*(3), 331–346.

Burnap, P., & Williams, M. (2016). Us and them: Identifying cyber hate on Twitter across multiple protected characteristics. *EPJ Data Science, 5*(1), 1–15.

Casey, M. (2004). De-dyking queer space(s): Heterosexual female visibility in gay and lesbian spaces. *Sexualities, 7*(4), 446–461.

Cavanagh, S. (2010). *Queering bathrooms: Gender, sexuality, and the hygienic imagination*. Toronto: University of Toronto Press.

Collins, P. H. (2004). *Black sexual politics: African Americans, gender, and the new racism*. New York: Routledge.

Colliver, B. (2020). Representation of LGBTQ communities in the Grand Theft Auto series. In C. Kelly, A. Lynes, & K. Hoffin (Eds.), *Video games, crime and next-gen deviance* (pp. 131–150). Bingley: Emerald Publishing.

Colliver, B., & Coyle, A. (2020). 'Risk of sexual violence against women and girls' in the construction of 'gender-neutral toilets': A discourse analysis of comments on YouTube videos. *Journal of Gender-Based Violence, 4*(3), 359–376. https://doi.org/10.1332/239868020X15894511554617.

Colliver, B., Coyle, A., & Silvestri, M. (2019). The online 'othering' of transgender people in relation to 'gender neutral toilets'. In K. Lumsden & E. Harmer (Eds.), *Online othering: Exploring digital violence and discrimination on the web* (pp. 215–237). London: Palgrave Macmillan.

Connell, R. W. (1995). *Masculinities*. Cambridge: Polity Press.

Crenshaw, K. (1989). Demarginalizing the intersection of race and sex: A Black feminist critique of anti-discrimination doctrine, feminist theory and anti-racist politics. *University of Chicago Legal Forum, 1*, 139–167.

Crenshaw, K. (1991). Mapping the margins: Intersectionality, identity politics, and violence against women of color. *Stanford Law Review, 43*(6), 1241–1299.

Davidoff, L. (2003). Gender and the 'great divide': Public and private in British gender history. *Journal of Women's History, 15*(1), 11–27.

Davidson, G. (2019, September 1). SNP's Mhairi Black says she's been challenged when using women's toilets. *The Scotsman*. Retrieved August 19, 2020, from https://www.scotsman.com/news/politics/snps-mhairi-black-says-shes-been-challenged-when-using-womens-toilets-1408822.

Doan, P. L. (2010). The tyranny of gendered spaces: Reflections from beyond the gender dichotomy. *Gender, Place & Culture, 17*(5), 635–654.

Faktor, A. (2011). Access and exclusion: Public toilets as sites of insecurity for gender and sexual minorities in North America. *Journal of Human Security, 7*(3), 10–22.

Fischel, J. (2019). *Screw consent: A better politics of sexual justice*. Oakland, CA: University of California Press.

Fletcher, T. (2013). Trans sex workers: Negotiating sex, gender, and non-normative desire. In S. Van de Meulen & E. M. Durisin (Eds.), *Selling sex: Experience, advocacy and research on sex work in Canada* (pp. 65–73). Vancouver: UBC Press.

Garrison, S. (2018). On the limits of "trans enough": Authenticating trans identity narratives. *Gender & Society, 32*(5), 613–637.

Greed, C. (2019). Join the queue: Including women's toilet needs in public space. *The Sociological Review Monographs, 67*(4), 908–926.

Hale, C. (1996). Fear of crime: A review of the literature. *International Review of Victimology, 4*(2), 79–150.

Hale, S., & Ojeda, T. (2018). Acceptable femininity? Gay male misogyny and the policing of queer femininities. *European Journal of Women's Studies, 25*(3), 310–324.

Hines, S. (2010). Introduction. In S. Hines & T. Sanger (Eds.), *Transgender identities: Towards a social analysis of gender diversity* (pp. 1–22). New York: Routledge.

Hoskin, R. A. (2019). Femmephobia: The role of anti-femininity and gender policing in LGBTQ+ people's experiences of discrimination. *Sex Roles, 81*(11), 686–703.

Jamel, J. (2018). *Transphobic hate crime*. London: Palgrave Macmillan.
Kaufman, M. (2007). The construction of masculinity and the triad of men's violence. In L. O'Toole, J. Schiffman, & M. Kiter-Edwards (Eds.), *Gender violence: Interdisciplinary perspectives* (pp. 33–55). New York: New York University Press.
Kehrli, K. (2016). Tropes as erasers: A transgender perspective. In M. Valentinelli & J. Gates (Eds.), *Upside down: Inverted tropes in storytelling* (pp. 314–329). Lexington: Apex Publications.
Kelly, L. (1988). *Surviving sexual violence*. Cambridge: Polity Press.
McCall, L. (2005). The complexity of intersectionality. *Signs, 30*(3), 1771–1800.
McKeown, E., Nelson, S., Anderson, J., Low, N., & Elford, J. (2010). Disclosure, discrimination and desire: Experiences of Black and South Asian gay men in Britain. *Culture, Health and Sexuality, 12*(7), 843–856.
Meyer, D. (2010). Evaluating the severity of hate-motivated violence: Intersectional differences among LGBT hate crime victims. *Sociology, 44*(5), 980–995.
Meyer, D. (2012). An intersectional analysis of lesbian, gay, bisexual, and transgender (LGBT) people's evaluations of anti-queer violence. *Gender and Society, 26*(6), 849–873.
Milton, J. (2020, June 14). Boris Johnson is scrapping long-overdue plans to allow trans people to self-ID despite overwhelming public support, report claims. *PinkNews*. Retrieved August 18, 2020, from https://www.pinknews.co.uk/2020/06/14/trans-self-id-uk-boris-johnson-liz-truss-gender-recognition-act-leak-sunday-times/.
Moran, L., & Sharpe, A. (2004). Violence, identity and policing: The case of violence against transgender people. *Criminal Justice, 4*(4), 395–417.
Murphy, P. (2001). *Studs, tools, and the family jewels: Metaphors men live by*. Wisconsin: University of Wisconsin Press.
Namaste, V. (2000). *Invisible lies: The erasure of transsexual and transgender people*. Chicago, IL: University of Chicago Press.
Nash, C. (2013). Queering neighbourhoods: Politics and practice in Toronto. *International E-Journal for Critical Geographies, 12*(2), 193–213.
Nash, J. (2008). Re-thinking intersectionality. *Feminist Review, 89*(1), 1–15.
Noble, B. (2012). Trans. Panic. Some thoughts toward a theory of feminist fundamentalism. In A. Enke (Ed.), *Transfeminist perspectives in and beyond transgender and gender studies* (pp. 45–59). Philadelphia, PA: Temple University Press.

Pain, R. H. (1997). Social geographies of women's fear of crime. *Transactions of the Institute of British Geographers, 22*(2), 231–244.

Pearce, R. (2018). *Understanding trans Health: Discourse, power and possibility.* Bristol: Policy Press.

Perry, B. (2001). *In the name of hate: Understanding hate crimes.* London: Routledge.

Perry, B. (2009). The sociology of hate: Theoretical approaches. In B. Levin (Ed.), *Hate crimes, volume 1: Understanding and defining hate crime* (pp. 55–76). Westport: Praeger.

Phua, V. C. (2007). Contesting and maintaining hegemonic masculinities: Gay Asian American men in mate selection. *Sex Roles, 57*, 909–918.

Pritchard, A., Morgan, N., & Sedgley, D. (2002). In search of lesbian space? The experience of Manchester's gay village. *Leisure Studies, 21*(2), 105–123.

Richardson, N. (2009). Effeminophobia, misogyny and queer friendship: The cultural themes of Channel 4's Playing it Straight. *Sexualities, 12*(4), 525–544.

Robertson, A. (2016, April 7). Girl, 16, claims McDonald's staff told her to leave when she used the women's toilets…because they thought she was a boy. *Daily Mail.* Retrieved August 19, 2020, from https://www.dailymail.co.uk/news/article-3527827/Teenage-girl-16-claims-humiliated-McDonald-s-staff-asked-leave-used-women-s-toilets-thought-boy.html.

Roen, K. (2001). Transgender theory and embodiment: The risk of racial marginalisation. *Journal of Gender Studies, 10*(3), 253–263.

Sánchez, F. J., & Vilain, E. (2012). "Straight-acting gays": The relationship between masculine consciousness, anti-effeminacy, and negative gay identity. *Archives of Sexual Behaviour, 41*(1), 111–119.

Sanders, J., & Stryker, S. (2016). Stalled: Gender-neutral public bathrooms. *South Atlantic Quarterly, 115*(4), 779–788.

Schilt, K., & Westbrook, L. (2009). Doing gender, doing heteronormativity: Gender normal, transgender people, and the social maintenance of heterosexuality. *Gender and Society, 23*(4), 440–464.

Serano, J. (2007). *Whipping girl: A transsexual women on sexism and the scapegoating of femininity*. Emeryville, CA: Seal Press.

Shuster, S. (2017). Punctuating accountability: How discursive aggression regulates transgender people. *Gender & Society, 31*(4), 481–502.

Stanko, E. (1985). *Intimate intrusions: Women's experience of male violence.* London: Routledge & Kegan Paul.

Stotzer, R. (2009). Violence against transgender people: A review of United States data. *Aggression and Violent Behavior, 14*, 170–179.

Stotzer, R., & Shih, M. (2012). The relationship between masculinity and sexual prejudice in factors associated with violence against gay men. *Psychology of Men & Masculinity, 13*(2), 136–142.

Stryker, S. (2009). We who are sexy: Christine Jorgensen's transsexual whiteness in the postcolonial philippines. *Social Semiotics, 19*(1), 79–91.

Vandello, J. A., Bosson, J. K., Cohen, D., Burnaford, R. M., & Weaver, J. R. (2008). Precarious manhood. *Journal of Personality and Social Psychology, 95*, 1325–1339.

Vera-Gray, F., & Kelly, L. (2020). Contested gendered space: Public sexual harassment and women's safety work. *International Journal of Comparative and Applied Criminal Justice*. Advance Online Publication.

Vipond, E. (2015). Resisting transnormativity: Challenging the medicalization and regulation of trans bodies. *Theory in Action, 8*(2), 21–44.

Wetherell, M. (2009). *Theorizing identities and social action*. London: Palgrave Macmillan.

Whitley, B. E., & Kite, M. E. (1995). Sex differences in attitudes toward homosexuality: A comment on Oliver and Hyde (1993). *Psychological Bulletin, 117*, 146–154.

6

The Role of (In)Visibility in Hate Crime Victimisation

Introduction

As outlined in Chap. 2 of this book, several theoretical frameworks have been dominant when exploring hate crime victimisation. Namely, Perry's (2001) concept of 'doing difference' and Chakraborti and Garland's (2012) critique and proposal of 'vulnerability'. In this chapter, I hope to contribute to our conceptual understanding of hate crime victimisation through a detailed and thorough conceptualisation of the ways in which (in)visibility functions within hate crime victimisation. In the data I present within this chapter, it will be clear that notions of 'difference' and 'vulnerability' certainly appeared in participant's narratives of their victimisation. Whilst I shall argue that there is nothing inherently flawed about existing concepts, it will be shown throughout this chapter that the overarching notion of both perspectives relates to (in)visibility. When discussing and conceptualising (in)visibility, I will demonstrate the fluctuating, fluid and unstable nature of (in)visibility. Our identities are continually being established and developed and we must therefore develop our understanding of (in)visibility beyond the current dichotomy. This is key as Stryker (2006) highlights that trans people's experiences and

B. Colliver, *Re-imagining Hate Crime*, Palgrave Hate Studies,
https://doi.org/10.1007/978-3-030-65714-7_6

presentations of gender are not isolated from other identity markers such as class and race. I conclude this chapter by highlighting the ways in which concepts of (in)visibility can be applied across hate studies more generally and allow for a deeper understanding of the ways in which identities are negotiated.

I have written around the role of (in)visibility in hate crime victimisation before (Colliver and Silvestri 2020), but in this chapter, I hope to expand on this initial conceptualisation. In particular, the initial conceptualisation ignored the role of (in)visibility within an online context, something which I address in this chapter. The development of the internet has created new spaces within which we can exist, and as such, has implications for how we negotiate our identities (Code 2013). As will be discussed throughout this chapter, participants in this study often felt that there was greater control over the levels of (in)visibility they could maintain in an online context, although this control was sometimes taken away from them as a result of being 'outed'. Alongside a more thorough conceptualisation of (in)visibility as it relates to the cyber-world, I also revisit my initial conceptualisation of (in)visibility and offer further critique and comment around these ideas. In doing so, I draw upon existing conceptualisations of (in)visibility from a range of disciplines, most notably Queer and Trans studies, to provide a strong contextualisation of what I hope to contribute. The often dichotomous conceptualisation of (in)visibility will be highlighted, which form the basis of critique provided in this chapter. Notions of 'passing' are highly contested within existing literature, with different perspectives offered on what it means to 'pass' and the complexities associated with this concept (Roen 2002; Serano 2007). Ideas of (in)visibility are often intrinsically linked to an individual's ability to 'pass', and given the messy nature of what it means to 'pass', it is unsurprising to find that (in)visibility is also not a clear-cut concept.

In this chapter, I seek to adopt a 'trans-centric' approach to exploring (in)visibility and its relationship to hate crime. This approach has often been overlooked within UK-focused hate crime literature. Three of the largest UK research projects which have centred on, or included, hate crime experiences do not centre the lives of transgender people. Youth Chances, The All Wales Hate Crime Project and The Leicester Hate

Crime Project all engaged with over 1000 participants regarding their experiences of hate crime, yet only 14%, 3.5% and 3% of participants were transgender respectively. Additionally, within these studies, the experiences of non-binary people were often overshadowed as there was a strong focus on trans men and trans women's experiences, reinforcing the dominant western gender binary. As a result, trans people have often been homogenised and the differences between transgender people's experiences are conflated. Additionally, the experiences of non-binary people are conflated within a binary understanding of trans identities. In this chapter, I hope to tease some of these sometimes subtle differences out and provide a more comprehensive reading of the way in which (in) visibility interacts with trans identities in relation to hate crime victimisation.

Throughout this chapter, four key arguments are engaged with. I firstly argue that whilst existing conceptualisations of (in)visibility that have been developed in other disciplines have been key in developing our understanding of victimisation, we must engage with this concept in a more complex way. Existing conceptualisations that suggest an increased level of visibility leads to higher rates of victimisation are certainly valid, but they may overshadow victimisation in which (in)visibility is less clear-cut. I therefore suggest that (in)visibility is significantly more complex than these conceptualisations through acknowledging the ongoing, fluctuating negotiation of identities. Secondly, through acknowledging the significance of occupying multiple, marginalised social positions (Mattias de Vries 2012), I draw upon the work of Crenshaw (1989, 1991) to explore how intersectional oppressions impact individuals relationship with, and understanding of (in)visibility. I will argue that an increased level of visibility does not always equate to an increased sense of risk of victimisation, or actual victimisation. Instead, a visible 'difference' may function in a preventative manner, reducing the likelihood of victimisation.

The third argument I engage with is that in order to fully understand (in)visibility as a concept, and how it operates, we must acknowledge and identify less tangible, discursive experiences of (in)visibility. As such, I engage with (in)visibility beyond what is 'see-able', which may be the most obvious understanding of how (in)visibility operates. In appreciating this conceptualisation, we can better understand the experiences of hate crime victimisation that do not fit dominant narratives that coincide with 'stranger danger' frameworks. As such, we can better identify and engage with the experiences of victims that happen in private spaces, perpetrated by those known to the victim. The final argument presented is that in order to fully realise the potential of (in)visibility in explaining hate crime victimisation, we must adopt a wider lens, in which we explore how (in)visibility relates to all those involved in hate crime, including victims, perpetrators and witnesses. In presenting these arguments, I conclude that (in)visibility provides a useful framework through which we can understand existing dominant concepts such as 'difference' and 'vulnerability'. The lens of (in)visibility allows for a deeper, more nuanced understanding of how hate crime is experienced, understood and particular contexts in which hate crimes occur. These arguments are significant to criminological thought, and hate crime scholarship, in advancing our understanding of the personal, political and spatial contexts in which hate crime occurs.

It is important to note that whilst the analyses of (in)visibility presented throughout this chapter are firmly grounded within the experiences and lives of trans people within the United Kingdom, the conclusions reached have international significance and can be applied beyond transphobic hate crime. Throughout this chapter I refer to (in)visibility to identify the dichotomous conceptualisation that relates to both the increasing and decreasing nature of this concept. I do, however, speak directly to both visibility, and invisibility, when outlining experiences or contexts which result specifically in either an increase or decrease in visibility, rather than a situation in which either could occur.

Existing Conceptualisations of (in)Visibility

The idea of (in)visibility is not a new concept in and of itself. Indeed, many scholars have engaged with this concept and applied it to various social issues (Perry 2015; Rundall and Vecchietti 2010; Wallengren and Mellgren 2015). In hate crime scholarship, the concept of (in)visibility has been engaged with to varying degrees of detail. As such, the conceptual engagement has varied from study to study, with some engaging with the concept at an individual level, and some at a wider, structural and political level (Mills 2019; Perry 2015; Wallengren and Mellgren 2015). Hate crime studies that have engaged with the concept of (in) visibility have largely been in relation to Islamophobia (Chakraborti and Zempi 2012; Mason-Bish and Zempi 2019; Perry 2015). Perry (2015) engaged with the concept of visibility in relation to Muslim communities in a broader structural, political, cultural and mediatised society. At the macro-level, she argues that the events of 9/11[1] led to Muslim identities becoming more visible because of media and political narratives associated with terrorism. It is argued that this heightened level of visibility positions Muslim communities under the social 'spotlight', and they may therefore be seen as legitimate targets for violence and hate. Perry's (2015) work is key in helping us understand how notions of (in)visibility relate to structural systems that perpetuate oppression. However, it does overlook the role (in)visibility plays at an individual level of identity.

On the other hand, Chakraborti and Zempi (2012) have engaged with this concept at an individual level in relation to the veil. The veil, in and of itself, and the process of 'veiling' has been conceptualised as a visual, and visible indicator of 'difference'. In this sense, they address the gendered nature of Islamophobia, in which the veil becomes a visible symbol of an individual's religious identity. Whilst this work is vital in addressing the gendered nature of victimisation, it is heavily centred on the public nature of victimisation that fits within existing frameworks that relate to 'stranger danger'. Perry and Dyck (2014) provide one of the few studies that adopt a 'trans-centred' approach to visibility and experiences of violence. However, as with other studies that centre visibility, this is largely done in relation to violence experienced within public spaces, and is contextualised heavily within the 'pass-not pass' dichotomy. As such, the specific spatial, and contextual dynamics of victimisation that occurs within the private spheres, such as the home, healthcare settings and romantic and/or sexual relationships is overshadowed. We attended to this oversight in our original conception of (in)visibility, but I hope to further

[1] The 9/11 attacks were a series of four coordinated attacks by the terrorist group al-Qaeda against the United States.

illustrate the complicated nature of (in)visibility and its relationship to space in this chapter (Colliver and Silvestri 2020).

As discussed previously in this book, the concept of 'stranger danger' is firmly established within hate crime studies (Gerstenfeld 2004; Lawrence 1999). The emphasis on 'stranger danger' contributes to the construction of hate crime as a public issue, an issue that is able to be contextualised in a particular spatial framework. This conceptualisation fails to acknowledge hate crimes that occur within the home, perpetrated by those closest to the victim including parents and carers, siblings and romantic and/or sexual partners. In the last chapter, I addressed some of these issues, highlighting the particular risks associated with disclosing ones trans identity in the context of romantic and/or sexual relationships, and previous research has also identified that a significant amount of transphobic hate crime is experienced inside the home (Stotzer 2009). Similarly, in the last chapter I challenged the idea that the public–private divide is a clear distinction and discussed spaces that may blur this boundary, including public toilets. I would argue that the prevalence of 'stranger danger' within victimisation studies has contributed to the overshadowing of those experiences perpetrated in 'private', by those known to the victim. Indeed, others have identified that victims of hate crime are likely to have a pre-existing relationship with those who perpetrate this form of victimisation (James et al. 2016; Mason-Bish 2010). Others have claimed that the focus on 'stranger danger' has dangerous implications for the stereotyping of racial and social class groups (Meyer 2014). It has been claimed by Walters (2011: 319) that 'cultures of prejudice are nurtured within families, friendship circles and by neighbours' and would therefore seems illogical to assume that hate crime perpetrators only victimise strangers. Although the studies discussed have tended to focus on Islamophobia, they have shown that the more visible a perceived 'difference' is, the higher levels of fear of victimisation are reported.

Whilst the engagement with (in)visibility as a concept within hate crime scholarship has not garnered significant traction, it has been considered more significantly within trans and queer studies (Kilian 2014; Lovelock 2017; Rundall and Vecchietti 2010). Research in this area has explored notions of (in)visibility in relation to media portrayals and media visibility (Lovelock 2017), within the arts (Kilian 2014) and within employment (Rundall and Vecchietti 2010). A significant amount of work has also focused on the 'pass-not pass' dichotomy and some of the complications associated with this (Fütty 2010; Roen 2002; Serano 2007). This has often been discussed in relation to the (in)visibility of a trans identity in relation to an individual's ability, or want, to 'pass'. At a time when gender identity is becoming increasingly politicised, the implications of 'passing' and what it means to 'pass' is an area of contention. Passing, or 'to pass', refers to whether a trans individual is perceived, or read, as trans by other people, and society more broadly. Those who are perceived to be cisgender may be referred to as being able to 'pass'. Whilst the complexities associated with 'passing' are beyond the scope, and not the purpose of this book to engage with, I felt it important to provide a brief summary of some of the key contentions associated with passing. It may be the case for some that to 'pass' is to live authentically (Sellberg 2012), as a method to avoid victimisation or may be seen in more socio-political terms as conforming to, and reinforcing rigid gender binaries (Roen 2002). However, 'passing' may not be as dichotomous a concept as initially perceived, and others have critiqued the simplicity often associated with 'passing' (Serano 2007). Passing may not always be in the control of a trans individual, and there are likely to be economic, political and cultural factors that influence whether an individual can, or wants to pass. The notion of passing is also heavily confined to discussions around the gender binary, and becomes even more complex in relation to non-binary individuals. People may or may not pass, with, or without intending to, in different spaces and at different times.

(In)Visibility and Hate Crime Victimisation

Whilst I have discussed that existing conceptualisations of (in)visibility have tended to be dichotomous in the way they are discussed, this is not to say that they offer no framework for understanding transphobic hate crime. Whilst existing conceptualisation often presents (in)visibility as a linear process, in which one travels from being 'visible' to 'invisible', it is often more complex than this. However, for some participants, particularly those who identified within the gender binary, this appeared to fit within their narratives. As was alluded to in the previous chapter, greater levels of visibility often resulted in higher levels of fear, and higher levels of actual victimisation. On the other hand, participants who were able to, and wanted their trans identity to remain invisible, reported significantly lower feelings of fear, and less experiences of actual victimisation. However, this was also heavily related to the public–private divide. In this sense, participants described higher levels of fear were primarily associated with victimisation in public. This conceptualisation of '(in)visibility' was also heavily interrelated in the sense of 'see-ability'. That is, physically visual indicators of an individual's trans identity were most commonly drawn upon to discuss the idea of (in)visibility and how it relates to fear of victimisation. Later in this chapter I complicate this conceptualisation of (in)visibility and extend our understanding beyond what is 'see-able'.

It was evident within participants' narratives that the fear of victimisation based upon their trans identity, particularly in public spaces, was minimal for those who perceived themselves to successfully 'pass'. In this sense, their perceived 'difference' has been rendered invisible as a result of meeting physical gendered expectations. In line with the dichotomous nature of (in)visibility that has been conceptualised to date, individuals who perceived themselves as unable to pass, or for those who consciously decided to live as 'visibly trans', feelings of fear were a more heightened concern. In this sense, their 'difference' is visible, particularly in the public sphere. As one participant explained, 'because I went through so many years of having testosterone in my body, it doesn't matter what I do, people will always read me as trans'. This sentiment was particularly present for trans people who felt conscious about their physical appearance and felt particularly vulnerable to the 'public gaze'. Levels of anxiety about an individual's physical appearance were often heightened when accessing sex-segregated spaces in public which have become subject to significant public debate (Colliver and Coyle 2020). This is intrinsically linked to the dominant western gender binary, and expected physical presentations associated with 'male' and 'female' (Namaste 2000).

Whilst the experiences that were briefly described above fit within some existing frameworks of transition being a linear process, in which one moves from 'visibly trans' to 'invisibly trans', this was not the case for all participants. 'Passing' was not necessarily the end goal for many participants, and for some, it was not considered achievable. This was particularly the case for many non-binary participants who did not recognise the importance of 'passing' for themselves, given their identity between, or outside the gender binary of 'male' and 'female'. As one non-binary participant Ty questioned, 'what am I supposed to pass as?'. This is not to say that the concept of 'passing' is completely redundant for non-binary, as Star explained, 'sometimes I dress more feminine for particular situations, so that people won't necessarily question my gender identity. Like, sometimes I am able to present in a more cis-normative way to avoid particular situations going bad'. For Star, they are able to adjust their physical presentation more in line with cis-normative expectations of gender presentation to avoid victimisation, and minimise the visibility of their trans identity. Research has shown that those with a visible 'difference' may adapt their lifestyle or appearance in an attempt to assimilate into 'mainstream' society (Ford et al. 2012). However, identity concealment is believed to negatively impact psychological distress in trans individuals (Rood et al. 2017). On the other hand, for some participants, being visibly trans was a personal, social, or political decisions and therefore no measures were taken to render their 'difference' invisible. Instead, sometimes measures were taken to emphasise the visibility of their trans identity, including the use of trans-affirmative slogan clothing or through tattoos. This relates to wider literature surrounding autonomy in relation to identity negotiation and presentation (Gressgård 2010) and the role of the individual in negotiating how their identities are read and perceived.

As discussed in the previous chapter, the concept of 'passing' is not universal within trans communities in relation to its importance. It is also important to note that the politicisation of 'passing' and surrounding debates may make assumptions about an individual's autonomy over people's perceptions of them. Claims that choosing to 'pass' perpetuates normative expectations of gender presentation and that choosing to live openly as a trans person is symbolic of radicalism and activism may therefore be unsubstantiated when we consider the narratives expressed in this research. Participants who did not consider themselves as 'passing' were often not consciously 'choosing' not to pass. Rather, many participants felt unable to meet cisnormative, gendered expectations in relation to the way they presented their gender identity. As such, living as 'openly trans' was a default position assigned to them as others perceived them to be trans, regardless of how they intended their gender presentation to be read. It is also important to note that the idea of 'passing' is not a static, achieved status. Indeed, it is an ongoing, relational process that has varying levels of importance and meaning based upon the cultural, spatial and situational context an individual occupies. However, as significant work has already been done on the concept of 'passing', I now want to complicate our understanding of how (in)visibility operates in relation to hate crime and victimisation and extend our understanding and engagement beyond the apparent dichotomy of invisible and visible.

(In)Visibility, Intersectionality and Victimisation

In moving beyond the dominant conceptualisation of (in)visibility as a binary concept, I will first outline the ways in which intersectional oppressions may complicate and compound our understanding of (in) visibility. Although I have previously written around intersectionality and (in)visibility (Colliver and Silvestri 2020), in this chapter I offer further empirical data to bolster this conceptualisation. In doing so, I suggest that (in)visibility is a fluid, unstable and continually negotiated concept. Through participants' narratives, it will become clear that (in)visibility, as it relates to an individual's 'difference' and 'vulnerability' may become more pronounced in particular contexts, spaces and contexts. Specifically in this research project, it became clear that the visibility of participants' trans identity fluctuated in different contexts, and this was also often compounded by other identity characteristics. Woods (2014) has claimed that experiences of oppression are shaped not only by an individual's gender identity, but also other identity markers such as race, religion, disability status and sexuality, although this is not an exhaustive list. In addressing how (in)visibility operates, I add to the literature on 'intersectional' difference, oppression and victimisation. In doing so, I hope to avoid the limitations associated with 'identity politics' that Crenshaw

(1989, 1991) previously outlined, including the tendency to conflate experiences of diverse communities.

Jamel (2018) highlights that a significant amount of western research into trans and gender-diverse identities is Eurocentric and white. Resultantly, relationships between intersecting oppressions are often overlooked. Whilst some research has explored this area (Meyer 2010, 2012), it is scarce within hate crime literature. This book attends to this gap within the literature, as the ways in which different aspects of identity impacted participants' experiences of victimisation were central in this research. As highlighted previously, some participants' narratives in this research spoke to existing literature which conceptualises an increasingly visible trans identity having a direct impact upon trans people's fear of transphobic victimisation, particularly in public spaces. However, I now want to address the ways in which trans identity, and other identity markers may become more dominant, or more visible in particular contexts and therefore mediate the risk of transphobic victimisation. Most commonly, this was perceived to be as a result of prejudiced stereotypes surrounding another identity marker. For Emmet, a 30-year-old man, it was stereotypical perceptions of Irish Traveller's that minimised his feelings of fear of transphobia. However, it is important that this was only in relation to victimisation in public, perpetrated by strangers. His identity as an Irish Traveller did not minimise his fear of transphobic victimisation in private, perpetrated by family and wider community members. When describing his interactions with strangers, Emmet describes how:

> When people have started abusing me and calling me a tranny and harassing me and then I say something, people shit themselves. Like, there are loads of stereotypes about traveller men, being violent and aggressive … So, sometimes being a traveller actually makes me feel safer.

Research has shown that there are a number of stereotypes associated with Irish Traveller communities that primarily relate to crime, aggression and violence (Council of Europe 2006; Tremlett 2014). Emmet perceives these stereotypes of violence and aggression to offset the perceived 'vulnerability' associated with his trans identity. It is important to note that this is not to say that Traveller communities do not experience oppression, violence and discrimination, as this is well documented (James 2020; James and Smith 2017; Wallengren and Mellgren 2015). However, in the scenario Emmet described, he perceived his Traveller identity as less likely to be seen as 'vulnerable', and actually may function as a barrier to victimisation due to the associated stereotypes. In the same interview, Emmet emphasised how in situations in which he felt particularly vulnerable he attempted to emphasise his Traveller identity to minimise the risk of victimisation. As noted earlier, although there are debates surrounding the use of the term 'vulnerable' due to its connotations of passivity, helplessness and lack of autonomy, Emmet's narrative alludes to a certain level of autonomy and control over which parts of his identity he chooses to be dominant at a particular time. This is not to say that others will read an individual's identity in the intended way.

The narrative discussed above demonstrates one of the ways in which identity negotiation is a complex, ongoing task. It also illustrates the ways in which (in)visibility is not a binary concept, and particular parts of an individual's identity may become more or less visible in particular contexts. Emmet's experiences also highlight the spatial and cultural implications that must be considered when conceptualising notions of (in)visibility. For example, when Emmet is around family and friends, his trans identity becomes dominant, and his Traveller identity does not compensate against his perceived 'difference' or 'vulnerability' in that particular context. However, when interacting with strangers, his Traveller identity may become more prominent than his trans identity and function to compensate against his perceived 'vulnerability' associated with being trans. However, it is important to note that although Emmet's Traveller identity may have reduced people's perception of his 'vulnerability', it does not conceal his 'difference', and in fact, his 'difference' may be exacerbated. It is also key to acknowledge that a perceived reduction in 'vulnerability' heavily relies on other individuals reading and perceiving another's identity in the intended way.

Allusions to physical dominance and aggression were key in some other participant's narratives when discussing their perceptions of vulnerability. Although those who were seen to be physically dominant reported that this often made them feel more 'different', they expected their identities to be read and perceived as less 'vulnerable', and therefore less at risk of experiencing transphobic hate crime, abuse and discrimination. Star, a 44-year-old non-binary individual described the ways in which their physical appearance and presentation reduced their feelings of fear and risk of victimisation:

> my appearance has actually helped me avoid being physically attacked. Like, punk aesthetic can be quite intimidating, and I am quite dominating physically, like I'm six foot two, I'm quite big built, and I'm a Queer Punk … So, yeah, I think in some ways, even though I stand out, sometimes it actually helps keep me safe.

As noted earlier in relation to Traveller communities, this is not to say that those who may be identifiable as belonging to a subculture do not experiences oppression, hate and violence, as this has been well documented (Garland 2010; Garland et al. 2015; Hodkinson and Garland 2016), most notably with the murder of Sophie Lancaster in 2007 (Minton 2012). It is not to say that Star no longer experiences oppression or discrimination, but Star's fear of physical violence is alleviated. It therefore becomes clear that for both Emmet and Star, the 'difference' that they both perceive to be most dominant, or visible, acts as a barrier to victimisation in their conceptualisation of risk. In this sense, Emmet and Star's understanding of their visible 'difference' is more complex than in the previous discussions of (in)visibility.

The experiences and understandings of Emmet and Star are different from other participants, and it becomes evident that it is not as simple as conceptualising (in)visibility in a dichotomous way. As such, this is one of the ways I challenge ideas of 'difference' being a fixed, constant indicator of an individual's 'vulnerability'. An alternative understanding of (in) visibility that can be offered relates to stereotypes. Stereotypical perceptions of those deemed 'different' that may be associated with aggression, violence and physical dominance function as a preventative factor in the victimisation of some people. In this sense, an individual may be able to draw upon routinely evoked stereotypes to emphasise a particular facet of their identity, thus minimising their perceived vulnerability. This challenges dichotomous understandings that suggest an increased visibility of 'difference' leads to an increased perception of 'vulnerability'.

Emphasising a particular facet of an individual's identity does not always equate to a decreased sense of risk. In fact, the very visibility of a different characteristic may indeed reduce feelings of fear of transphobic victimisation, but does not minimise the feelings of risk more generally. As discussed in the last chapter, a 'master identity' may be imposed upon us, that does not necessarily accord with our own understanding of our identities. Our identities are fluid and under constant negotiation (Wetherell 2009), in conjunction with how others perceive and read our identities. In this sense, another identity marker may be more visible, thereby increasing an individual's feeling of fear of victimisation more generally, although this may not be directly linked to their gender identity. This is most clearly emphasised by Sam, a 31-year-old trans man, who when reflecting upon their experiences of victimisation claimed that:

> I do find that I experience more racism than transphobia. I am so visibly Asian and I can't hide that. I can walk with my head down so people can't see my face, but I can't disguise my colour and I think that is what stands out instantly about me, my brownness.

Sam recounts the practical measures he can employ to minimise the visibility of his trans identity, through concealing as much of his face as possible when in public. However, it becomes clear that the same techniques cannot be used to minimise the visibility of all of his identity markers. It is clear that the visibility of his Asian heritage is the more significant factor in his accounts of risk. The approaches to emphasise or conceal particular identity traits are not universal and therefore different approaches may be necessary in relation to different identity traits. Issues related to racism were common in some participant's narratives. In particular, the experiences of Ty, a 21-year-old non-binary individual below show the ways in which particular identity characteristics may be brought to the fore in different spatial and situational contexts. Ty describes the way in which the visibility of their racial identity increases their feelings of risk of experiencing abuse.

> I think because people can see I'm Black and I can't cover that up, people tend to focus on that. I mean don't get me wrong, I usually experience

> transphobia with racism, but I think it is the colour of my skin that makes people initially notice me.

Although Ty experiences transphobia, it is not the visibility of their trans identity that they associate with risk. Rather, the transphobia they experience is often a secondary form of victimisation. As such, it is Ty's racial identity that is most visible and therefore their racial identity may be imposed upon them as their master identity, and their trans identity becomes secondary. This also demonstrates that one visible 'difference' may then result in hate and abuse, targeting a less visible 'difference'. As Ty explains, it is usually racism that they experience first, and transphobia is often secondary. However, this is context specific, and Ty does highlight a particular space in which they feel more at risk of transphobia than racism:

> I get anxious that I will be singled out because I look completely different to all of the other Black boys on the estate.

The residential area where Ty lives is a space of heightened anxiety of gender policing. Ty's belief that they fail to meet racialised gender expectations results in increased levels of anxiety around experiencing transphobia. The experience described above alludes to the fact that Ty's gender presentations fall outside the realms of what is expected of peers from the same background. Research relating to homosexuality has shown that various communities consider homosexuality as 'something that white people do' (Carbado 2001: 250). Despite not focusing on issues of gender, it could be argued that similar parallels may be present given the intrinsic relationship between gender and sexuality. Ty evidently experiences a matrix of oppression, in which a multitude of identity markers amalgamate to create a unique experience of gender. It becomes clear in this instance that Ty experiences a reduced autonomy in relation to others' perception of their identity and expected presentation. Therefore, feelings of risk are felt in a broader sense for failing to meet gendered expectations, but this also speaks to a specific failure to conform to racialised expectations of gender. This demonstrates the way that understandings and expectations of gender identity and expression are culturally and racially situated and this has implications for trans people who may also belong to other marginalised groups (Archer 2003).

Not only do intersecting oppressions contribute to both increased and decreased levels of (in)visibility in particular spaces and contexts, but there are also significant implications for trans people enacting a specific, culturally configured presentation of masculinity or femininity. White-western cultural expectations of gender identity and presentation are entrenched within heteronormative, white-normative ideals (Collins 2000). Therefore, expectations of how gendered bodies should be presented, based upon their sex assigned at birth, is created, maintained and perpetuated within western cultural configurations of masculinity and femininity, and intrinsically linked to whiteness (Schippers 2007). As a result, culturally configured expectations of gender presentation, and appropriate gendered behaviour, impact the level of (in)visibility trans people are able to achieve. There may therefore be culturally and racialised expectations of gender presentation which may make transition between masculine and feminine presentations and behaviours more complex, whilst for some trans people, transition between masculine and feminine presentations may be seemingly linear based upon white-western expectations of gender. Consequently, trans people may 'pass', or successfully be read in accordance with their intended gender presentation within 'white spaces', but the visibility of their trans identity may become more prominent within specific spaces in which cultural or racial gendered expectations take precedence. Clearly, for Ty, and other non-binary people this may be compounded and complicated even further as a result of not trying to meet a western configuration of gendered expectations.

In participants' narratives, it was not just racial identities that exacerbated feelings of risk of victimisation. Age and physical ability were also highlighted as significant contributing factors to perceptions of risk. As discussed earlier, in the case of Star, it was their physically dominant appearance which reduced the feelings of risk of victimisation. However, for Rose, a 67-year-old trans woman, it is the associated weakness of her physical appearance that *increases* her feelings of risk. Rose stated that:

> People target me because I am older, I walk with a stick, I'm wrinkly and so people think I'm an easy target. I can't run away, I can't defend myself,

> so people think I will be easy to abuse. To be fair, they are right, I lose my balance easily. I can't physically defend myself, so I am open to all sorts of abuse.

For Rose, it is a culmination of her visible 'difference' in relation to her trans identity, and the perceived vulnerability that is associated with her visible physical frailty that she perceives to be the reason why she experiences transphobic abuse. In discussing her experiences of verbal abuse, harassment and physical violence targeting her trans identity, the implication made is that if she was perceived as younger, and less physically vulnerable, she may be targeted less. As such, Rose's experiences of the ways in which her physical appearance are read and interpreted by others differ from that of Star. Therefore, it is key to acknowledge and interrogate the ways in which (in)visibility and 'vulnerability' interact to create unique readings of an individual's identity. Participants' feelings of risk were also impacted by intersectional oppressions as evidenced in the online survey conducted. Binary logistic regression was conducted on the data collected and a number of identity characteristics revealed statistically significant results. Those who considered themselves to have a disability had 2.087 times the predicted odds of feeling at risk of experiencing a hate crime than those who did not consider themselves to have a disability. Furthermore, as shown in 'Table 6.1', participants who were not 'white British' had 1.839 times the predicted odds of feeling at risk of experiencing a hate crime.

In comparison to the very dichotomous manifestation of (in)visibility that was presented at the beginning of this chapter, it is clear that intersectional oppression and multiple marginalised identity characteristics

Table 6.1 Regression analysis—predicted odds of feeling at risk of experiencing a hate crime

		B	S.E.	Wald	df	Sig.	Exp(B)
Step 1[a]	Ethnicity	0.609	0.284	4.597	1	0.032	1.839
	Religion	0.098	0.279	0.122	1	0.727	1.102
	Gender	0.787	0.340	5.368	1	0.021	2.198
	Sexuality	-0.240	0.285	0.713	1	0.399	0.786
	Disability	0.736	0.304	5.864	1	0.015	2.087
	Constant	-2.779	0.454	37.489	1	0.000	0.062

complicate notions of (in)visibility. An individual's trans identity may become either more or less visible in different spaces and contexts as a result of the ways in which other visible identity markers are read by others. Identity markers such as age, race and disability status operated by either overshadowing an individual's trans identity, or drawing attention to their trans identity as a form of secondary victimisation. This adds complexity to the notion of (in)visibility, as whilst an individual's trans identity may be invisible, through passing successfully, they may still experience victimisation based on the visibility of another marginalised identity characteristic. This demonstrates the ways in which oppression, abuse and victimisation do not manifest in a silo manner, but often operate as part of a matrix of oppression, in which victimisation is motivated by several prejudices.

Discursively Constructed Visibility

Now that I have outlined the ways in which notions of (in)visibility manifest in tangible ways, in relation to the 'see-ability' of an individual's identity, it is important to consider how (in)visibility operates in less tangible ways. In doing so, I reflect upon the ongoing negotiation of (in) visibility and the way in which (in)visibility is not a stable, static of fixed status. In this sense, I conceptualise (in)visibility *beyond* what can be seen. In this section, I also challenge dominant narratives of 'stranger danger', which reinforces ideas that strangers pose the biggest threat to an individual's safety. The narratives that are explored in this section demonstrate the ways that transphobia, hate crime and victimisation may occur within private sphere such as the home. Perpetrators in these spaces are more likely to have known the victim, and may be those considered closest to them, such as family, friends and colleagues. Often, victimisation in private spheres results from an individual 'coming out', disclosing their trans identity, and therefore rendering their 'difference' visible. As such, it is not a physically visible 'difference' or 'vulnerability' that results in victimisation. Rather, the 'difference' imposed on an individual's identity is less tangible and less 'see-able'. In this sense, an individual's trans identity can be discursively made visible.

When this occurs within family units, the consequences of discursively rendering a 'difference' visible can be life changing. It can often result in homelessness, unemployment and a loss of contact with family members and children. Existing research has shown that trans people experience higher levels of homelessness, employment discrimination and hate crime than their cisgender counterparts (Grant et al. 2011; METRO Charity 2014; Rosich 2020). As discussed earlier, there may be particular cultural configurations of gender expression and presentation that are expected of an individual. These expectations may be heightened within family units and a failure to meet these expectations may be seen as an 'assault' on family values. As Corrina, a 21-year-old woman from an Irish Traveller background describes:

> I had to run away when I came out, I brought shame into my family, I embarrassed my family. I was abused and abused by family and who I thought were friends and then I finally had enough and escaped.

At the point of 'coming out' to her family, Corrina had been presenting her gender in more 'traditional' ways associated with her sex assigned at birth and in-line with her family's cultural expectations of gender presentation. The abuse that she experienced, including physical assault, verbal abuse and harassment was the result of 'coming out', thereby rendering a previously invisible difference, visible. This was a common narrative in which experiences of transphobia, abuse and violence are heightened around times in which trans people 'come out'. Sam, a 31-year-old trans man described a particularly violent incident:

> My dad and my brother viciously attacked me, I mean literally beat me to a pulp, I was left with broken ribs, black eyes, a swollen jaw … I just saw it as something I expected to happen because of my culture and faith and the reactions that I knew would come.

Sam's description is of his family's reaction when he 'came out' as trans. Until this point, Sam had been discussing incidents of verbal and emotional abuse that he had experienced from his family in response to his failure to conform to culturally prescribed gender norms. However, this abuse significantly escalated at the transitional moment in which Sam's family's perception of him changed from failing to meet gender expectations, to actively rejecting gendered expectations. In this sense, 'coming out' is a crucial time in relation to risk escalation and risk management. The reason an individual may 'come out' are plenty and varied. This may be as a result of feeling internal pressure, to live openly, or from an external pressure, such as family, friends or society more broadly. However, it is this particular moment that often renders an individual's 'difference' visible and can subsequently result in victimisation.

It is well-documented that 'coming out' is an ongoing and cyclical process which may see an individual 'come out' at different times in different spaces (Zimman 2009). Research has shown that periods of time associated with 'coming out' may be especially high-risk for gender and sexual minorities (Wandrey et al. 2015), and based on the conceptual lens adopted for this research, I would argue that this is a result of the increased visibility afforded to an individual's 'difference' at this particular time. As a result, (in)visibility is a fluctuating, fluid and continually negotiated concept that is spatially and socially contextualised. For those with a concealable 'stigma', there may be ongoing decisions made that relate to which spaces, and to whom, it is safe to 'come out'. Therefore, whilst the rigidly dichotomous conceptualisation of (in)visibility can be applied within the context of what is see-able, it overlooks the complexity and nuanced nature of (in)visibility more generally. As the process of 'coming out' is an ongoing process, there is not one static point in time in which an individual may be at risk. It may be unknown at what times, and in which contexts an individual may feel the need to, or want to, 'come out'. At the same time, there is no guarantee as to what time an individual may be 'outed', in the sense that someone else discloses their trans identity, therefore rendering their 'difference' visible. Due to the complicated, and messy nature of identity formation, negotiation and interpretation, it is not possible to neatly conceptualise (in)visibility as it relates to identities, 'difference' and 'vulnerability'.

Ideas around 'coming out' are intrinsically linked with notions of 'autonomy', and the control an individual has over which spaces, and which contexts, their identities are read by others as trans. This is particularly pertinent for an individual who 'passes', whose 'difference' may not be instantly visible, or see-able. As discussed in the previous chapter, notions of 'passing' are often tied up within political and activist debates. However, the decision to disclose a trans identity is not always associated with these reasons. In particular contexts, an individual may feel the need to disclose their trans identity because of the unique situational context. This demonstrates the complex and multifaceted relationship individuals have with the idea of (in)visibility. Previous work regarding 'visibility' has often overlooked the way this operates within private spheres, such as the home, in which victimisation is often perpetrated by partners, family and friends.

The Role of (In)Visibility in Online Victimisation

Notions of (in)visibility were not only apparent in the physical world. They were very much present in participants' narratives regarding their online presence and interactions. In this sense, participants' descriptions of their experiences in an offline context are mirrored within their description of victimisation online. It became clear throughout the interviews conducted that for many trans people the internet, and social networking in particular, had become engrained as part of their daily routine. Consequently, victimisation and transphobic abuse became part of their 'everyday'. With the rise in popularity of social networking sites, there has been a growth in research that identifies the similarities and differences between hate speech targeting minoritised groups in online and offline contexts (Banks 2010; Brown 2017; Chetty and Alathur 2018). These studies have been key in developing our understanding of how the internet has developed as an unregulated site for the dissemination of discriminatory, prejudicial and hateful views. The global reach of the internet permits the spread of dominant, social ideologies (Weaver 2013). However, whilst there is a growing body of research exploring online hate speech, the interest in the online victimisation of trans people has trailed significantly behind the interest of more socially recognised victim groups relating to race, sexuality and religion (Awan 2014; Cmeciu 2016; Weaver

2013). Resultantly, very little is known about the victimisation of trans people in an online context, although I have begun to address the gap previously (Colliver et al. 2019; Colliver and Coyle 2020).

I have previously written on the ways in which transgender people are constructed in online 'debate' surround public toilets. I have highlighted how notions of 'mental health', 'unnaturalness', 'religion' and 'technology' have all been drawn upon to delegitimise trans identities (Colliver et al. 2019). More specifically, in the context of public toilets, trans people are often constructed as potential perpetrators of physical and sexual violence against 'weak' and 'vulnerable' cisgender women and children (Colliver and Coyle 2020). Despite the lack of research exploring trans people's experiences of hate speech online, some scholars have begun to address this issue. Findings by METRO Charity (2014) identified that 25% of their LGBTQ+ sample had experienced some form of cyberbullying. This finding was starkly different to the results of this research study, in which 77% of participants identified that they had experienced online abuse targeting their trans identity.

Nevertheless, it is important to note that participants in this study also highlighted a number of benefits they associated with using the internet. The ability to connect with a global trans community was often highlighted as a key feature of social networking sites. Other research has highlighted how the internet can be used to produce visual records of transition (Stein 2016) and facilitate the organisation of activists (Shapiro 2004). Despite the fact that many incidents of online hate speech and/or hate crime are not reported, the internet has allowed a number of initiatives to be developed and circulated that intend to encourage the reporting of hate crime victimisation (Jamel 2018). However, these initiatives are not without criticism, as Williams and Tregidga (2013) argue that online initiatives fail to consider the needs of those with limited, or no access to the internet. Furthermore, Chakraborti (2018: 394) claims that 'very few of the research participants in any of the studies were familiar with the idea of third party reporting'.

In understanding how participants relate to their own experiences and interactions in an online context, notions of (in)visibility proved to be key in relation to building and maintaining a global network of trans friends. In this context, (in)visibility operated in a number of ways.

Firstly, in a similar manner to that of the linear conceptualisation of (in)visibility discussed earlier in this chapter, those whose trans identity was invisible in their online interactions reported experiencing minimal incidents of transphobia. On the other hand, those whose trans identity was visible within an online context reported significantly more incidents of transphobic abuse. However, for those whose trans identity was visible in an online context, this was not always the result of disclosing their trans identity, or intentionally being visible. For some, this resulted from people making assumptions about an individual's gender identity based on the content an individual engaged with. For those who actively followed, discussed or engaged with issues of gender identity online were often assumed to be trans. Finally, (in)visibility also proved key for many participants' journey, in which they could remain invisible, but receive substantial support from visibly trans individuals and networks.

The participants who were able to and wanted to remain invisible in an online context reported significantly lower experiences of transphobic abuse than those who were unable to, or chose not to. However, in ensuring, or attempting to ensure that an individual's trans identity remained invisible in an online context, quite often their behaviours and interactions were severely restricted. Resultantly, some participants were unable to benefit from the vast connectivity the internet can offer. As Bushra, a 29-year-old trans woman explains:

> I have not really [experienced abuse online], I am very careful that I do not put any pictures of myself online and I only talk about being transgender in very private and safe places ... Because of this people do not really abuse me online because of being transgender ... I don't talk to many trans people online, because I want to avoid being targeted.

Bushra feels unable to connect with many other trans people, particularly on public platforms, as she feels that this will make her a more visible target for online abuse and harassment. In this sense, it is the fear of victimisation that prevents Bushra from benefitting from the global connectedness that the internet provides. Not sharing photographs was a common narrative for participants, particularly for those who felt that their physical appearance would be read as transgender. For some, meticulously removing old photos from social media was also a key task in rendering their trans identity less visible in an online context. As Elaine, a 48-year-old trans woman notes:

> I have created all brand new profiles, I don't have pictures of me before I transitioned on there, so I live very much as a woman online and I pass, so I don't really get any abuse online anymore ... I also have really strict controls over my social media and who gets to see it. Since I made new profiles, I don't follow any pages that are about trans issues, as I don't want to be clocked ... Sometimes I wish I could join some online networks and stuff, but I just feel like the potential abuse outweighs the potential support.

Due to the nature of the internet, many participants felt it was key to create new social media profiles that were completely disconnected from any previous profiles. In doing so, it is hoped that they would no longer be associated with a trans identity in an online context. Identifying safe and supportive spaces may prove difficult, particularly in an online context, and the unknown may result in hypervigilance in order to avoid victimisation (Rood et al. 2016). This may be because an individual perceives themselves to 'pass'. Alternatively, this may be a conscious decision aimed at reducing the likelihood of victimisation. Research has shown that the internet can be a vital tool in network building for gender and sexual minorities (Cipolletta et al. 2017). However, for Elaine, she is unable to benefit from these opportunities due to fear of victimisation. As a result, Elaine does not connect with other trans people in an online context as part of a risk-reduction strategy. Elaine also referred to maintaining stringent privacy and security settings on her social media profiles. This is a preventative measure that forms part of a wider risk-reduction strategy and also contributes to maintaining an 'invisible presence' online, particularly in relation to their trans identity. However, some participants did note that this could often create a false perception of invisibility. Lia, a 17-year-old woman discussed that:

> Even on like Facebook, my privacy settings are quite strict so only friends can see stuff, and it gives you a false sense of security, because even if only your friends can see it, if they share it then all of their friends can see it ...

> If two of their friends share it, all of theirs can and before you know it thousands of people can see a photo or a post that you have put on.

The excerpt presented above illustrates the measures that some participants take to minimise their online visibility, which may be associated with a false sense of security. Similarly, self-censorship is utilised and engaged in to minimise the risk of experience abuse and hate speech. Whilst individuals may engage in self-censorship in order to minimise the risk of experiencing transphobic abuse online, Lia complicates notions of security and (in)visibility by alluding to the false sense of security that can be experienced as a result of monitoring 'privacy settings'. As such, having access to a wide range of privacy options can lead to the perception that participants have minimised their visibility online; however, actual and perceived invisibility may differ. This may be the result of snowball sharing of online content directly from the victim, or may be the result of more malicious intentions by someone an individual trusts. Resultantly, trans people may experience online abuse that is not anticipated or expected as a result of perceived invisibility.

Alternatively, some participants anticipated high levels of abuse, discrimination and hate speech in an online context because of publicly disclosing their trans identity across a number of social media platforms. Resultantly, their online interactions, coupled with their visible trans identity resulted in higher levels of risk. As Lia goes on to say, by posting trans content on social media, trans people 'open themselves up to being trolled'. Lia clarifies that this does not mean that trans people who experience trolling are to blame for their victimisation. However, ideas of self-blame permeated participants' narratives in which they associate online victimisation with their own online behaviours. This is particularly pertinent in cases where trans people throw themselves 'to the wolves', as Isa, a 58-year-old woman explains, that she is 'so often a target because [she is] vocal online about what [she] thinks and feels and disagrees with someone and essentially throws [herself] to the wolves.' For Isa, a personal need to advocate for trans rights means that she often finds herself in a position in which she engages with people posting transphobic content. Whilst not justifying the behaviour of those who abuse her, Isa appears to believe that it is her choice to engage in these conversations that lead to her own personal abuse. However, for others, simply posting trans-positive content results in victimisation. In this sense, abuse can result from engaging with either trans-positive or transphobic content. Irrespective of the perspective of the poster, engaging with any content deemed to be associated with trans issues may result in experiencing transphobic victimisation. As Sam, a 31-year-old trans man explains:

> I am very much an activist within the community, so I often receive lots of attention, and lots of it is negative, it is just part of being active online. I am quite well known in the trans community, so I am a constant target for TERFs. I speak out about trans issues and as a result become a very public target.

For Sam, it is his notoriety as a trans activist, and the resultant visibility this affords him, that he perceives to be the underlying reason as to why he is targeted in an online context. In this sense, visibility is conceptualised as a causal reason for victimisation and is perceived to be a result of participants' actively choosing to engage in online discussions. As such, notions of self-blame underpin participants' accounts of their victimisation online because of choosing to be visible. When visible in an online context, participants' experiences of abuse range from name-calling and misgendering to the incitement to self-violence in which trans people are encouraged to engage in self-harm or suicidal behaviour. These experiences are mirrored by research that explores the ways in which trans people are constructed and delegitimised in an online context (Colliver et al. 2019). As discussed earlier in this book, in relation to experiences of micro-crimes, a process of rationalisation and normalisation occurs in which participants anticipate experiencing online trolling. Participants in this research often attributed the experiences and frequency of online abuse to the relative invisibility of those who perpetrate these forms of victimisation.

> I think this is the hardest [dealing with online abuse in comparison to abuse in the physical world] because it normally comes in such huge volumes, like you get involved in a conversation and within twenty-four hours you have received maybe one hundred, two hundred, three hundred inbox

messages and comments … Most of them are from anonymous accounts. Being online allows you to keep your real self invisible from others, you can be who you want to be, even if that means being a faceless, nameless profile. (Isa, 58, female)

The increased levels of anonymity that the online sphere provides is perceived as contributing to the higher frequencies of abuse that trans people may encounter online. In this sense, a fundamental difference between online and offline victimisation is the frequency and instantaneousness of such abuse. Research has already established clear differences between online and offline hate speech, primarily concerning the given anonymity, immediacy and lack of established regulations to monitor online hate speech (Brown 2017; Cohen-Almagor 2011). This is compounded by the interplay between visibility and invisibility, in which victims may be those who are most visibly trans and may be perpetrated by those who are able to keep their own identity invisible. Again, this demonstrates the complexity of '(in)visibility' as a concept. I argue that we cannot understand (in)visibility as a singular concept that can be applied to one individual, without considering the relationship that perpetrators, or potential perpetrators also have with (in)visibility.

Conceptualising (In)Visibility

Now that I have presented some empirical data, I'd like to engage with the notion of (in)visibility at a more conceptual level, highlighting the importance of acknowledging how (in)visibility operates when engaging with hate crime victimisation. Perry's (2001) concept of 'doing difference' and Chakraborti and Garland's (2012) conceptualisation of 'vulnerability' have been key in hate crime scholarship for developing our understanding of the causes and consequences of hate crime. Ideas of 'difference' were clearly apparent throughout this study and participants regularly made reference to their own 'difference', sometimes explicitly and sometimes implicitly. This was most commonly discussed and conceptualised as a causal reason and motivating factor for victimisation they experienced. By engaging with intersectional oppression, this becomes even clearer, as participants' understanding of their own multiple, minoritised identity markers were conceptualised as increasing the level of 'difference' associated with them. Therefore, the findings of this research support the framework provided by Perry (2001) and I would argue that 'difference' does indeed play a significant role in the victimisation of trans people.

Similarly, participants' accounts of victimisation also invoked notions of 'vulnerability' and provided support for claims made by Chakraborti and Garland (2012). They argue that 'a vulnerability-based approach acknowledges the heightened level of risk posed to certain groups or individuals that can arise through a complex interplay of different factors, including hate, prejudice, hostility, unfamiliarity, discomfort or simply opportunism or convenience' (2012: 506). The opportunistic nature of victimisation was certainly apparent in participants' narratives in this study and opportunistic victimisation was often perceived to be the result of particular 'vulnerabilities' imposed on the victim by the perpetrator(s). Age and disability status were conceptualised as significant indicators of an individual's 'vulnerability' and being visibly trans was often understood as being associated with 'weakness' and 'vulnerability'. In this sense, trans people often considered themselves to be perceived as 'easy targets', and this may be exacerbated by other identity markers. Notions of 'vulnerability' were also evident in the narratives of this research in relation to social, cultural, political and economic power inequalities in which trans people's marginalisation in society results in the label 'vulnerable' being imposed upon them. In this sense, the narratives collected in this study lend support for Chakraborti and Garland's (2012) claim that understanding how 'vulnerability' operates is key in developing our understanding of hate crime victimisation.

Whilst there is nothing inherently problematic with either of these contributions to hate crime scholarship, and indeed, they have been central to developing our understanding of the dynamics associated with hate crime victimisation, I would argue that engaging with (in)visibility allows us to extend our knowledge of these concepts and of hate crime more broadly. Through engaging with the concept of (in)visibility in relation to intersectional oppressions experienced, we are able to fully understand how 'difference' can function as both an indicator of 'vulnerability', but also function as a protective barrier against victimisation. In focusing solely on the role of 'difference' in the motivation and perpetration of hate crime, Perry (2001) didn't explore how stereotypes related to 'difference' can actually minimise people's fear of victimisation. Stereotypes may be culturally specific, or may just relate to physically dominant presentations of identity. In this sense, when perceived 'difference' is understood by potential perpetrators of hate crime as decreasing a potential victim's vulnerability, a more balanced power dynamic in relation to physicality may be established, and therefore 'difference' may serve as a preventative factor. Factors such as age, disability status, race, religion, dress and gender presentation were regularly discussed as increasing or decreasing an individual's visible 'difference' or 'vulnerability'. However, it is important to note that these identity markers complicate our understanding of (in)visibility, in that the presence or absence of these does not always equate to a trans identity becoming more visible. Indeed, disability status, dress, race and religion were often seen as increasing the visibility of 'difference', but not necessarily in relation to an individual's trans identity. In some instances, the presence of multiple oppressed identity markers did increase feelings of fear of transphobic victimisation, but in some cases, the fear of transphobic victimisation was decreased in place of a fear of victimisation targeting a more visible characteristic. This was particularly the case for individuals who believed that their race was more visible than their trans identity, and therefore felt greater risk of experiencing racist hate crime, although often racism and transphobia were simultaneous.

I would therefore argue that whilst both 'difference' and 'vulnerability' are useful, both are dependent upon the way in which (in)visibility operates. I would therefore call for a much stronger engagement with this concept when exploring hate crime victimisation and perpetration. (In)visibility therefore plays a central role in both perceptions of 'difference' and perceptions of 'vulnerability'. In this sense, 'difference' and 'vulnerability' that are invisible or undetectable are at less risk of being targeted, whereas those 'differences' or 'vulnerabilities' which are visible, or seeable, are more likely to result in targeted abuse. In this study, for those who felt visibly trans, either through choice or otherwise, felt much more at risk of experiencing transphobic hate crime and reported significantly more incidents of actual victimisation. This has also been reflected in the ways that cisgender people discuss and construct trans people, with no problems associated with those who 'appear' to be cisgender accessing sex-segregated spaces (Colliver et al. 2019). However, it is also important to understand how (in)visibility operates beyond what is 'see-able'. Participants in this study who felt that they 'passed' frequently reported experiencing victimisation as a consequence of disclosing their trans identity, thereby increasing the visibility of their 'difference'. In highlighting the discursively constructed nature of (in)visibility, we are better able to understand how this concept functions at critical moments of victimisation. Utilising ideas that relate to less tangible forms of 'visibility' also provides a counter narrative to dominant frameworks that focus on 'stranger danger' and adds to the literature that challenges this concept (Mason 2005; Mason-Bish 2010). This allows for a greater appreciation of hate crime victimisation experienced in private spheres, perpetrated by those closest to the victim such as intimate partners, family and friends. This is key in addressing barriers to reporting hate crime and encouraging victims to recognise their experiences as criminal, and therefore reportable.

The concept of (in)visibility is therefore a reciprocal one, in which we must consider (in)visibility as it relates to both victims, perpetrators and witnesses or onlookers. The level of (in)visibility of each of these 'actors' within any given situation may have implications on the likelihood that victimisation occurs. This was most evident in discussions around online victimisation. The internet provides unprecedented opportunities for individuals to have ultimate control over the level of visibility associated with an individual's identity. It is therefore key to engage with the fluid nature of (in)visibility in an online context, in which individuals can rapidly alter privacy settings and access to content and information associated with them. There may be specific combinations of (in)visibility that result in higher levels of victimisation, particularly when the victim's 'difference' is visible, whilst the identity of the perpetrator is invisible. Indeed, participants in this study often reflected on the anonymous nature of much abuse directed at them online. The ability for perpetrators to remain anonymous, their identities rendered invisible to other users was understood as a central reason as to why online hate speech was so prevalent. Those who considered themselves to be visibly trans online, particularly through activism and content engaged with, described experiencing significantly more hate speech than those who attempted to, or kept their trans identity invisible in online spaces. As such, we cannot simply apply and interrogate notions of (in)visibility as they apply to the victim; we must consider the relationship between victims and perpetrators and the unique ways in which (in)visibility operates for both.

Conclusion

In this chapter I have engaged with the concept of (in)visibility as a complex, fluid and ongoing process and applied this to individual accounts of victimisation. I hope to have provided a more nuanced account of the nature of (in)visibility and the various ways it operates. I have highlighted how individuals engage and understand their own feelings of risk of victimisation based on differing levels of 'visibility' associated with their 'difference', or 'vulnerability'. In doing so, I have drawn upon dominant frameworks within hate crime scholarship and advocate for greater attention to be paid to the role of (in)visibility, and its relationship to 'difference' and 'vulnerability' when engaging with hate crime. The level of 'visibility' associated with an individual's perceived 'difference' has implications for which space they can access safely, and by whom they are likely to experience abuse. Managing identities is an intricate, context-dependent and fluid process that is achieved and fully realised both individually and in relation to others and their readings of an identity. Identity formation and negotiation is context-specific in that the emphasis placed on a particular aspect of an identity may shift through time and space, and may be culturally, politically or socially situated.

There are four key claims I have made in this chapter. Firstly, from a criminological perspective, we must consider how (in)visibility operates when investigating hate crime victimisation and perpetration. This should be done alongside notions of 'difference' and 'vulnerability', and I argue that (in)visibility provides a useful framework for which 'difference' and 'vulnerability' can be understood. Participants in this study often understood their trans identity as visibly 'different' in particular spaces and as a signifier of 'otherness'. This is then conceived to be a significant motivator in their victimisation. Secondly, understanding the discursively constructed and less tangible nature of 'visibility' is key in developing our understanding of pivotal moments which may be particularly high risk in relation to potential victimisation. In recognising the different ways in which (in)visibility manifests, we can move beyond polarised and dichotomous conceptualisations of 'passing' and its relationship with (in)visibility. Furthermore, a greater emphasis on the notion of (in)visibility can contribute to current debate surrounding which 'groups' are afforded legislative protection and whether these should be expanded. Visibility, as it relates to what is see-able, and also less tangible forms of visibility that may be result from 'coming out', or disclosing an aspect of an identity, may be useful in determining which groups are most at risk. Utilising an (in)visibility approach would be useful in building a case for the inclusion of people involved in various aspects of sex work, people who are homeless, and people who belong to or identify with alternative subcultures.

Thirdly, (in)visibility must be considered in relation to intersectional oppressions. I have demonstrated in this chapter that the relationship between (in)visibility, vulnerability and difference is not simple or linear, but is a complex relationship. Within particular spaces, a heightened level of visibility in relation to difference may lead to either an increase or decrease in feelings of risk. Additionally, (in)visibility may operate to reduce the risk of experiencing transphobia, but increase the risk of experiencing a hate crime targeting another identity marker. Finally, I have highlighted the importance of considering (in)visibility as it relates to victims and perpetrators. The level of (in)visibility afforded to each of these 'actors' within any given situation may have implications for the likelihood that a hate crime will occur.

It is at this point that it is key to remember that (in)visibility is clearly linked to individuals' understanding of the likelihood of experiencing hate crime victimisation. I therefore argue that it is problematic to discuss hate crime victimisation without acknowledging the role (in)visibility plays. However, the discussion presented in this chapter has focused on (in)visibility at an individual level, and it may be necessary for future work to explore and interrogate the relationship between (in)visibility at both the micro- and macro-levels. As outlined at the beginning of this book, recent years have seen an increased level of visibility for trans communities, particularly in mainstream media. Future work on (in)visibility should seek to understand the relationship that individuals have with an increased social and political visibility, and how this affects their own understanding of victimisation.

References

Archer, L. (2003). *Race, masculinity and schooling: Muslim boys and education*. London: Open University Press.

Awan, I. (2014). Islamophobia and twitter: A typology of online hate against Muslims on social media. *Policy and Internet, 6*(2), 133–150.

Banks, J. (2010). Regulating hate speech online. *International Review of Law, Computers and Technology, 24*(3), 233–239.

Brown, A. (2017). What is so special about online (as compared to offline) hate speech? *Ethnicities, 0*(0), 1–30.

Carbado, D. (2001). *Black men on race, gender and sexuality: A critical reader*. New York: New York University Press.

Chakraborti, N. (2018). Responding to hate crime: Escalating problems, continued failings. *Criminology and Criminal Justice, 18*(4), 387–404.

Chakraborti, N., & Garland, J. (2012). Reconceptualizing hate crime victimization through the lens of vulnerability and difference. *Theoretical Criminology, 16*(4), 499–514.

Chakraborti, N., & Zempi, I. (2012). The veil under attack: Gendered dimensions of Islamophobic victimization. *International Review of Victimology, 18*(3), 269–284.

Chetty, N., & Alathur, S. (2018). Hate speech review in the context of online social networks. *Aggression and Violent Behavior, 40*, 108–118.

Cipolletta, S., Votadoro, R., & Faccio, E. (2017). Online support for transgender people: An analysis of forums and social networks. *Health and Social Care in the Community, 25*(5), 1542–1551.

Cmeciu, C. (2016). Online discursive (de)legitimation of the Roma community. *Journal of Media Research, 9*(1), 80–98.

Code, J. (2013). Agency and identity in social media. In S. Warburton & S. Hatzipanagos (Eds.), *Digital identity and social media* (pp. 37–57). Pennsylvania: Information Science Reference.

Cohen-Almagor, R. (2011). Fighting hate and bigotry on the internet. *Policy and Internet, 3*(3), 1–25.

Collins, P. (2000). *Black feminist thought: Knowledge, consciousness, and the politics of empowerment* (2nd ed.). New York: Routledge.

Colliver, B., & Coyle, A. (2020). 'Risk of sexual violence against women and girls' in the construction of 'gender-neutral toilets': A discourse analysis of comments on YouTube videos. *Journal of Gender-Based Violence, 4*(3) 359–376. https://doi.org/10.1332/239868020X15894511554617.

Colliver, B., & Silvestri, M. (2020). The role of (in)visibility in hate crime targeting transgender people. *Criminology and Criminal Justice*, [online first]. https://doi.org/10.1177/1748895820930747.

Colliver, B., Coyle, A., & Silvestri, M. (2019). The 'online othering' of transgender people in relation to 'gender neutral toilets'. In K. Lumsden & E. Harper (Eds.), *Online othering: Exploring digital violence and discrimination on the web* (pp. 215–238). London: Palgrave Macmillan.

Council of Europe. (2006). *Is this a stereotype? A tool for fighting stereotypes towards Roma.* Strasbourg: Council of Europe, European Commission.

Crenshaw, K. (1989). Demarginalizing the intersection of race and sex: A black feminist critique of antidiscrimination doctrine, feminist theory and antiracist politics. *University of Chicago Legal Forum, 140,* 139–167.

Crenshaw, K. (1991). Mapping the margins: Intersectionality, identity politics, and violence against women of color. *Stanford Law Review, 43*(6), 1241–1299.

Ford, E., Bergmann, M., Boeing, H., Li, C., & Capewell, S. (2012). Healthy lifestyle behaviors and all-cause mortality among adults in the United States. *Preventative Medicine, 55*(1), 23–27.

Fütty, J. (2010). Challenges posed by transgender-passing within ambiguities and interrelations. *Graduate Journal of Social Science, 7*(2), 57–75.

Garland, J. (2010). 'It's a mosher just been banged for no reason': Assessing targeted violence against goths and the parameters of hate crime. *International Review of Victimology, 17*(2), 159–177.

Garland, J., Chakraborti, N., & Hardy, S.-J. (2015). 'It felt like a little war': Reflections on violence against alternative subcultures. *Sociology, 49*(6), 1065–1080.

Gerstenfeld, P. (2004). *Hate crimes: Causes, controls, and controversies.* London: Sage Publications Ltd..

Grant, J., Mottet, L., Tanis, J., Harrison, J., Herman, J., & Keisling, M. (2011). *Injustice at every turn: A report of the National Transgender Discrimination Survey.* Washington, DC: National Center for Transgender Equality and National Gay and Lesbian Task Force.

Gressgård, R. (2010). When trans translates into tolerance—Or was it monstrous? Transsexual and transgender identity in liberal humanist discourse. *Sexualities, 13*(5), 539–561.

Hodkinson, P., & Garland, J. (2016). Targeted harassment, subcultural identity and the embrace of difference: A case study. *The British Journal of Sociology, 67*(3), 541–561.

Jamel, J. (2018). *Transphobic hate crime*. London: Palgrave Macmillan.

James, Z. (2020). Gypsies' and Travellers' lived experience of harm: A critical hate studies perspective. *Theoretical Criminology, 24*(3), 502–520.

James, Z., & Smith, D. (2017). Roma inclusion post Brexit: A challenge to existing rhetoric? *Safer Communities, 16*(4), 186–195.

James, S., Herman, J., Rankin, S., Keisling, M., Mottet, L., & Anafi, M. (2016). *The report of the 2015 US transgender survey*. Washington: National Center for Transgender Equality.

Kilian, E. (2014). Claiming space: Transgender visibility in the arts. In C. Zabus & D. Coad (Eds.), *Transgender experience: Place, ethnicity, and visibility* (pp. 85–107). New York: Routledge.

Lawrence, F. (1999). *Punishing hate: Bias crimes under American law*. Cambridge: Harvard University Press.

Lovelock, M. (2017). Acceptance, humanity and emotional excess: The politics of queer suffering in big brother UK. *European Journal of Cultural Studies, 20*(4), 449–463.

Mason, G. (2005). Hate crime and the image of the stranger. *British Journal of Criminology, 45*(6), 837–859.

Mason-Bish, H. (2010). Future challenges for hate crime policy: Lessons from the past. In N. Chakraborti (Ed.), *Hate crime: Concepts, policy, future directions* (pp. 58–77). Collumpton: Willan Publishing.

Mason-Bish, H., & Zempi, I. (2019). Misogyny, racism, and Islamophobia: Street harassment at the intersections. *Feminist Criminology, 14*(5), 540–559.

Mattias de Vries, K. (2012). Intersectional identities and conceptions of the self: The experience of transgender people. *Symbolic Interaction, 35*(1), 49–67.

METRO Charity. (2014). *Youth chances*. London: METRO Charity.

Meyer, D. (2010). Evaluating the severity of hate-motivated violence: Intersectional differences among LGBT hate crime victims. *Sociology, 44*(5), 980–995.

Meyer, D. (2012). An intersectional analysis of lesbian, gay, bisexual and transgender (LGBT) people's evaluations of anti-queer violence. *Gender and Society, 26*(6), 849–873.

Meyer, D. (2014). Resisting hate crime discourse: Queer and intersectional challenges to neoliberal hate crime laws. *Critical Criminology, 22*, 113–125.

Mills, C. (2019). Gay visibility and disorganized and strained communities: A community-level analysis of anti-gay hate crime in New York City. *Journal of Interpersonal Violence*, 1–22. https://doi.org/10.1177/0886260519848784.

Minton, S. (2012). Alterophobic bullying and pro-conformist aggression in a survey of upper secondary school students in Ireland. *Journal of Aggression, Conflict and Peace Research, 4*(2), 86–95.

Namaste, V. (2000). *Invisible lives: The erasure of transsexual and transgender people*. Chicago: The University of Chicago Press.

Perry, B. (2001). *In the name of hate: Understanding hate crimes*. London: Routledge.

Perry, B. (2015). 'All of a sudden, there are Muslims': Visibilities and Islamophobic violence in Canada. *International Journal for Crime, Justice and Social Democracy, 4*(3), 4–15.

Perry, B., & Dyck, D. (2014). 'I don't know where it is safe': Trans women's experiences of violence. *Critical Criminology, 22*(1), 49–63.

Roen, K. (2002). 'Either/or' and 'both/neither': Discursive tensions in transgender politics. *Signs, 27*(2), 501–522.

Rood, B., Reisner, S., Surace, F., Puckett, J., Maroney, M., & Pantalone, D. (2016). Expecting rejection: Understanding the minority stress experiences of transgender and gender nonconforming individuals. *Transgender Health, 1*, 151–164.

Rood, B., Puckett, J., Resiner, S., Maroney, M., Berman, A., & Pantalone, D. (2017). Identity concealment in transgender adults: A qualitative assessment of minority stress and gender affirmation. *American Journal of Orthopsychiatry, 87*(6), 704–713.

Rosich, G. (2020). Sexual citizenship theory and employment discrimination among transgender-identified people. *Societies, 10*(1), 1–17.

Rundall, E., & Vecchietti, V. (2010). (In)visibility in the workplace: The experiences of trans employees in the UK. In S. Hines & T. Sanger (Eds.), *Transgender identities: Towards a social analysis of gender diversity* (pp. 127–152). New York: Routledge.

Schippers, M. (2007). Recovering the feminine other: Masculinity, femininity, and gender hegemony. *Theory and Society, 36*(1), 85–102.

Sellberg, K. (2012). Transgender identity and passing authentically. In D. Cooley & K. Harrison (Eds.), *Pro-passing, transgender identity and literature: (Post)-transsexual politics and poetics of passing* (pp. 211–219). Farnham: Ashgate.

Serano, J. (2007). *Whipping girl: A transsexual woman on sexism and the scape-goating of femininity*. Emeryville, CA: Seal Press.

Shapiro, E. (2004). Transcending barriers: Transgender organizing on the internet. *Journal of Gay and Lesbian Social Services, 16*, 165–179.

Stein, A. (2016). Transitioning out loud and online. *Contexts, 15*(2), 40–45.

Stotzer, R. (2009). Violence against transgender people: A review of United States data. *Aggression and Violent Behaviour, 14*, 170–179.

Stryker, S. (2006). (De)subjugated knowledges: An introduction to transgender studies. In S. Stryker & S. Whittle (Eds.), *Transgender studies reader* (pp. 1–18). New York: Routledge.

Tremlett, A. (2014). Demotic or demonic? Race, class and gender in 'gypsy' reality TV. *The Sociological Review, 62*(2), 316–334.

Wallengren, S., & Mellgren, C. (2015). The role of visibility for a miniority's exposure to (hate) crime and worry about crime—A study of the traveller community. *International Review of Victimology, 21*(3), 303–319.

Walters, M. (2011). A general theories of hate crime? Strain, doing difference and self-control. *Critical Criminology, 19*, 313–330.

Wandrey, R., Mosack, K., & Moore, E. (2015). Coming out to family and friends as bisexually identified young adult women: A discussion of homophobia, biphobia, and heteronormativity. *Journal of Bisexuality, 15*(2), 204–222.

Weaver, S. (2013). A rhetorical discourse analysis of online anti-Muslim and anti-Semitic jokes. *Ethnic and Racial Studies, 36*(3), 483–499.

Wetherell, M. (2009). *Theorizing identities and social action*. London: Palgrave Macmillan.

Williams, M., & Tregidga, J. (2013). *All Wales hate crime research project*. Cardiff: University of Cardiff.

Woods, J. B. (2014). Queer contestations and the future of a critical "Queer" criminology. *Critical Criminology, 22*(1), 5–19.

Zimman, K. (2009). 'The other kind of coming out': Transgender people and the coming out narrative genre. *Gender and Language, 3*, 53–80.

7

Concluding Thoughts

Reimagining Hate Crime: Transphobia, Visibility and Victimisation has documented the various ways in which transphobia, cisnormativity and transphobic hate crime operate to oppress and marginalise trans and non-binary communities. This book is unique in that it is the first of its kind within the United Kingdom to provide an empirical account, which focuses exclusively on transphobic hate crime. The aim of this book was to provide a more detailed account of the experiences of trans and non-binary people in relation to hate crime. In doing so, I have challenged popular discourse that often presents hate crimes as single, isolated incidents of extreme behaviour, contextualising participant's narratives within the social and political context which legitimises trans and non-binary people as appropriate targets for victimisation. In drawing on intersectional oppressions and acknowledging identities as complex, fluid and unstable, I have challenged the 'silo-approach' to hate crime (Mason-Bish 2015). I hope that this work can be utilised for future research to highlight the importance of challenging our single-axes approach to exploring victimisation.

In this chapter, I emphasise the key concepts that have been developed throughout this research project and highlight the applicability of these

B. Colliver, *Re-imagining Hate Crime*, Palgrave Hate Studies,
https://doi.org/10.1007/978-3-030-65714-7_7

concepts beyond transphobic hate crime, and hate crime studies more generally. I draw particularly on the concepts of 'micro-crimes' and '(in) visibility' as concepts with wider utility. I then explore the potential implications that this research has for policy and practice, paying particular attention to improving the 'victim experiences' within criminal justice systems, from initial reporting through to prosecution. I end this chapter with some suggestions for future research, particularly in looking to further explore some of the key ideas put forth throughout this book. It is with these suggestions that I hope significantly more empirical research is conducted that explores transphobic hate crime, with the purpose of improving policy and practice and contributing to a more equal and just society.

Academic Contributions

Whilst the research that informed this book has made a number of contributions to the sparse literature that focuses exclusively on transphobic hate crime, it is here that I want to emphasise two key conceptual contributions. In emphasising these, I hope that they will have applicability outside the realms of transphobic hate crime, to hate crime scholarship more broadly. Furthermore, I believe that the conceptualisations I have offered throughout this book relating to micro-crimes and (in)visibility will have applicability outside of hate crime scholarship. In reflecting on these contributions, I will highlight specific areas in which I see transferability to other areas within Criminology and the Social Sciences more broadly.

Criminology has long had an interest in the lives of minoritised genders and sexualities. Ball (2014: 544) argues that 'criminological knowledge has been used to regulate queer lives in unjust ways, and for many years, queer people were spoken about by criminologists, sexologists, and others seeking to "know" about those considered sexually deviant'. Despite a historic interest, Criminology has also largely neglected the experiences of trans people and their victimisation. The publication of this book sees a significant contribution to a growing body of literature that pays explicit attention to the ways in which trans people experience, understand and respond to victimisation targeting their gender identity (Chakraborti et al. 2014; Jamel 2018; Kidd and Witten 2008). Not only has this research provided an in-depth understanding of participants' experiences, I have also engaged in a more complex discussion around inclusion and exclusion within trans communities. In doing so, I have challenged dominant Criminological perspectives that often tend to the needs of the least marginalised trans people and contribute to the politicisation of language that is used to police who 'belongs' in communities and who is 'othered'.

In addressing these issues, I have identified three distinct, yet interconnected, forms of victimisation that many trans people experience: micro-aggressions, micro-crimes, and socially recognisable forms of hate crime. In challenging dominant frameworks through which hate crimes are most commonly understood, we are better able to understand the social and situational dynamics that victimisation occurs in. It is not the case that identifying victimisation within these three categories serves to reinforce a hierarchy of victimisation, as all three forms of victimisation have implications for how, when and where victims can engage in social spaces. Repetitive, targeted micro-crime victimisation is likely to have similar practical and emotional consequences for victims as more socially recognisable forms of victimisation. It is key to acknowledge different forms of victimisation if issues of underreporting are to be addressed. Only through acknowledging micro-crime victimisation as a legitimate form of criminal victimisation can victims be recognised as such and encouraged to report these experiences.

In acknowledging micro-crime victimisation, it is likely that this concept will have utility outside of research in transphobic hate crime. Whilst a significant amount of work that explores racist and anti-religious hate crime has been completed (Awan 2014; Bowling 1999; James and Smith 2017), it is likely that much of this work focuses on more socially recognisable forms of victimisation, and therefore overshadows the experiences of micro-crime victimisation. Research into hate crime targeting people with, or perceived to have, a disability is a growing area of study (Healy 2020; Wilkin 2020) and the concept of micro-crime victimisation will arguably have utility in developing research in this area. Outside of hate crime research, the concept of distinguishing between the 'visibility' of particular forms of victimisation will help challenge dominant frameworks and narrow definitions of 'violence' across Criminology that often focus on victimisation and harm associated with physically violent crime (Tombs 2007). In doing so, this will encourage criminological perspectives to look outside of traditional conceptualisations of violence and victimisation.

The second specific contribution I have made with this research is reconceptualising hate crime victimisation through the lens of '(in)visibility'. In building on the work of Perry (2001) and Chakraborti and Garland (2012), I have offered another conceptual tool through which to investigate hate crime. As discussed earlier, I find nothing inherently problematic about acknowledging and understanding how both 'difference' and 'vulnerability' operate, and these concepts were certainly present in participants' narratives. However, in this research, the idea of (in)visibility was the overarching concept within which 'difference' and 'vulnerability' can be understood to operate. Those who were able to render their 'difference' or 'vulnerability' invisible reported significantly lower levels of anxiety regarding victimisation. Therefore, I would argue that in order to fully understand existing concepts which are utilised in hate crime scholarship, we must continue to engage in interrogating the way (in)visibility operates for different groups in different spatial and social contexts.

Although the notion of (in)visibility has been engaged with before, in hate crime scholarship and wider queer studies (Chakraborti and Zempi 2012; Mills 2019; Perry 2015), I have offered a more complex reading of this concept. Existing research that utilises (in)visibility as a tool by which to understand social phenomena have tended to adopt a dichotomous approach, in which one is either invisible or visible. Through exploring intersectional oppressions, I have demonstrated how an individual, and their perceived 'difference' or 'vulnerability', can be simultaneously visible and invisible. This concept warrants further attention outside of transphobic hate crime to explore how applicable this is to other minoritised communities. Additionally, in complicating our understanding beyond the dichotomy of visible or invisible and its relationship with difference and vulnerability, I have demonstrated the ways in which increased visibility can result in a decrease of perceived vulnerability.

When a 'difference' is strongly associated with negative, harmful stereotypes relating to aggression, violence and physical dominance, a potential victim's perceived 'vulnerability' may decrease. In acknowledging that identities are multiple and fluid, the notion of (in)visibility has important implications for future research that looks at victimisation targeting a specific identity. As was demonstrated in this research, and that I have written about previously (Colliver and Silvestri 2020), sometimes the visibility of another identity marker contributed to transphobic victimisation and sometimes overshadowed transphobic victimisation in the place of racism, Islamophobia and misogyny, amongst other things. In this sense, we often experience a 'master identity' being imposed on us, and this may be attributed to our most 'visible' identity marker. Finally, in complicating our understanding of (in)visibility, I have moved beyond what is 'see-able' to consider the discursively constructed nature of (in) visibility.

This has implications and applicability for those working in other areas of hate crime. This may be a particularly useful concept for exploring how anti-disability hate crime operates, particularly in the context of disabilities which may be 'invisible'. Using this framework would allow for a more complex understanding of the ways in which 'difference' is perceived. Additionally, those working outside of the five centrally monitored strands of race, religion, sexual orientation, disability status and transgender identity may find this concept useful. Whilst work focusing on sex workers as victims of hate crime has begun to emerge (Corteen 2018), this concept may be useful in addressing the similarities and differences in experiences between 'indoor' and 'outdoor' sex workers and the implications that (in)visibility has in this context. Whilst I acknowledge that there is likely to be an overlap between sex workers who would be described as 'street sex workers' and those who work from a private residence, the 'public gaze', and therefore 'visibility' of their identity as a sex worker may be different. Similarly, this concept could be useful for those working in the area of homelessness, and whilst research is being conducted that explores violence against the homeless within a hate crime framework (Al-Hakim 2015), it could benefit from interrogating how (in)visibility operates. This would help identify similarities and differences between the experiences of individuals who may be 'street homeless' and those who may be in temporary accommodation or 'sofa-surfing'. For research into both areas of sex workers and people who are homeless as victims, the ideas presented around 'discursively constructed visibility' would be useful, particularly when investigating how those who occupy a marginalised social position experience hate crime, abuse and discrimination as a result of disclosing a social status that may not as easily be identified by the 'public gaze'. Through utilising this perspective, I also identified a number of implications for policy and practice, outside of academia.

Policy and Practice Implications

In completing this research, I have identified a number of implications for policy and practice. The publication of this book is the first step in using the findings from this research to make positive changes to the ways in which trans and non-binary people are positioned within social hierarchies. What became clear through participants' narratives was that significantly higher levels of micro-crime victimisation were experienced at the beginning of their transition journey, often attributed to having a visibly gender incongruent presentation. Whilst I acknowledge that medical transition will not be the most appropriate option for all trans people, for those who wish to pursue this option waiting times must be reduced. The process of obtaining legal recognition of an individual's gender, and the process for accessing a Gender Identity Clinic are extremely long, with some trans people reporting a wait of over five years for an initial appointment (Vincent 2018). In order to address this, waiting lists for initial appointments at Gender Identity Clinics must be reduced significantly to allow trans people timely opportunities to progress their transition. It is hoped that recent announcements from Liz Truss, which indicate the government's intent to open at least three new Gender Identity Clinics in 2020, will reduce waiting times and also provide greater geographic coverage, as current Gender Identity Clinics are distributed sparsely across the country. It is key that this commitment is delivered and to acknowledge that this is the first step in improving the process for accessing a Gender Identity Clinic. However, it is likely that further investment will be needed to streamline and prioritise trans people's health and safety.

Given notions of 'transnormativity' discussed earlier in the book, which reinforce medical transition and delegitimise non-binary identities, it is imperative that the government seek to change the options available for gaining legal recognition of an individual's gender identity (Vipond 2015). A number of other countries already recognise non-binary identities as valid, to varying degrees, including New Zealand, Denmark and Nepal. Whilst the usefulness of such recognition has been debated (for example, see Aboim 2020), many non-binary participants in this study felt that the lack of legal recognition perpetuated stereotypes and delegitimised the authenticity of their identity. In this sense, the failure to legally recognise gender identities outside or between the western gender binary may constitute a form of symbolic ham, in which this omission perpetuates these identities as inauthentic. In order to address these concerns, and to also challenge the perception that only those who identify within the western gender binary and follow a medical model of transition are authentic, steps should be taken to allow non-binary people to have their gender legally recognised. Whilst this may prove challenging in a society that is built largely around a binary gender system, the UK should follow the lead of other countries that have moved to recognising non-binary identities.

The findings of this research also indicate that current legislation, the Criminal Justice Act (2003) specifically, should be reviewed for a number of reasons. In October 2018, the Law Commission announced it would conduct a review of current hate crime policies and legislations in an attempt to make the process more effective. Given the hierarchies of protected characteristics discussed in Chap. 4, I would recommend that current legislation be amended to provide equal legislative protection across all officially monitored strands of hate crime. Current legislation provides punishments that are more punitive for racially and religiously aggravated offences. Symbolically, this perpetuates and reinforces hierarchical perceptions of victimisation and contributes to the underreporting of transphobic hate crime. It is key to deconstruct this hierarchy of victimisation in order to assign legitimacy to trans people as victims.

Existing legislation and the process for prosecuting should also be reviewed in order to formally recognise victimisation that is motivated by more than one prejudice. In order to recognise intersectional oppressions (Crenshaw 1989, 1991), the process for considering an aggravating factor must be more fluid to appreciate the complex nature of identity. Failure to do this perpetuates a simplistic conceptualisation of how identities are lived, and this can have negative consequences for victims. Criminal justice systems are not designed to centre the victim in criminal proceedings (Davies 2007), and acknowledging more than one form of oppression may contribute to a better sense of 'justice' for victims. Whilst 'justice' is likely to mean different things to different people, having formal recognition of all motivations of a crime may be a useful step in providing justice. As such, a holistic approach should be taken to legislation in which the nuanced experiences of minorities can be appreciated.

In acknowledging that 'justice' means different things to different people, the use of restorative justice in hate crime cases may prove beneficial. Whilst I suggest that legislation should be reviewed to ensure all protected strands are afforded the same level of protection, this does not necessarily indicate an increase in punitive responses. There is already a strong case building for the use of restorative justice (Mayor's Office for Policing and Crime 2014; Walters 2014). Given the significant emotional impact upon victims of hate crime, a restorative justice approach may address some of the harms caused more effectively than an increased prison sentence. This is particularly pertinent as many participants conceptualised their micro-crime victimisation as a result of ignorance, misunderstanding or lack of knowledge on behalf of the perpetrator. A restorative justice approach in which the victim and perpetrator have an opportunity to discuss the incident may not only reduce the harm caused to the victim but also increase the awareness of trans identities for the perpetrator. However, it should be noted that existing research on the effectiveness of restorative justice is inconclusive and is often based on relatively small sample sizes (Walters 2014). If restorative justice is to be implemented nationally, it should be standardized, as the perceived effectiveness is related to the context in which it is conducted. Walters (2014) found that impromptu meetings hosted by police officers resulted in victims being significantly less satisfied than when meetings were conducted by a third party in a neutral space.

I would also recommend a number of initiatives are developed to encourage the reporting of hate crime. Many participants did not report incidents of micro-crime victimisation as there was a lack of clarity as to what types of incident could be reported as well as the process associated with reporting. This has been discussed before and Chakraborti et al. (2014) suggest that this is particularly relevant to communities who are socially and politically marginalised. In order to address this issue that contributes to the underreporting of transphobic hate crime, an accessible, easy to understand policy should be developed. The policy should outline what can be reported to the police as a hate crime, what victims can expect when reporting a hate crime in terms of the process and the behaviour from police officers, with clear guidance on how to make a complaint in the event of experiencing further discrimination. Clear guidance should be developed in cooperation with communities who are most affected by hate crime, and I would recommend that support services and charities are consulted in the development of guidance, as this will help ensure the guidance is accessible.

Furthermore, for participants who did report, they often experienced a number of microaggressions from those they reported to, including incidents of misgendering and dead-naming, which undermined the credibility and trustworthiness of the police in their eyes. This signified to participants a lack of awareness of gender identity from police officers and made them cautious of reporting again. Despite police initiatives to build confidence within minority communities and encourage the reporting of hate crimes, these are often seen as tokenistic gestures with the aim of appeasing trans communities. In order to address this, a standardized 'Gender Identity Awareness' training should be available for all public-facing police roles, which should be facilitated by an organisation working with trans people. To address financial and time constraints, the training could be delivered as a phased model, in which small cohorts of police officers are trained at a time, so as not to drain police resources. The police have made efforts in relation to strengthening relationships between the police and LGBT communities, for example, the introduction of LGBT Liaison Officers in every London borough. However, this is not without criticism, in that the introduction of LGBT Liaison Officers was primarily on an ad-hoc basis in areas which had a visible, commercial LGBT 'scene' (Moran 2007). Additionally, there has been no consistency in relation to the roles and responsibilities of LGBT Liaison Officers and the requirements to be one, in relation to necessary training and self-identification as a member of the LGBT community (Moran 2007). Therefore, the police should engage with trans communities and hold meaningful conversations around transphobic hate crime that are often not feasible at existing events that police attend, such as Pride events, due to the public nature and lack of confidentiality available to trans people at such events. Finally, if LGBT Liaison Officer roles are to continue, they must be advertised more publicly and reach out to the most marginalised groups of LGBT communities. Funding should be made available to ensure an LGBT Liaison Officer is available in every police force, in a paid, full-time capacity to engage in community relationship development, safety initiatives and to encourage the reporting of transphobic micro-crimes.

The other significant factor that was identified by participants as a barrier to reporting incidents of transphobic micro-crimes was the frequency of victimisation, in which participants felt they experienced victimisation too frequently to report every incident. As a result of this, and to ensure that all incidents of victimisation can be reported conveniently, it is suggested that an online reporting system be developed, in which victims of hate crime can upload statements relating to victimisation and attach any evidence. This will help victims of hate crime log and record incidents of micro-crime. As discussed earlier, victimisation is often a systematic, ongoing process and not a one-off incident. The online statements and evidence could be reviewed remotely by police officers who could contact the victim if it was believed that the incident met the threshold for police intervention. This removes the onus from the victim to follow up with reports and will also be more convenient for victims in reporting. However, in order to avoid the pitfalls associated with third-party reporting, an official online reporting service would need to be sufficiently advertised, explained and made accessible to as many marginalised people as possible. It has been argued that third-party reporting systems are often poorly publicised and are therefore not as effective as they should be

(Chakraborti 2018). Therefore, the online reporting system should be facilitated through police forces, rather than through third-party reporting.

This research has contributed to this literature and identified sex-segregated toilets as sites of significant risk to trans people. The use of sex-segregated toilets can have significant consequences for trans people in their everyday lives. Considering this, it is recommended that public buildings are encouraged to provide 'gender-neutral' toilets. There are arguably a number of benefits to installing gender-neutral toilets relating to carers, parents and individuals with a gender incongruent presentation. As there would be significant financial implications, this could be phased in with new buildings rather than demanding that all buildings restructure to accommodate the installation of a gender-neutral toilet. Furthermore, gender-neutral toilets have been advocated on the grounds that, depending on how they are implemented, they can reduce queuing times for women and be less costly to the public purse (Anthony and Dufresne 2007). This would also make it easier for non-binary people to engage in social life, in which the currently dominant provision of toilets may cause anxiety and a withdrawal from social life.

Considerations for Future Research

There is a growing body of literature exploring microaggressions targeting LGBTQ communities, which often incorporates incidents of micro-crimes, and a significantly larger amount of existing literature exploring hate crime targeting LGBTQ communities which often overshadows micro-crimes. Future research should seek to build upon the conceptualisation of micro-crimes as a recognisable form of criminal victimisation. Specifically, future research should seek to identify the perpetrators of micro-crimes using a large data set to make confident conclusions relating to participants' experiences of victimisation and their conceptualisation of stranger danger, which I challenged in Chap. 4. Despite the wider literature addressing the victimisation of LGBTQ people more broadly, trans people's experiences are often overshadowed by or conflated with sexuality, and therefore future research should aim to highlight the experiences of trans people specifically. In doing so, the interrelated nature of microaggressions, micro-crimes and more socially recognisable forms of hate crime should be explored. In exploring the concepts of micro-crimes further, future research should seek to explore perpetrator's motives and conceptualisations of hate crime offence.

This research has also drawn upon Perry's (2001) notion of doing difference and highlighted how a visible difference can function as both a facilitator of hate crime victimisation, whilst also serving as a protective barrier, potentially limiting the amount of victimisation trans people experience based on their perceived difference. The role of difference as a protective barrier for victimisation has not been explored extensively and raises interesting questions around notions of difference in explaining hate crime victimisation. Therefore, this is an area that warrants further exploration both empirically and theoretically. Given the theoretical contributions I have made in relation to the role of visibility in trans people's experiences of micro-crimes, future research should seek to gain more empirical data to investigate the role of visibility in victimisation. In doing so, consideration should be given to other potential influencing factors that may predict the victimisation of those deemed 'different' and 'vulnerable' by perpetrators. Although existing research has explored the role of visibility in relation to victimisation, none has done so specifically in the context of trans people's victimisation, and when visibility is discussed, it is often done in a simplified manner, neglecting the intersectional nature of visibility. Future research should seek to explore a more complex conceptualisation of (in)visibility.

This research has considered some of the ways in which occupying multiple, marginalised social positions affects the ways people experience, and respond to, hate crime. I would suggest that future research into transphobic hate crime adopts an intersectional framework to better understand the experiences of trans people who experience abuse. Additionally, this approach should be adopted to further explore intra-community discrimination and exclusion. Whilst some work has been done that explores hate crime through an intersectional lens (Meyer 2010, 2012, 2014), there is still much work to be done in this area. I would suggest that other characteristics which are often overshadowed are put at the forefront of research agendas, specifically looking to explore the victimisation experiences of trans people living with a disability. Despite this suggested focus, it is also important that any future research exploring trans people's experiences of discrimination, micro-crimes and victimisation be pursued through an intersectional lens to avoid further marginalising the most oppressed sectors of trans communities.

Concluding Thoughts

Whilst in this chapter I have focused on the contributions of this research to academia and to policy and practice, I wish to end with a personal reflection. Some three years after this research project was completed, I am now more than ever aware of the need to draw attention to unjust systems, policies and practice that marginalise and oppress trans and non-binary people. Since data collection ended for this research project, the social visibility of trans and non-binary communities has increased significantly. This increased visibility has also resulted in toxic online 'debates', regular delegitimisation of trans and non-binary people and a political and social climate in which 'difference' has often become intolerable. Having spoken with many participants since the research project finished, I am reminded of the need to continue working in this field, to continue challenging discrimination and hate.

In a social climate in which highly influential people reinforce harmful and transphobic narratives and stereotypes, I am starkly reminded of the need for strong allyship. I urge everyone to speak out against transphobia, and against discrimination, prejudice and hatred more broadly. Trans and non-binary people have the right to live their lives free from discrimination, fear and harassment, and this must be the starting point for moving equality forward. It is important to remember that we are all different, and in difference, we find unity and strength. Attempts to roll-back the rights for trans and non-binary people is an attempt to roll-back human rights. I end this book with the conclusion that in a world that dehumanises those who are 'different', we must always look to find humanity in others.

References

Aboim, S. (2020). Gender in a box? The paradoxes of recognition beyond the gender binary. *Politics and Governance, 8*(3), 231–241.

Al-Hakim, M. (2015). Making a home for the homeless in hate crime legislation. *Journal of Interpersonal Violence, 30*(10), 1755–1781.

Anthony, K. H., & Dufresne, M. (2007). Potty parity in perspective: Gender and family issues in planning and designing public restrooms. *Journal of Planning Literature, 21*(3), 267–294.

Awan, I. (2014). Islamophobia and Twitter: A typology of online hate against Muslims on social media. *Policy and Internet, 6*(2), 133–150.

Ball, M. (2014). What's queer about queer criminology? In D. Peterson & V. Panfil (Eds.), *Handbook of LGBT communities, crime, and justice* (pp. 531–555). New York: Springer.

Bowling, B. (1999). *Violent racism: Victimisation, policing and social context.* Oxford: Oxford University Press.

Chakraborti, N. (2018). Responding to hate crime: Escalating problems, continued failings. *Criminology and Criminal Justice, 18*(4), 387–404.

Chakraborti, N., & Garland, J. (2012). Reconceptualizing hate crime victimization through the lens of vulnerability and difference. *Theoretical Criminology, 16*(4), 499–514.

Chakraborti, N., Garland, J., & Hardy, S.-J. (2014). *The Leicester hate crime project: Findings and conclusions.* Leicester: University of Leicester.

Chakraborti, N., & Zempi, I. (2012). The veil under attack: Gendered dimensions of Islamophobic victimization. *International Review of Victimology, 18*(3), 269–284.

Colliver, B., & Silvestri, M. (2020). The role of (in)visibility in hate crime targeting transgender people, Criminology and Criminal Justice, [Online First] Available at: https://doi.org/10.1177/1748895820930747.

Corteen, K. (2018). New victimisations: Female sex worker hate crime and the 'ideal victim'. In M. Duggan (Ed.), *Revisiting the 'ideal victim': Developments in critical victimology* (pp. 103–122). Bristol: Policy Press.

Crenshaw, K. (1989). Demarginalizing the intersection of race and sex: A Black feminist critique of anti-discrimination doctrine, feminist theory and antiracist politics. *University of Chicago Legal Forum, 1*, 139–167.

Crenshaw, K. (1991). Mapping the margins: Intersectionality, identity politics, and violence against women of color. *Stanford Law Review, 43*(6), 1241–1299.

Davies, P. (2007). Criminal (in)justice for victims? In P. Davies, P. Francis, & C. Greer (Eds.), *Victims, crime and society* (pp. 251–278). London: Sage Publications.

Healy, J. (2020). 'It spreads like a creeping disease': Experiences of victims of disability hate crimes in austerity Britain. *Disability & Society, 35*(2), 176–200.

Jamel, J. (2018). *Transphobic hate crime*. London: Palgrave Macmillan.

James, Z., & Smith, D. (2017). Roma inclusion post Brexit: A challenge to existing rhetoric? *Safer Communities, 16*(4), 186–195.

Kidd, J., & Witten, T. (2008). Transgender and transsexual identities: The next strange fruit—Hate crimes, violence and genocide against the global trans-communities. *Journal of Hate Studies, 6*(1), 31–63.

Mason-Bish, H. (2015). Beyond the silo: Rethinking hate crime and intersectionality. In N. Hall, A. Corb, P. Giannasi, & J. Grieve (Eds.), *The Routledge international handbook on hate crime* (pp. 24–33). London: Routledge.

Mayor's Office for Policing and Crime. (2014). *A hate crime reduction strategy for London*. London: Mayor's Office for Policing and Crime.

Meyer, D. (2010). Evaluating the severity of hate-motivated violence: Intersectional differences among LGBT hate crime victims. *Sociology, 44*(5), 980–995.

Meyer, D. (2012). An intersectional analysis of lesbian, gay, bisexual, and transgender (lgbt) people's evaluations of anti-queer violence. *Gender and Society, 26*(6), 849–873.

Meyer, D. (2014). Resisting hate crime discourse: Queer and intersectional challenges to neoliberal hate crime laws. *Critical Criminology, 22*, 113–125.

Mills, C. (2019). Gay visibility and disorganized and strained communities: A community-level analysis of anti-gay hate crime in New York City. *Journal of Interpersonal Violence*, 1–22. https://doi.org/10.1177/0886260519848784.

Moran, L. (2007). Invisible minorities: Challenging community and neighbourhood models of policing. *Criminology and Criminal Justice, 7*(4), 417–441.

Perry, B. (2001). *In the name of hate: Understanding hate crimes*. London: Routledge.

Perry, B. (2015). 'All of a sudden, there are Muslims': Visibilities and Islamophobic violence in Canada. *International Journal for Crime, Justice and Social Democracy, 4*(3), 4–15.

Tombs, S. (2007). 'Violence', safety crimes and criminology. *British Journal of Criminology, 47*(4), 531–550.

Vincent, B. (2018). *Transgender health: A practitioner's guide to binary and non-binary trans patient care*. London: Jessica Kingsley Publishers.

Vipond, E. (2015). Resisting transnormativity: Challenging the medicalization and regulation of trans bodies. *Theory in Action, 8*(2), 21–44.
Walters, M. (2014). *Hate crime and restorative justice: Exploring causes, repairing harms*. Oxford: Oxford University Press.
Wilkin, D. (2020). *Disability hate crime: Experiences of everyday hostility on public transport*. London: Palgrave Macmillan.

Appendix: Interview Participant Demographic Information

Name	Age	Gender	Sexuality	Ethnicity	Religion
Brian	20	Male	Pansexual	Black British	Christian
Jae	21	Non-Binary	Pansexual	White British	No Religion
Deena	34	Female	Heterosexual	Black British	Muslim
Laura	57	Female	Heterosexual	White British	Christian
Callum	19	Demi-Male	Pansexual	White British	No Religion
Corrina	21	Female	Heterosexual	Irish Traveller	Christian
Ryan	17	Male	Gay	White British	No Religion
Piper	42	Female	Bisexual	White British	No Religion
Dilip	45	Male	Gay	Asian British	Sikh
Melody	17	Non-Binary	Pansexual	White British	No Religion
Bushra	29	Female	Heterosexual	Asian Bangladeshi	Muslim
Joe	28	Gender-Queer	Pansexual	Black British	Christian
Elaine	48	Female	Lesbian	White British & Black Caribbean	Christian

(*continued*)

B. Colliver, *Re-imagining Hate Crime*, Palgrave Hate Studies,
https://doi.org/10.1007/978-3-030-65714-7

(continued)

Name	Age	Gender	Sexuality	Ethnicity	Religion
Lia	17	Female	Bisexual	White British & South American	No Religion
Rachel	18	Female	Heterosexual	White British	No Religion
Emmet	30	Male	Bisexual	Irish Traveller	Christian
Ashley	34	Male	Asexual	White British	No Religion
Star	44	Non-Binary	Asexual	White British	No Religion
Monica	30	Female	Heterosexual	White British	No Religion
Sam	21	Male	Gay	Asian Pakistan	Muslim
Nastasia	26	Female	Bisexual	White European	No Religion
Cody	29	Male	Heterosexual	White American	No Religion
Joby	17	Gender-Fluid	Pansexual	White British	No Religion
Isa	58	Female	Heterosexual	White British	Christian
Peter	41	Male	Gay	White British	No Religion
Simon	47	Male	Bisexual	White British	Christian
Ty	21	Non-Binary	Pansexual	Black African & White British	No Religion
Madee	24	Female	Heterosexual	Thai	No Religion
Ruby	52	Female	Heterosexual	White British	No Religion
Tom	19	Male	Bisexual	White British	No Religion
Rose	67	Female	Bisexual	White British	No Religion

Index[1]

[1] Note: Page numbers followed by 'n' refer to notes.

B. Colliver, *Re-imagining Hate Crime*, Palgrave Hate Studies,
https://doi.org/10.1007/978-3-030-65714-7

The manufacturer's authorised representative in the EU is Springer Nature Customer Service Centre GmbH, Europaplatz 3, 69115 Heidelberg, Germany. If you have any concerns regarding our products, please contact ProductSafety@springernature.com

Printed and bound by CPI Group (UK) Ltd, Croydon, CR0 4YY

30/09/2026

02225453-0004